MYSTERIES OF MIND SPACE & TIME

The Unexplained

VOLUME
14

Originally published in the United Kingdom in weekly parts as The Unexplained **Mysteries of Mind Space and Time** is a study of the paranormal, mystical and psychic phenomena commonly referred to as the Supernatural. It is not intended to justify or persuade, but to describe the unexplainable phenomena and occurrences experienced by men and women—events that defy normal human experience.

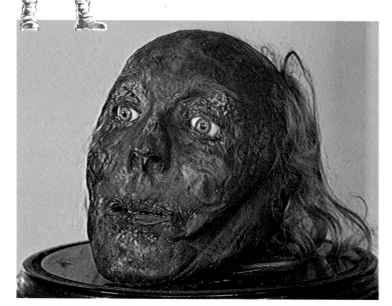

MYSTERIES OF MIND SPACE & TIME

The Unexplained

VOLUME
14

H. S. STUTTMAN INC. *Publishers*   Westport, Connecticut 06880

CONTENTS

Cover illustration, Andy Zito - The Image Bank

Published by H. S. STUTTMAN INC.
Westport, Connecticut 06880
© Orbis Publishing Limited 1992

No part of this book may be reproduced in any form or by any electronic or mechanical means, including information storage and retrieval devices or systems, without prior written permission from the publisher, but brief passages may be quoted for reviews.

PRINTED IN THE UNITED STATES OF AMERICA
3P(2125)20-60

Library of Congress Cataloging in Publication Data

Mysteries of Mind, Space & Time - The Unexplained
    p.   cm.
    Includes index.
    Summary: A twenty-six-volume study of the paranormal, mystical and psychic phenomena commonly referred to as the supernatural
    ISBN 0-87475-575-1
    1. Curiosities and wonders. 2. Supernatural.
[1. Supernatural—Encyclopedias.
2. Occultism—Encyclopedias.]
I. Title. Mysteries of mind, space and time.
AG5.M97 1992   91-21268
031.02—dc20   CIP
                                                AC

Some people believe that images produced by Kirlian photography are proof of the existence of the 'astral body'. This photograph of a normal hand shows a strong blue aura

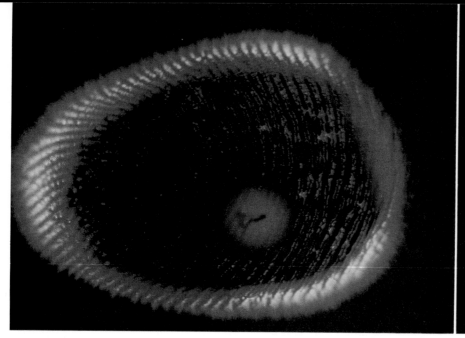

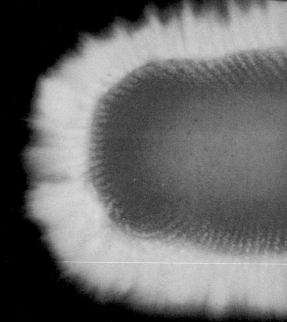

Images of the unseen

Do we have a spiritual body that exists separately from our physical body? For centuries mystics and clairvoyants have claimed that there is a halo of brightly-coloured light surrounding the human body. Then, in 1970, news was received that Russian scientists had photographed this 'aura'. BRIAN SNELLGROVE reports on their revelations

IN 1939 A RUSSIAN engineer, Semyon Kirlian, was repairing an electro-therapy machine in a research laboratory in the Ukrainian town of Krasnodar. Accidentally he allowed his hand to move too close to a 'live' electrode. The shock he received was accompanied by a brilliant flash of light given off by a large spark of electricity. His curiosity aroused, Kirlian wondered what would happen if he placed a sheet of light sensitive material in the path of the spark. Placing his own hand behind a piece of light-sensitised paper, Kirlian found on developing the film strange streamer-like emanations surrounding the image of his fingertips. On closer inspection, Kirlian found that each emanation was seen to have a different radiation pattern.

Fascinated by his 'discovery', Kirlian set up a laboratory in his tiny two-roomed flat and spent all his spare time investigating this phenomenon. Kirlian's research into high-voltage photography over the next 40 years led to intense scientific speculation and debate, and the claim, by some, that the strange emanations captured on film by Kirlian were proof of the existence of the so-called 'astral body'.

For centuries mystics and clairvoyants had claimed that they were able to see a brilliant halo of light surrounding the physical body of all living organisms. This 'halo', they believed, was the spiritual 'double' of our physical selves, but independent of it and surviving the death of the body.

Was the image that Kirlian was able to photograph that of the 'astral body'? Some

have believed so. But at present it is not at all clear what causes the brilliant glow surrounding the hands, feet, plant leaves and other objects that have been photographed using the Kirlian technique.

Nor indeed were the effects that Kirlian thought he had discovered entirely new or unknown. In the 1890s, Nikola Tesla, a Serbian scientist working in the USA, had

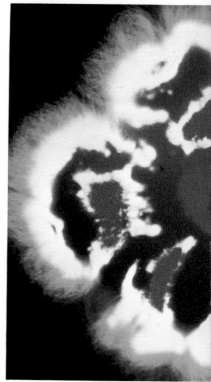

Top left: a fingertip photographed by the Kirlian method, which shows the surrounding radiation pattern. The vivid colour is not in fact significant. The colour of the aura tends to vary according to the type of film used

Left: Semyon and Valentina Kirlian, the husband and wife team who spent over 40 years developing a technique to capture on film the strange streamer-like emanations that, in varying degrees of strength, surround. almost all objects

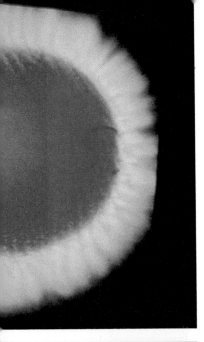

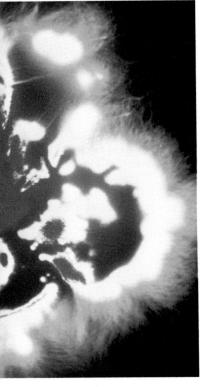

An amazing inventor

Born in Smiljan, Yugoslavia, 9 July 1856, Nikola Tesla became a driving force in the invention of electrical devices and equipment, as well as being something of a prophet.

Unable to interest European engineers in a new alternating current motor he had conceived, Tesla went to the United States in 1884 and joined Thomas Edison in the designing of dynamos. But the two men soon fell out. Tesla left his employ and set up his own laboratory dedicated to showing the feasibility of Alternating Current.

In 1891 Tesla unveiled his famous coil, which is still widely used today in electronic equipment, including television and radio. Tesla's coil is an electrical device for producing an intermittent source of high voltage. It consists of an induction coil with a central cylindrical core of soft iron onto which are wound two insulated coils: an inner (primary) coil of a few turns of copper wire, and a surrounding, secondary coil with a large number of turns of thin copper wire. An interrupter is used for making and breaking the current in the primary coil automatically. This current magnetises the iron core and produces a large magnetic field through the induction coil. For experimentation with the high voltage output of power from his coil, Tesla produced a gas-filled, phosphore coated tubular light – forerunner of today's fluorescent light.

A measure of Tesla's inventiveness can be seen by his tele-automatic boat of 1898 which was guided by remote control. Then in 1900 he made what many have claimed as his finest discovery – terrestrial stationary waves. He proved with this discovery that the earth could be used as a conductor and would be as responsive as a tuning fork to electrical vibrations of a certain pitch. He also lighted 200 electric lamps without wires from a distance of 25 miles and created man-made lightning, producing flashes of some 135 feet. Tesla was convinced at one time that he was receiving signals from another planet at his Colorado laboratory. But his claims were met with derision from the scientific press.

His ideas later became even more speculative. He asserted that he was able to split the world in half like an apple and that he had invented a 'death ray' that could destroy aircraft 250 miles away. His ideas concerning communication with other planets met with incredulity. Yet in 1917 he accurately forecast the coming of radar.

Top: a brilliantly illuminated Kirlian picture of a fingertip. A strong 'aura' is said to show ESP powers, sometimes latent, in the subject of the photograph

Above: as this picture of an oleander leaf shows, plants also respond to the Kirlian method. This fact has been taken by some to prove that all life is essentially spiritual

used high-voltage photography, with much the same results as those achieved by Kirlian. In the early 1930s an English researcher, George de la Warr, discovered the existence of weak 'electromagnetic force fields' surrounding areas of the human body and at a distance from it. These fields extended in a lattice-like formation and contained voltage peaks as high as 70 millivolts. The vividness of these fields was also seen to fluctuate according to the physical and emotional state of the subject.

But undoubtedly the major advances in the field of high voltage photography were indeed made by Kirlian himself. Some of his most interesting contributions were made quite by chance. On one occasion, Kirlian was preparing his equipment for a demonstration he was giving to a distinguished visitor. To his dismay, on the day the visitor was to arrive the machine failed to produce the normal clear results. Kirlian took his machine apart, checked for faults and made further tests, but with the same negative results. In frustration he asked his wife, Valentina, to be the subject. To their mutual surprise, a perfect image was produced. A few hours later, Kirlian discovered what he believed to be the cause of his failure to produce a clear image. He developed a particularly virulent form of influenza, and to Kirlian it seemed reasonable to suppose that his illness had caused the weak image. The photograph, Kirlian claimed, had in some way given warning of the influenza.

A further possible use of the Kirlian method was revealed when the chairman of a major scientific research institution arrived. He brought with him two apparently identical leaves for the Kirlians to photograph, the

Controlling the Kirlian aura

From the age of 11 Matthew Manning, below left, has been aware of possessing a wide range of psychic powers. Powers that he could, with practice, turn on at will. In 1974 a group of 21 scientists met to investigate these powers. Was Matthew being used by supernatural forces outside himself, or could his 'gift' be explained in terms of science? The evidence remains inconclusive. But Kirlian photographs taken of Matthew's fingertips produced startling results. The picture on the left shows Matthew's 'normal' corona, but the picture below, taken when he had 'switched the power on', shows a remarkably intense aura.

A Kirlian photograph of a rose petal (top right) shows a characteristic aura. But when a portion of the petal is cut away (below right) the Kirlian photograph still shows, quite clearly, the section that has been removed. This is known as the 'phantom leaf effect' and Russian investigators say that it proves that 'bioplasma' surrounds all living things

Below: a 50p coin with the characteristic outer 'glow'. If, as some claim, this glow is really the 'aura', then it would imply that even inanimate matter has some form of spiritual existence

Bottom: the same coin photographed after two psychic healers had placed their hands 4 inches (10 centimetres) above the coin for five minutes. The outer glow is noticeably brighter

two samples had been taken from the same species of plant, torn off at the same time. From one leaf the husband and wife team obtained the characteristic flare patterns surrounding the leaf. But from the other leaf, no clear patterns were obtained. The Kirlians adjusted their machine in every possible way, but with the same inconsistent results. Next morning they related their failure to produce the same results to their visitor. To their surprise he was delighted. The leaf with the weak pattern, he told them, had been taken from a plant that had contracted a serious disease. The other leaf, with the clear pattern, had been taken from a perfectly healthy plant. The experiment seemed to confirm Kirlian's hypothesis: his machine was able to give warning of disease. The high voltage photograph had detected illness and disease in advance of any physical symptoms appearing on the surface.

Further experiments seemed to produce equally startling results. If a section of a leaf was cut off and photographed an image of the outline appeared on the photograph. This phenomenon, known as the 'phantom leaf', seemed to confirm the claims of clairvoyants that they could see clearly the 'phantom limb' on people with an amputated limb, but who continued to feel pain from the severed limb.

Though the Kirlians themselves did not describe the results of their investigations as evidence for the existence of an 'astral body', many were only too eager to do so. What other explanation was there, they asked, for the startling pictures Kirlian was able to take? But in one sense even the clairvoyants were disappointed with the results of Kirlian photography. Even the richly colourful images achieved by Kirlian lacked the subtlety of the 'aura' seen by clairvoyants.

While working at St Thomas's Hospital in London at the turn of the century, Dr Walter Kilner found that if he observed his patients through a glass screen coated with a blue dye,

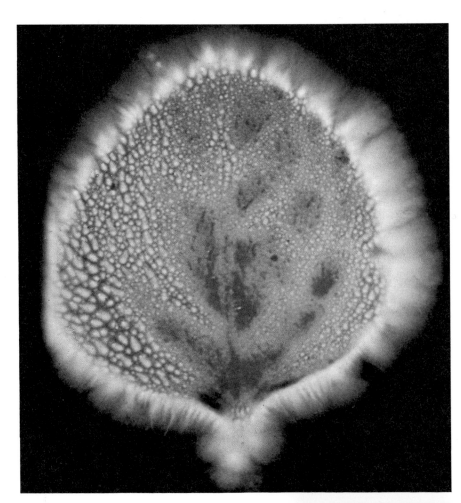

but also a counterpart body of energy'.

Much evidence already exists, claim the enthusiasts, to support Inyushin's theory. And there is also evidence that the nature and extent of these fields of energy, surrounding every living organism, corresponds to the image on the Kirlian print. Not so, reply the critics. Kirlian photography cannot be considered of scientific interest, since it is not repeatable under stringent laboratory conditions; a necessary requirement of all scientific phenomenon. Also, they argue, those experiments that have been conducted produce different results every time, not as the result of underlying physical or psychological causes, as Kirlian claimed, but due, simply, to such factors as sweat secretion and the primitive nature of the equipment used in Kirlian photography.

The debate continues. No one knows for certain what the images the Kirlians photographed are. Some, while rejecting the spiritual aspects of Kirlian, accept that, whatever the emanations mean, they can be used to achieve insight into the physical and psychological condition of the subject. Others, including practising scientists, claim far more. But all are agreed that the Kirlians opened up a hitherto invisible world, once known only by the exceptional and privileged few, for everyone to see.

he could see a 'faint cloud' surrounding them that seemed to vary according to the physical and mental state of the patient. The dye had, Kilner later came to believe, acted as a stimulant to his own innate ability to perceive the 'glow' without any artificial aid. But the ability of those like Kilner to see this 'aura' clearly is of little help to scientists. Because it is such a personal quality, it is difficult to measure, control, analyse and subject to scientific scrutiny in the laboratory.

Research in the West into the possible cause of Kirlian photography is still in its infancy. Certainly, no definite conclusions have been reached. Research in Russia has been of much longer duration and has contributed many interesting theories as to the possible cause of the Kirlian effect. Working at the University of Alma Atta, Dr Victor Inyushin has spent several years investigating Kirlian photography. As a result of his investigations, Inyushin has come to the conclusion that the 'aura' effect shown in Kirlian photography is evidence of what he calls 'biological plasma' and not the result of any electrical state of the organism. Dr Inyushin describes 'biological plasma' in terms that closely resemble those used by clairvoyants to describe the 'astral body'. 'All living things' writes Dr Inyushin '– plants, animals and humans – not only have a physical body made of atoms and molecules,

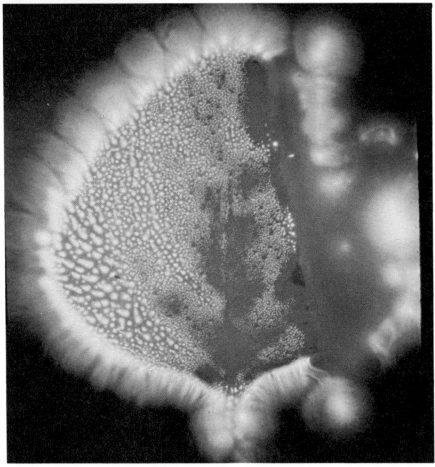

Reading between the lines

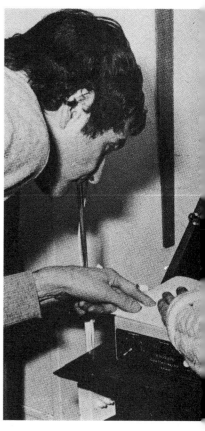

Left: the bright glow surrounding this gold cross is attributed to the influence of the wearer's 'aura'. Gold is able to retain the 'aura' indefinitely

Above: the author, Brian Snellgrove (left), operating a Kirlian machine. The regularity of the corona produced by the subject's hand can provide information about his personality and state of health

Can Kirlian photographs reveal the early stages of cancer? Does a disturbed 'corona' indicate stress and anxiety? What else can Kirlian photography detect? BRIAN SNELLGROVE investigates

WHEN RUSSIAN SCIENTISTS announced the discovery of an 'energy body' composed of 'bioplasma' existing quite separately from the physical body, few scientists in the West were prepared to take them seriously. What evidence was there, they asked, to substantiate such a claim?

And the question, despite much scientific investigation, still awaits a conclusive answer. What the Russians believed to be the 'energy body' turned out to be the curious corona shown by Kirlian photography to surround almost all living things. But, as sceptics in the West asked: what exactly is the strange corona effect that Kirlian photography is able to capture on film? Does it really constitute, as some have claimed, positive scientific evidence for the existence of an 'energy body'? Is the corona effect, perhaps, a picture of the 'aura' that has been described by mystics and clairvoyants? Or is there some other, perfectly ordinary, explanation?

Recent research has been concerned to show that whatever Kirlian photographs may mean, they can be used to achieve practical benefits in medical diagnosis and insights into the human mind. For example, a relationship has been found to exist between the various patterns of Kirlian photographs of the human hand and the physical and psychological condition of the subject.

The left hemisphere of the brain corresponds to the right hand, and radiations from it detected by Kirlian photography provide clues to the logical ability of the subject. The intuitive potential of the subject can also be discovered by a reading of the corona effect of the left hand, which correlates with the right hemisphere of the brain. Both hands in a state of balance show a well-balanced personality.

Characteristics that can be recognised by

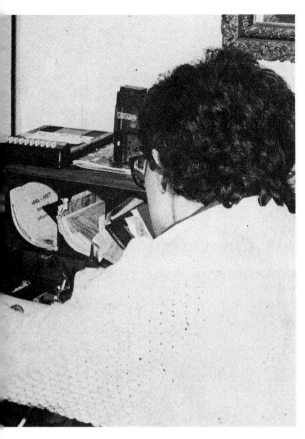

this method of analysis – characteristics that the subject himself may not realise he possesses – include healing ability, creative potential and qualities of leadership. Kirlian photographs are also said to show the nature and extent of conflicts arising from professional and emotional life and also the existence of physical tension.

Initial investigations into the diagnostic possibilities of Kirlian photography have revealed a wide range of possibilities. Studies on rats carried out by Dr Thelma Moss and Dr Margaret Armstrong of the University of Rochester, New York, indicate that marked changes occur in the corona discharge of the tails of cancerous rats as compared to those of non-cancerous rats. Similar corona patterns have been found in cancerous plants and in the fingertips of cancerous humans. Virtually all areas of the body photographed by the Kirlian method have yielded some information about the physical and mental condition of the subject. However, areas where the clearest corona pictures are obtained are the hands and feet.

The basic equipment used in Kirlian photography is simple, and consists of a high voltage 'Tesla coil', which is connected to a metal plate, and which is insulated from the subject by a non-conductive layer. A sheet of light-sensitive material – bromide paper or film, for example – is placed between subject and machine.

The Kirlian machine radiates a high-voltage, high-frequency field. The 'energy body' of the hand or object to be photographed repels the field and causes a pattern of interference to be established. This 'energy body', or whatever it is that creates the pattern, varies. When the 'energy body' is in a balanced condition a regular interference pattern is produced when the field of the machine and that of the subject interact. When there is an imbalance in the field of the subject, irregularities appear in the corona. And it is these irregularities, as research has shown, that can often be correlated to some physical or mental ailment.

Energy of the soul?

Despite the quite beneficial results that have been achieved, Kirlian photography is still beset with many theoretical and practical difficulties. Perhaps the most controversial area of Kirlian photography centres on the interpretation of results.

There are at present four broad views taken of Kirlian photography. According to the cynical view, the so-called Kirlian effect is merely the result of normal discharge between the subject, film and the machine. Any accurate diagnosis produced is purely coincidental and is due solely to the intuition of the researcher. Accepting that Kirlian photography can monitor physical symptoms such as the activity of the sweat glands and temperature, more sympathetic critics say that it still needs to be shown that these changes reflect changes in the physical or psychological state of the subject before proper diagnosis can be made.

Parapsychologists, however, insist that although purely physical causes, such as sweat, may play a part in the production of

Above: a Kirlian picture of a slice of wholewheat bread. Russian experts on nutrition are said to have used the Kirlian process in improving the quality of grain and other foodstuffs

Right: a photograph of a healthy geranium leaf taken with a conventional camera

Far right: the same leaf photographed by the Kirlian method. The corona surrounding the body of the leaf can be seen quite clearly

Below right: a Kirlian photograph of the same geranium leaf taken after the leaf has died. The corona effect has almost completely disappeared, leaving only the image of the leaf

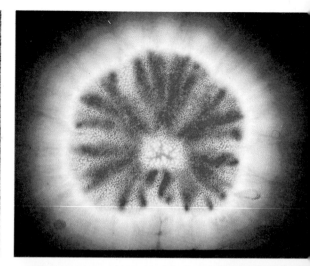

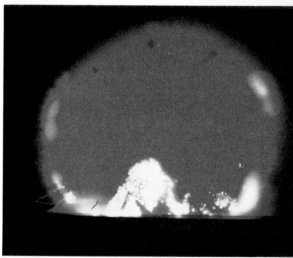

Below: the strong corona surrounding the foot of this subject suggests good health. But notice the absence of the corona around the big toe. This indicates that the subject is suffering from a headache. By massaging the toe, it is claimed, the headache will be eased

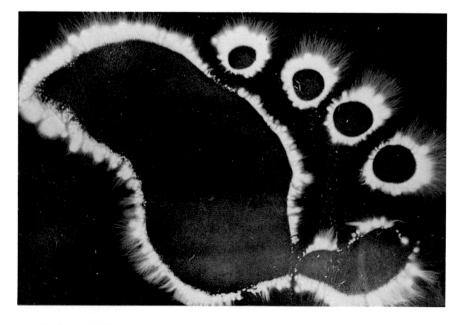

the corona effect, these causes by themselves do not provide a full explanation. According to parapsychologists, Kirlian photography can only be fully understood if the existence of an 'energy body', 'aura', 'bioplasmic body' or some other 'paranormal' phenomenon is accepted.

The most radical interpretation is that of the 'enthusiast' who claims that Kirlian photography has nothing to do with such mundane physical causes such as sweat. It shows, quite clearly, the energies of the soul. The colours and shapes revealed by Kirlian photography are what mystics and clairvoyants have been talking about for centuries.

Before being able to say which of these four competing views is most likely to be correct, there are a number of factors that the serious researcher has to take into account. The Kirlian machine used must conform to a certain standard to ensure that skin resistance, sweat, and other physical manifestations do not interfere with the corona. The subject being investigated must be relaxed. It has been found that when the majority of people try consciously to project their 'aura', the result is a weaker and more

irregular radiation. A similar effect is caused by anxiety or fear on the part of the subject. But, on the other hand, the researcher must be experienced enough to be able to distinguish between cases where the result is caused by anxiety, sweat, or some other temporary physical manifestation owing to nervousness, and those effects that indicate deeper physical or psychological significance.

There are, in addition, six areas where the Kirlian photographer needs to exercise caution if he is to avoid the more common criticisms levelled against Kirlian photography.

The area to be photographed needs to be chosen with care. A fingertip when photographed alone presents a different image from that of the finger when photographed as part of the hand. When photographing a single fingertip only the most acute abnormalities show up, so fingertip photography does have a limited usefulness in medical diagnosis. But for psychological diagnosis the larger the area photographed, the better the diagnosis.

There is a temptation to correlate the colours of the corona with an emotional state. The colour cast, however, depends solely on the type of film used. Ektakrome 35 mm film, for example, produces reds or yellows, while

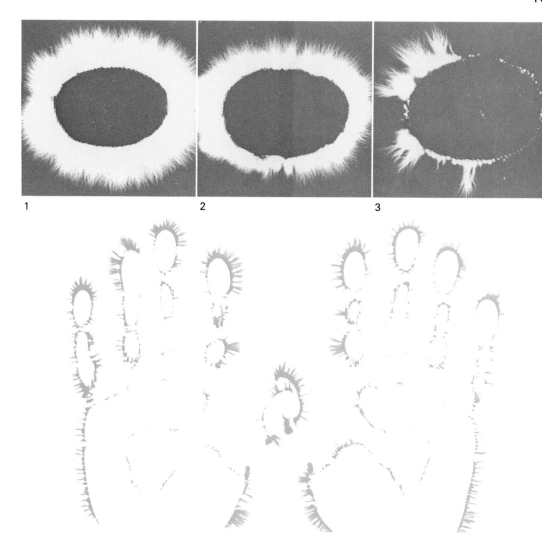

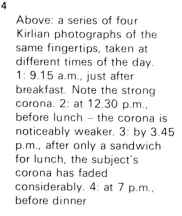

Above: a series of four Kirlian photographs of the same fingertips, taken at different times of the day. 1: 9.15 a.m., just after breakfast. Note the strong corona. 2: at 12.30 p.m., before lunch – the corona is noticeably weaker. 3: by 3.45 p.m., after only a sandwich for lunch, the subject's corona has faded considerably. 4: at 7 p.m., before dinner

Left: the 'spiky' nature of the streamers surrounding these hands is typical of tense subjects and indicates a lack of emotional flow. A well-balanced personality, on the other hand, has a softer, more regular corona

Polaroid film produces a red outer corona with a white inner band. Resin-coated paper produces blue and little else. The colours themselves are not important. What is important is the regularity and extent of any colour effects and what stimuli causes them.

Operator effect also needs to be taken into account. The ability of the mind to cause structural and emotional changes in both living and inanimate objects has been observed on many occasions. An aggressive attitude on the part of observers can inhibit the performance of ESP subjects; voltage patterns of wired-up plants change when disharmonious thoughts are projected. In order to exclude any possible effect of this nature, the operator should stand at least 4 feet (1.5 metres) away from the subject in a relaxed and open frame of mind.

Excessive voltage produces an artificially bright corona and the researcher needs to be able to recognise voltage and waveform characteristics. The golden rule is to use the minimum voltage required to produce a readable pattern.

The energy body takes time – sometimes a matter of days – to settle down after therapy. Results can also be misleading when photographing a subject after, for example, a session of meditation. In many cases the corona will have completely disappeared.

Too long or too short an exposure time can also produce misleading results. There appear to be slow cycles of activity that can be missed if exposure time is too short. For fingertip photographs, one second is sufficient; for the whole hand, two seconds.

In recent years Kirlian photography has been used successfully in a number of applications. In a study commissioned by a commercial firm in the USA, for example, Dr Thelma Moss was able to predict the incidence of germination of soya bean seeds with almost 100 per cent accuracy. The implications for agriculture are immense. Other areas where Kirlian methods of interpretation might be used include personnel selection and evaluation by employers of prospective employees, compatibility assessment and the estimation of the effect of parental conflict, particularly on children. When used in conjunction with acupuncture, counselling or homeopathy, Kirlian photography can produce accurate medical diagnoses.

While the practical benefits of Kirlian photography have been clearly shown, doubt remains as to whether it proves the existence of the 'aura'. There seems to be a 'flow of energy' surrounding almost all living things. But *what* that energy is remains unknown.

Further reading
Walter Benjamin, *Beyond the body*, Routledge and Kegan Paul 1974
Henry Gris and William Dick, *The new Soviet psychic discoveries*, Sphere 1980
Stanley Krippner and Daniel Rubin (eds), *The energies of consciousness: exploration in acupuncture, auras and Kirlian photography*, Gordon and Breach 1975
Sylvan Muldoon and Hereward Carrington, *The projection of the astral body*, Time-Life 1990
Rhea A. White (ed.), *Kirlian photography bibliography*, Parapsychology Sources of Information Centre 1987

A crack in Kirlian's halo

Its champions claim that Kirlian photography can reveal a subject's character, emotional state, medical condition – even his very soul. But, says A.J. ELLISON, there is very little about the process that is strictly paranormal

IN THE MID 1960s I received from an academic staff member at a certain university a set of photographs – so-called Kirlian photographs. One was of a freshly cut leaf, the second was of the leaf after a piece had been cut out of it, the third was of a dead leaf. He told me how the photographs had been produced – in the way now known as Kirlian photography. His accompanying letter referred to the pattern of 'vital forces' shown by the bright tracks, spots of light and radiation surrounding the living leaf, the shadowy signs of an 'etheric body' of the part of the leaf that had been cut off, and the complete loss of all life and fire of the dead leaf, all the 'vital forces' having disappeared with death. He asked me, as an electrical engineer having some familiarity with high voltage discharge phenomena, and also as a Theosophist having a background of many years of study of etheric and astral bodies, of prana and such like, if I did not agree that the electric discharge was showing up remarkably clearly these 'subtle forces of life'.

I looked at the Kirlian photographs carefully, with an open mind. And the explanation seemed quite clear to me. As an independent check I consulted a colleague having a particularly distinguished reputation in the field of high voltage electrical discharge phenomena. It seemed quite clear to him too and we agreed. The differences between the photographs of the living and dead leaves were due entirely to the presence of the sap in the living leaf.

An 'etheric body' explained

But what of the etheric body of the cut leaf? The likeliest explanation of this was that the electrodes had not been carefully cleaned between the taking of the two photographs of the whole and cut leaf. So I looked (the opportunity occurred later) for evidence of this. A competent experimenter would know that the electrodes had to be cleaned carefully between the taking of the two photographs to remove all traces left during the first exposure, and he would have referred in his report specifically to this careful cleaning and inspection of the electrodes. No such reference was to be found.

So we had a perfectly good explanation of the pictures, which agreed with the description of how they had been made. We also had reason to suspect the competence of the experimenter.

I replied to my academic colleague to the

Above: Arthur J. Ellison has had a distinguished career as a psychical researcher and as a scientist. The president of the Society for Psychical Research, he is professor of electronic and electrical engineering at the City University, London

Above right: a detail from Matthias Grünewald's 16th-century altar painting in Isenheim, Alsace, showing the Virgin Mary surrounded by a halo. Artists have long signified the holiness of saints by portraying them emitting a heavenly radiance, which has been identified with the human aura or 'etheric body'. Some sensitives are apparently able to see the human aura, and it has been claimed that the Kirlian photographic process captures it on film

Right: this Kirlian photograph shows a rose leaf from which a small section has been cut – yet its 'ghost' remains visible. This has been described as scientific proof of a non-physical dimension to life – but the appearance of the 'spirit' of the leaf is probably due to physical traces of the whole leaf on the electrodes

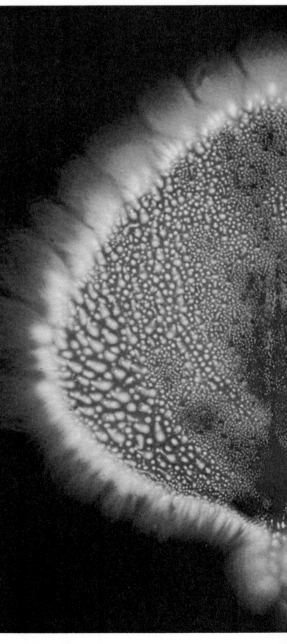

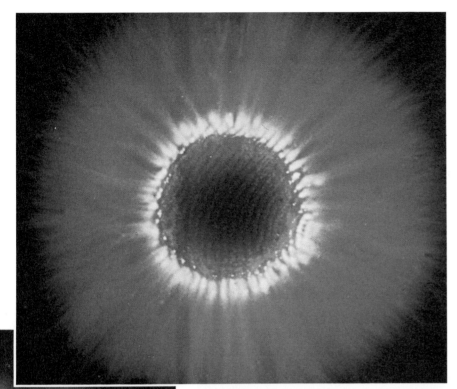

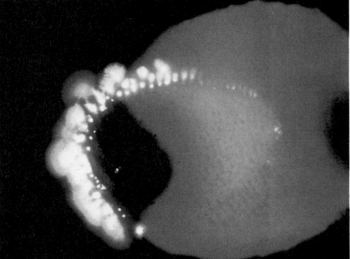

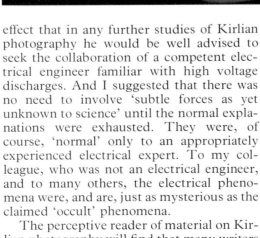

scientific method, either.

Most, if not all, writers on Kirlian photography, describing and evaluating their own 'researches' or those of others, are not competent to evaluate high voltage electrical discharges. Why should they be? This is a very specialised area of work involving a long professional training. It is clear why, to such writers, electric fields and discharges are just as mysterious as the etheric body is to the ordinary down-to-earth scientist who does not interest himself in such matters.

Further, such writers have not studied the scientific literature on the 'subtle bodies'. The term 'subtle body' is used by psychical researchers to describe bodies other than the physical body, which exist in a number of interpenetrating levels of consciousness. The first subtle body is the 'etheric' body, which – unrecognised by conventional science – is believed to carry 'life energies' of various kinds. It acts as a kind of bridge between the dense physical body and the more subtle astral body. Subtler still is the mental body, or mind; and there are supposed to be yet subtler bodies.

These subtle bodies are not made of some

Some vivid examples of Kirlian photography made by Thelma Moss, a respected American researcher:

Top: high frequency corona discharge from the finger of a relaxed person

Centre: photograph of the same finger of the same subject while under emotional stress

Below: fingertips of a subject who had taken marijuana

effect that in any further studies of Kirlian photography he would be well advised to seek the collaboration of a competent electrical engineer familiar with high voltage discharges. And I suggested that there was no need to involve 'subtle forces as yet unknown to science' until the normal explanations were exhausted. They were, of course, 'normal' only to an appropriately experienced electrical expert. To my colleague, who was not an electrical engineer, and to many others, the electrical phenomena were, and are, just as mysterious as the claimed 'occult' phenomena.

The perceptive reader of material on Kirlian photography will find that many writers on the subject have no knowledge of electrical engineering, even though high voltage discharges are the basis of Kirlian photography. Many have no knowledge of the kind of 'subtle matter', which interpenetrates the physical body and projects all round. This is an entirely misguided way of looking at the matter. The subtle bodies are in 'other spaces', despite the fact that to the 'clairvoyance' of a psychic they do appear to interpenetrate the physical body.

A comparison might be made to 'waking dreaming'. The objects in the dream space are not to be considered as interpenetrating the physical world space and having position in it. This is quite easy for anyone to understand and has been shown clearly by experiments in which the position of someone's physical body has been screened while the psychic observed the etheric body. A psychic is unable to tell the position of the physical body by observation of a 'subtle body'. The experiments were carried out with the willing collaboration of some 20 experienced psychics and the results all agreed. It is most unlikely that there will ever be any physical way of making the etheric body visible to ordinary sight.

The unscientific writers also go wrong as a

Below: Kirlian apparatus employs this 'sandwich' arrangement. When an object such as a leaf is to be photographed, it is placed between the upper (earthed) plate and the film surface. When a fingertip, hand or some other part of the body is photographed, no upper electrode is required since the subject is, in normal conditions, earthed. If he is not properly earthed, however – perhaps because he has shoes with rubber soles, or is on a carpet with a rubber underlay – there may be a loss of quality in the Kirlian picture obtained

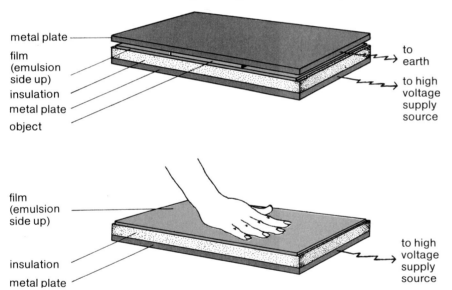

metal plate
film (emulsion side up)
insulation
metal plate
object
to earth
to high voltage supply source

film (emulsion side up)
insulation
metal plate
to high voltage supply source

result of not understanding how to apply the scientific method, especially how to remove from experiments, and their evaluation, the biases and preconceptions of the observer by using double-blind techniques. And they use *post hoc* reasoning: because a particularly dull picture happened to be followed by the illness of the subject, therefore the dullness was due to the incipient illness. They often select evidence that agrees with their preconceptions and ignore the rest. Some examples will illustrate mistakes listed above.

It is becoming quite common these days to get Kirlian photographs of fingertips or indeed of larger areas of the body. The Kirlian apparatus consists of a 'sandwich' made up of a flat metal electrode, a sheet of insulating material, a piece of colour film, and a second, earthed, electrode. In this case the finger is the second electrode, and is placed on the piece of film (emulsion side

Controlling the experiment

Dr Yoshiaki Omura proposes that these 24 points should be carefully specified in reports of Kirlian experiments:

1. High voltage frequency, measured at the power source and at the subject.
2. Oscilloscopic photograph showing waveform of the source.
3. Approximate range of output impedance of the source.
4. Approximate maximum voltage or voltage ranges, as well as waveform, polarities, duration, rise-and-fall time and repetition rate of the pulses.
5. Minimum and maximum distance between electrode plate and subject.
6. Details of the insulator between the electrode and the subject, with its size and geometrical arrangement.
7. Parameters of high voltage electrode plates (including shape, size and kind of metal and surface condition).
8. Name and characteristics of the film.
9. Electrode-to-film and specimen-to-film distances.
10. Exposure time for film and subject.

upwards), the sheet of insulation material below it forming the sandwich filling, with the metal plate below it connected to the high voltage supply source. The owner of the finger is at earth potential and the frequency is made sufficiently high so that he does not receive shock.

Earlier articles (see pages 1618 and 1622) showed several such fingertip pictures, some of which are claimed to indicate vibrant health (a bright discharge with lots of 'vital subtle forces flowing') and others to show illness or disease, real or potential, indicated by a very dull pattern of discharges. There were also photographs produced by psychics, first with the psychic doing nothing special, and second with the psychic 'force' switched on.

Important variables

Such claims involve comparisons among Kirlian pictures. A basic principle of the scientific method is that every variable except the one being compared must be the same, or at least controlled so that the effects of variations in these other variables are known. What variables are important as likely to influence the fingertip Kirlian picture when that picture is produced in the way described? Clearly, first the pressure of the finger. This would appear to be the most important variable of all, because the spaces under and around the finger and between the other members of the Kirlian 'sandwich' can crucially affect the form of the discharge.

11. Grounding conditions and approximate current through the subject.
12. Range of surface temperatures of the subject.
13. Electrical conductivity of the surface areas of the subject and the method used for measurement.
14. Whether (and how) the surface of the subject has been washed and cleaned.
15. Environmental conditions, including atmospheric pressure, room temperature, humidity, and degree of air pollution.
16. Pressure (approximate) exerted on the subject and the area of contact of subject with the surface of the film.
17. Vital signs (biological activity) before and after Kirlian photography.
18. Safety precautions.
19. Experimental set-up, shown in photographs or schematic diagram.
20. Voltage-current curves recorded by oscilloscope during photography.
21. Blood chemistry of subject.
22. Factors influencing circulatory conditions of various parts of the body.
23. Micro-circulatory states of the area of the body to be photographed.
24. Other pertinent information about subjects or procedure.

Other factors are clearly of importance too, such as the temperature, humidity of the air, voltage waveform and consistency, the duration of the discharge with its frequency, and the consistency of the film. There are, according to Professor Omura of the International Kirlian Research Association, 24 different variables that should be controlled. If at least the more important of these are not controlled then any comparison of Kirlian pictures is *meaningless.*

Some users of the Kirlian technique do not even measure and control the pressure of the subject's finger on the film. Their results are valueless and any deductions made from them are unlikely to be useful.

Let us take another example. Several years ago claims were made that, if a single Kirlian photograph were taken of the fingertips of two people who had not previously met, then each would show the 'normal' pattern; but if the experiment were repeated using two subjects who loved each other then their 'auras' (shown by the discharges) would be seen at least partially to merge. This claim was illustrated by striking Kirlian photographs. However, it would seem that the photographs had been selected from a large number of photographs that were not shown, probably because many of these did not show the desired effect.

Let us look at the way in which all the variables can be properly controlled so that pictures in which only one variable is changed can be compared. The controls should be

checked by repeated photographs in which nothing has been changed: an artificial finger should be used with all the other variables unaltered. The photographs will then depend only on the type of film (the nature and distribution of the emulsions), the waveform and magnitude of the voltage, the thickness and material of the sandwich layers, and the number of discharges used on each occasion.

Reactions of the skin
When everything has been controlled and checked, the subject's finger may be placed on the pad. The changes in the picture will now depend on the physical/electrical parameters of the finger. The most important of these will be the electrical skin resistance, known to change with certain psychological variables, and the presence of sweat will clearly be a factor. Changes in electrical skin resistance are known to doctors and psychologists as the 'psychogalvanic skin reaction' or GSR. It will indicate changes in arousal, and it may also indicate the presence of disease. It can be changed by heavy breathing (resulting in over-oxygenation of the blood) and altered radically by deep relaxation, the skin resistance increasing greatly in a state of trance.

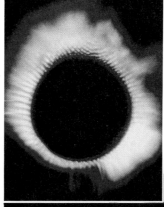
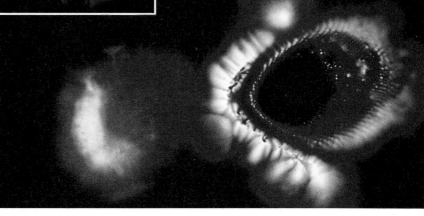

Above: fingertip Kirlian photographs obtained from a famous sensitive – Uri Geller. The upper picture shows the pattern obtained when Geller was at rest; the lower one, allegedly showing a burst of 'psychic energy', was taken after he had been invited to use his peculiar powers. What is perhaps more likely is that Geller, in concentrating, exerted extra pressure on his fingertips – or simply perspired more – and so altered the corona discharge around his finger

It is clear that properly controlled scientific experiments by competent people may well indicate that Kirlian photography has some diagnostic potential. But the emphasis has to be on proper control of the variables and sufficient experiments to be amenable to statistical evaluation, all human beings varying over a wide range in almost every respect. Such a study requires the collaboration of researchers from several disciplines – at least from electrical engineering and physiology – and is not easy. It has some possible value when carried out by trained people, but it is difficult to see any value at all in much of the material that is now being produced and published by experimenters who appear to have no qualifications to undertake such a difficult multi-faceted scientific study.

More than meets the untrained eye

Are all the claims made for Kirlian photography the result of exaggeration or wishful thinking? In his second article, A. J. ELLISON explains what happens during the process – and what it can really tell us about a subject

IN THE PREVIOUS article I explained briefly how the 'etheric' body does not appear to be in physical space. This is a mysterious concept, and Kirlian experimenters propose to make the etheric body physically visible by means of something that, to those who are not electrical engineers, is equally mysterious – an electrical discharge. This is like trying to make the body you find yourself 'occupying' while dreaming visible to ordinary physical sight in a similar way.

There are, of course, 'force fields' around the human body. The body is an electrochemical machine: electric currents flow through it and the body is surrounded by weak magnetic and electric fields. There are also temperature differences between the body and its surroundings, so it is surrounded by a radiating thermal field; this is the basis of medical diagnosis by thermography. The body is surrounded by a field of moving air, which is due to these temperature differences.

In addition there is a 'field' of small particles being continually thrown off the body surface. Perspiration appears on the skin and evaporates. This perspiration contains various chemical substances depending in kind and concentration on the body's metabolism and general health, which are major factors in determining the electrical resistance of the skin. The nature and quantity of these substances is affected by psychological states, and can change very rapidly; it

Right: a heat picture or 'thermograph' of the human body, which can be used in medical diagnosis. The cool parts show blue, the warmest white or yellow

Far right: the environmental chamber used at the Polyclinic Medical Center to ensure that variables are kept constant during the Kirlian process. Among the instruments are a barometer, thermistor, pulse detector, oscilloscope, hydrometer and a room thermometer

Bottom: human skin, shown at 5000 times life size. Each tiny crevice will affect the high voltage electrical field in a Kirlian photograph

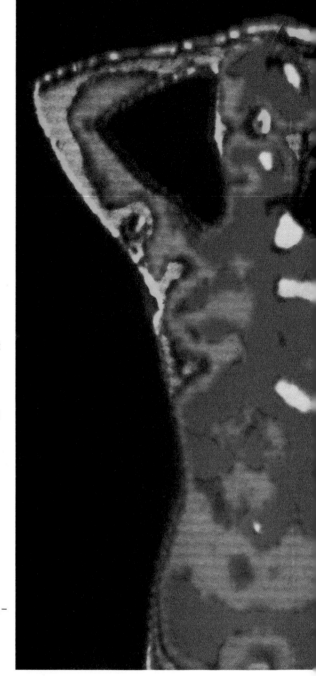

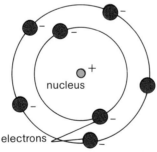

nucleus

electrons

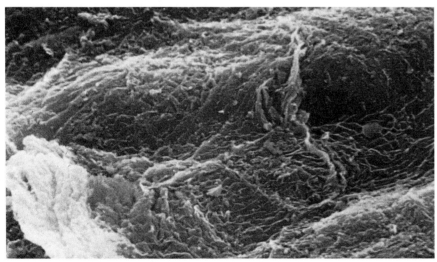

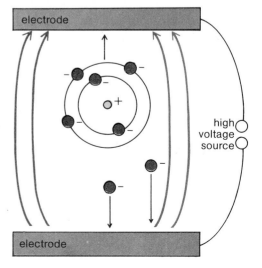

electrode

high voltage source

electrode

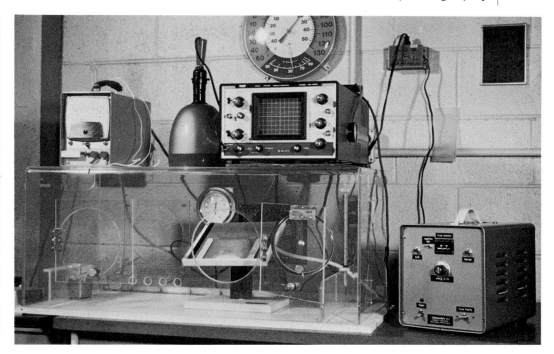

Above left: every atom consists of a nucleus around which electrons – particles of negative electricity – circle. Their charge balances the positive charge of the nucleus. A very intense electric field (left, shown by pink arrows) can pull electrons away from the atom. The free electrons and the incomplete atom are called ions, and move in opposite directions. In Kirlian photography, the ions create patterns when they strike the film. Though complex, the patterns are not mysterious

can also be affected by drugs.

Now let us look at what happens when an electrical discharge takes place between a finger pad and a high voltage electrode. The kind of glow produced in Kirlian photography is known as a corona discharge, and it is very different from a spark. Air is normally quite a good insulator, but if the voltage is sufficiently high the insulation may break down, and a single or continuous spark jumps the gap. When the current is small – as, for instance, in the spark produced by an induction coil – the spark can give one an intense shock, but it is not particularly harmful; on the other hand, a stroke of lightning, for example, carries very high current and is usually fatal.

Colour and form

The corona discharge occurs at lower strengths of electric field – that is, in essence, at lower voltages – than that required for spark breakdown, and it carries a low current; it is, therefore, harmless. It is caused by intermittent ionisation of the air around the fingertip, and it is therefore affected by irregularities in the electric field strength due to the ripples and folds and other irregularities of the skin. Other factors that will affect the nature of the corona include the nature of the insulating material between the finger and the plate, and the pressure and composition of the surrounding air.

The colours in the corona discharge result from the light produced by the ionisation of atoms and molecules, and the subsequent recombination of ions and electrons; and each substance will produce a characteristic colour. Everybody is familiar with the colour of a sodium discharge lamp or a mercury vapour light. Yellow is the characteristic discharge colour for sodium, and blue-violet for mercury. Air, which is made up of mostly nitrogen and oxygen, normally has a blue-purple discharge corona; but a finger that is sweating heavily may well produce yellow streaks, since the sweat will be rich in sodium chloride, or salt.

The colour of the corona will also depend upon the variation of voltage with time, and upon whether the finger is the negative or positive pole of the discharge. And, finally, the nature of the photographic film used is also of importance. Colour film has three layers of emulsion, each of which will behave independently as part of the Kirlian 'sandwich': the current itself will directly affect the colours of the final picture, and the magnitude and distribution of this current will be affected by the nature and structure of the layers of film. It is quite clear that a photograph of the corona taken with a normal camera will be very different from the picture obtained on the film actually involved in the discharge process.

In scientific studies of the Kirlian discharge with so many different parameters, all affecting the result to varying degrees, it is necessary to keep all of them except one constant, so far as is possible, and then to vary that one and observe the effect.

It is a fact of some importance that the Tesla coil, used by so many investigators, produces a very unstable voltage supply, varying randomly in waveform and frequency. Serious scientific work needs a more controlled arrangement such as would be provided by an oscillator with an adjustable and stable frequency and fixed waveform. Differences in Kirlian photographs from eastern Europe and from the West, or between researchers in the West, are not surprising as there is as yet no standardisation of equipment: both the frequency and waveform – and also the time the discharge is passed for a photograph – vary according to

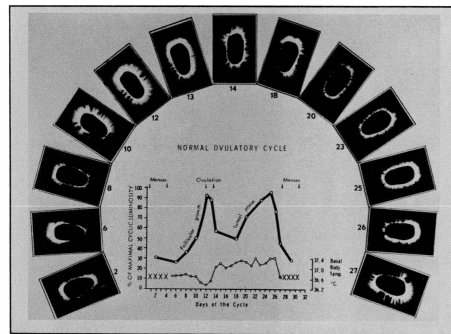

The fingertip test

Shown here are some results of the research into menstrual cycles conducted by Leonard W. Konikiewicz's team. On the left is a series of Kirlian images taken from a woman with a normal cycle; on the right they are from a woman taking Lo-Ovral birth control pills. The thick line on the graphs shows the relative luminosity of the Kirlian images, while the thin line on the left shows body temperature. There seems to be no correlation between the images and body temperature, but there *is* a relation between ovulation and the intensity of the corona; and the 'steady state' of the body, maintained as the pill prevents ovulation, is reflected in the consistent intensity of the Kirlian images in the set on the right.

the arrangement of the experiment.

Let us suppose that a suitable stable finger pad electric discharge has been produced and all other parameters kept appropriately constant and then comparisons are made between photographs of sick subjects before and after 'healing'. Should there be normal differences? Of course there should. 'Healing' most certainly affects the chemicals appearing in the sweat ducts – the primary cause of the large changes in electrical skin resistance when a subject becomes more tranquil and relaxed. Merely sitting quietly with someone's hands gently resting on one's forehead, particularly if it is accompanied by a belief that mysterious healing 'forces' are also flowing, will cause enormous changes in chemical secretion. If the comparison of Kirlian pictures before and after healing is confused by variations in an unstable electric supply source, in the finger pressure and ambient temperature and perhaps in the humidity, too, the comparison is well nigh worthless. Almost every comparison of Kirlian photographs available is quite invalid for these reasons.

Some researchers have noticed similarities between traditional eastern descriptions of the flow of 'prana' and 'vitality globules' and the appearance of 'bubbles' and stream lines in the corona discharge. The interchange of 'rose-coloured prana' between healthy and sick people has been suggested as a possible explanation of differences between finger pad Kirlian photographs of such people before and after healing. It would appear as yet to be far too early to take such similarities seriously.

So what should be done? Kirlian research requires a team involving, ideally, an electrical engineer, a psychologist, a physicist or chemist (expert in spectroscopy) and a physiologist. The experiments must involve

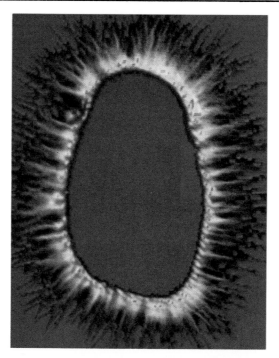

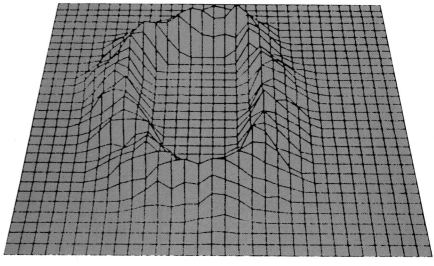

Top: two computer-processed Kirlian images show the difference between a healthy subject (left) and a patient suffering from cancer (right). Most cancer patients show a higher than usual light emission around the fingertips – marked here by the computer in red

Bottom: three-dimensional histograms made by computer analysis of Kirlian images. The control image above is thus seen as a regular series of 'bumps' (left), while a patient suffering from cystic fibrosis produces spikes on the graph (right). These correspond to high sweat emissions that show up brightly on the Kirlian image

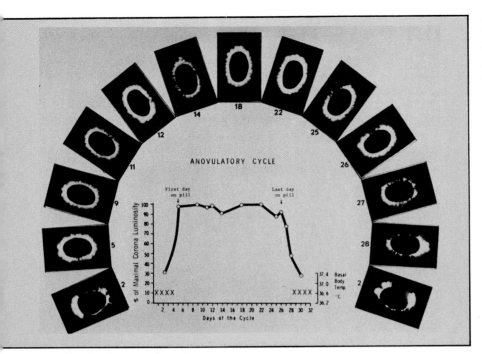

ANOVULATORY CYCLE

proper control of the parameters, double-blind comparisons, and a statistical evaluation, using a sufficient number of subjects and results from each. This research, as is the case with so many matters often considered parapsychological, *must* involve experts in many disciplines because no one person could be sufficiently expert in all the areas of knowledge involved.

The Objects of the International Kirlian Research Association of New York City seem to be on the soundly scientific lines needed to get to the bottom of this most interesting and perhaps very important phenomenon. Those lines are well exemplified by current work in the Polyclinic Medical Center, Harrisburg, Pennsylvania, USA, directed by Leonard W. Konikiewicz, who has produced a valuable book and a number of papers. In his work he uses all the controls referred to above, including an environmental chamber. He has verified the significance of a number of factors and discovered others previously unknown. For example, a rotary movement of the finger prior to exposure records a 'phantom image' by altering electron scattering.

Research makes the difference

Konikiewicz has found it essential to use special retainers to keep the film flat. Subjects must refrain from drugs and, two hours before tests, cleanse their thumbs with distilled water, dry them in air and then wear cotton gloves up to the test, to prevent contamination. In two blind studies involving 140 subjects, Konikiewicz correctly identified cystic fibrosis in 16 out of 18 CF patients and carriers of the gene in 37 out of 48. He could not differentiate controls from carriers if the relative humidity in his electrode environmental chamber (in which the hands are inserted through airtight openings) fell below 60 per cent, but he could still recognise CF patients. Earlier problems showed how the original Kirlian equipment (based on x-ray machine practice) with its very high frequency, stimulated the nerves controlling the sweat glands of the fingers – not always desirable. Konikiewicz solved these and other problems. Other work by this investigator shows, statistically of course, the variations in maximum luminosity of the corona discharge from finger pads of female subjects according to the day of the menstrual cycle. The day of ovulation, with other features, can be clearly seen. The patterns are quite different for subjects taking 'the pill' (see box).

It is clear, then, that while scrupulously conducted research like this may well vindicate the Kirlian process as a diagnostic tool, the information it provides is very much of *this* world and no other. Similarly, only research that maintains the highest professional standards will be of any use. The more widely these points are understood, the less likely it is that Kirlian's 'enthusiasts' will be able to mislead the uninformed.

Further reading
H. S. Dakin, *High-voltage photography*, H. S. Dakin 1978
Sylvan Muldoon and Hereward Carrington, *The phenomena of astral projection*, Sun Publishing Co. 1981
Leonard W. Konikiewicz, *Introduction to electrography*, Leonard's Associates (Harrisburg) 1979

At death's door

Terminally ill patients have gained reassurance from a remarkable woman doctor who believes she has experienced the process of dying and now has no fear of death. LYNN PICKNETT recounts her extraordinary story

ALMOST EVERYONE in the Western world is afraid of dying. The fear is so widespread and has such profound effects that the medical profession has coined a word for it: thanatophobia (*thanatos* is the Greek for 'death').

The fear itself is natural enough – but what exactly are we afraid of? The answer differs greatly from one person to another. One fears the pain and the indignities that terminal illness may bring; another fears divine judgement, while someone else, on the contrary, is afraid that there is nothing after death but oblivion; someone else is anxious not for himself but for the dependants left behind. But to most people death is simply 'the unknown', too fearful to be contemplated. The result is a taboo on the discussion of our own deaths. How many people make preparations for this inevitable event?

Figures of angels and the symbol of the cross, found in profusion in every Christian graveyard, express a profound hope for a life beyond the grave – a hope that goes hand in hand with a deep fear of death. Yet some who have been on the very brink of dying claim to *know* that there is an afterlife

This conspiracy of silence adds to the burdens of those who are approaching their deaths. Today in the developed countries most terminally ill patients are sent to hospital – removed from home to endure painful and frequently embarrassing treatment, and finally to die among strangers. They are facing the greatest trauma of their lives, yet all too often no one will even talk about their imminent death. Visitors try to maintain the fiction that all will be well; discussing the making of a will is considered to be in dubious taste. Even if surrounded by people, the dying patient is appallingly isolated.

A new profession has been created to meet the needs of the terminally ill: counsellors to the dying. Naturally, a name has been coined for this aspect of medical and psychological care: thanatology. One of the most remarkable workers in this field is Dr Elisabeth Kübler-Ross, an American who has been counselling the dying, from tiny children to old people, since the 1960s. But what is probably the most important result of her work is a source of embarrassment to her fellow professionals. In 1974 Dr Kübler-Ross made this uncompromising statement: 'Before I started working with dying patients, I did not believe in life after death. I now believe in it beyond a shadow of a doubt.'

Extraordinary personal experiences convinced her of this. But before they occurred, what she had seen of the deaths of others sometimes suggested that they marked the transition to a new life.

Five stages of dying

She observed that there are five stages that a terminally ill person, with only a few months to live, can go through – though they may not reach the last stage before death comes. The first is denial, accompanied by avoidance of other people: 'It can't happen to me – and I won't talk to anyone.' This is followed by anger: 'Why me – why not someone older, less well-educated, less useful?' The third stage is bargaining: 'If I do as I'm told, you will make me better, won't you?' Then comes depression: 'I really am dying – *me, dying*!' Finally comes the stage of acceptance.

It is at this last stage that nurses often report that the patient's behaviour changes drastically. He may hear voices, or see visions of dead friends and relatives who seemingly have come to escort him into a new existence. (Consequently they are dubbed 'take-away visions' by the thanatologist Dr Raymond Moody.) He may speak of recurring images of tunnels, lights and feelings of peace, like those occurring during out-of-the-body experiences (see page 2149).

In her work Dr Kübler-Ross encountered many such cases. She also talked to many patients who had clinically 'died' and been resuscitated. Their stories of leaving their bodies and experiencing great happiness and

Dr Elisabeth Kübler-Ross was born in Switzerland but now works in the United States. She applied her psychiatric training to the stresses endured by terminally ill patients, and is now acknowledged as a world authority on the counselling of the dying

even excitement were remarkably consistent. Few wanted to 'come back', and those few did so only out of a sense of responsibility for a loved one. And most significantly, almost everyone who had experienced a short period of 'death' had no fear of dying finally. As one doctor who resuscitated a woman patient remarked, 'I have worked with people many times to get them to accept their death; but this was the first time I have ever had to get someone to accept life.'

Of course, not everyone dies peacefully, without pain or distress. In many people the will to live is very strong and death is a battle. Sometimes the battle is won, as in the case of Wallace Abel, who in 1975 found himself in the Scottsdale Memorial Hospital in Arizona, USA, suffering from a heart attack. During his stay his heart stopped twice, and both times he was resuscitated. Recalling the second occasion, he said:

Suddenly there was a tugging at my midsection. A transparent figure of me was struggling to leave my body. I recognised it immediately, but my body seemed to refuse to let go of this cloud of me. My image struggled, twisted, pulled. Suddenly I realised I was witnessing my own struggle for life.

Not all thanatologists believe that these experiences are valid evidence of some kind of life beyond death. Another American, Dr Russell Noyes, a psychiatrist at the University of Iowa Medical School, studied the stories of 114 resuscitated patients – their out-of-the-body experiences, their floating sensations, freedom from pain, sense of joy – and has concluded that they merely represent 'depersonalisation', an 'emergency

mechanism, a sort of reflex action', genetically programmed into us to help us over our greatest trauma, death. He does not see that any of the tales of the dying are anything more than hallucinations.

The strength of her conviction, however, rests on her own amazing personal experiences. In the early 1970s, after a tiring day in which she had counselled several dying patients, Dr Kübler-Ross lay down to rest. Suddenly she had the experience of leaving her body. She learned later that someone checked her pulse and respiration at this time and thought she was dead.

When Dr Kübler-Ross 'returned' to her body, she felt that she had discovered that consciousness can leave the body under certain circumstances in life – and presumably does so at death, permanently. She felt that she now knew what it was like to die.

An even stranger and far more traumatic experience was to follow, transforming her outlook on life – and especially death. One night she was finding it difficult to sleep when suddenly:

I had one of the most incredible experiences of my life. In one sentence: I went through every single death of every single one of my thousand patients. And I mean the physical pain, the . . . agony, the screaming for help. The pain was beyond description. There was no time to think and no time for anything except that twice I caught a breath, like between two labour pains. I was able to catch my breath for a split second and I pleaded – I guess with God – for a shoulder to lean on, for one human shoulder, and I visualized a man's shoulder that I could put my head on.

And a thunderous voice came: 'You

A soul joyfully and trustingly leaves its body, escorted by angels, in William Blake's picture *The death of the good old man*. People near death often see beings – usually deceased loved ones – who have apparently come to act as guides into the next stage of existence

The souls of the dying in a New York hospital of the 19th century (left), as seen by the clairvoyant Andrew Jackson Davis, the 'seer of Poughkeepsie'. Davis claimed to be able to see into the world of spirits, which he called 'Summerland'. The departure from life could be blighted by the grim conditions of the hospitals of the time. The problem can be equally bad today: the patient can be intolerably lonely, though surrounded by medical staff (below). A counsellor may be required to help him come to terms with his fate

shall not be given'. Those words. And then I went back to my agony and doubling up in bed. But I was awake, it wasn't a dream. I was reliving every single death of every one of my dying patients.

Again the voice thundered 'You shall not be given.' Gasping for breath, she raged at it: 'I have helped so many and now no one will help me.' But at that moment the realisation came to her that she must 'do it alone, no one can do it for you'. In place of the unimaginable suffering came 'the most incredible rebirth experience'.

Everywhere I looked in the room – my legs, the closet, the window – everything started to vibrate into a million molecules. Everything vibrated at this incredible speed . . . Behind was a sunrise, the brightest light you can imagine . . . the light was full and open, like the whole sun was there . . . the vibrations stopped, and the million molecules, including me . . . fell into one piece . . . and I was part of that one. And I finally thought, 'I'm okay, because I'm part of all this.'

She began to see every pebble, leaf and bird – everything that is – as being part of a whole 'alive universe'. She had experienced what the mystics have termed 'cosmic consciousness'. In some way the experience gave her an insight into the continuity of all things, including the spirit before and after death.

This dreadful, yet enlightening, experience was not the end of the paranormal events in her life. Some time later, as she sat in her office in the hospital in Chicago, a former patient of hers walked in to thank her

Further reading
Roberta Halporn (ed.), *Thanatology thesaurus*, Center for Thanatology Research and Education 1990
Elisabeth Kübler-Ross, *On life after death*, Celestial Arts 1991
Maurice Rawlings, *Beyond death's door*, Bantam 1991

for all she had done and to encourage her to continue in her good work. Dr Kübler-Ross recognised Mrs Schwartz instantly – and thought she was hallucinating. Mrs Schwartz was dead. Then the doctor's scientific training asserted itself: she presented the apparition with a pen and paper and asked her to write a note, dated and signed. Mrs Schwartz duly did so and went away. The handwriting has been compared with the dead woman's and vouched for as hers.

On another occasion Dr Kübler-Ross tape-recorded the voice of another deceased patient, Willie. She says:

I understand that this is very far out, and I don't want people to be less sceptical. I am sceptical myself. The scientist in me needed Mrs Schwartz to sign a paper, though I knew she was in my office. And I needed a tape-recording of Willie's voice. I still listen to it and think it's one big, incredible dream. I am still filled with this incredible sense of awe and miracle.

The acknowledged pioneer in the growing field of thanatology, Dr Kübler-Ross has written a major work, *On death and dying* (1970), which is essential reading for doctors, nurses, social workers and others who are continually faced with the problems of coping with the dying. Yet her certainty about the afterlife, her out-of-the-body experiences and her descriptions of cosmic consciousness have proved a shocking embarrassment to the medical profession. Her work is freely quoted and her vast practical experience is drawn on, but very few students care to discuss her spiritual discoveries.

The dying patient who is lucky enough to be counselled by Dr Kübler-Ross may well never hear her speak of an afterlife unless she is specifically asked to do so. But to her five stages in the process of dying, she has privately added a sixth: the afterlife.

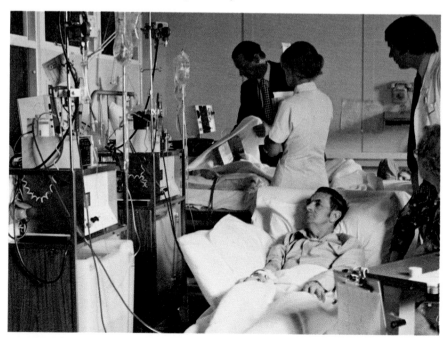

Last exit for the lost

The spiralling pattern of the maze or labyrinth is found all over the world. Are mazes designed merely for entertainment – to entrap and bewilder – or do they have an altogether deeper and more ancient significance? PETER JAMES probes the mystery

SCATTERED ACROSS the face of Europe, parts of Africa, Asia and the Americas lie hundreds of mazes and labyrinths. Sometimes made of turf, sometimes of hedges, stone or brick, or sometimes simply two-dimensional pictures on mosaic floors, paintings or rock, mazes can be found in almost every kind of setting. The more recent ones, like the ever-popular hedge-maze at Hampton Court or the great picture maze on the floor of Chartres Cathedral, are often displayed in grand and public places. Others are found on remote mountainsides and in hidden spots, like the superb turf-cut spiral Mizmaze near Breamore, Hampshire, which occupies a hidden clearing in the woods. Local traditions suggest that the Breamore Mizmaze, of unknown date but certainly of great antiquity, was once a prominent centre of folk rituals. Yet despite the fading of its original significance, the Mizmaze has retained its fascination and

The Mizmaze near Breamore, Hampshire, England – a superb turf-cut maze that occupies a hidden woodland clearing. It is impossible to get lost in the maze – the turfs are so low that the exit route is always visible. It seems that the Mizmaze was designed instead for ritual purposes. There was, for instance, a custom of running the maze – it was said that one person could run from here to Gallows Hill, some half a mile (800 metres) away, and back again in the time that it took another runner to complete the circuit of the Mizmaze

has been dutifully tended and preserved over uncounted generations into the 20th century. In an age of materialism and high technology, the maze has somehow survived as a delightfully irrational and enjoyable symbol of an essential characteristic of the human condition – bewilderment.

Sadly, we are at present far from an understanding of the reasons behind the building of the mazes. The modern fascination with mazes seems to spring largely from the sheer adventure of becoming completely lost, voluntarily, and finding one's way out only after a thrill of fear that one will never do so. An experiment conducted by Ralph Selby in Nottingham in July 1971 highlights the experience: he set up a complex three-dimensional maze. Invited to crawl through one, or both, floors of a two-storey complex (one lit, the other completely dark), built on a tiny site measuring a mere 34 by 17 feet (10 by 5 metres), visitors were bombarded with disorientating information, including bizarre readings from *Alice in Wonderland* and encounters with self-propelling steel spheres. Seven thousand people participated in the experiment; its designer afterwards summarised their reactions:

I was surprised by the way a usually cynical public was prepared to suspend

maze myth, the Greek story of Theseus and the Minotaur, will perhaps elucidate the problem. Theseus was one of seven youths and seven maidens demanded as tribute by the overlord of Athens, the tyrannical King Minos of Crete. The captives were to be fed as sacrificial victims to the Minotaur, a bull-headed monster who lived at the heart of a gigantic maze, the Cretan labyrinth. This was so complex that even its builder, the legendary architect and inventor Daedalus, had difficulty in finding his way around it; the Athenian victims, once in the labyrinth, would wander hopelessly until the Minotaur caught up with them and devoured them.

Theseus, however, was favoured by the gods, and when he arrived on Crete with the other captives, Minos's daughter Ariadne fell in love with him. Ariadne persuaded Daedalus to reveal the secret of the labyrinth, and at his suggestion gave Theseus a ball of thread, which he trailed from the door of the labyrinth as he entered its sinuous passages. Already an experienced monster-killer, Theseus found the Minotaur in its lair, beat it to death and retraced his steps, following the thread, bringing the other Athenians

their disbelief – and of course it was the most confident who found themselves more quickly trapped than the cautious. Most visitors reported that moment of heightened awareness of their own reaction, when they realised they couldn't find an immediate exit.

It is possible that heightened awareness obtained in this way is akin to the euphoric giddiness produced by some drugs and was a factor in the religious function of mazes. Certainly spontaneous excitement with a controlled 'unknown' must have stimulated ancient users of maze sites, at which we know the ritual cults involved dance, drama, music and other stimuli. But to attribute the prolific maze-cults of the ancient world simply to a desire to 'get high' may be taking too lightly a solemn cult of ancient Man.

It is just possible to discern, behind the disorderly variety of mazes and labyrinths produced by our ancestors, a meaningful common factor. The main purpose, it seems, was to provide limited access, an entry to a centre cunningly hidden from casual prowlers and penetrable only by the initiated. In the words of Oxford classicist Jackson Knight, 'the primary idea of the labyrinthine form . . . is the exclusion of hostile beings or influences.' In one sense mazes were a symbol of protection, a token 'guard' over the churches, temples, tombs and other sacred places they decorated. Evidently ancient mazes were not simple amusements. But what were they supposed to be guarding? What force, object or idea was potent enough to result in the building of mazes of such similar design over several millennia, from Denmark to South Africa, Spain to India?

The oldest and most famous European

Above: a visitor to a maze in an experiment conducted by designer Ralph Selby encounters confusing distortions of himself. Crawling through the complex two-storey maze, many of the participants reported experiencing a moment of heightened awareness when they realised that they could not easily find their way out. Some ancient mazes seem designed to produce the same feeling – perhaps as part of a religious ritual

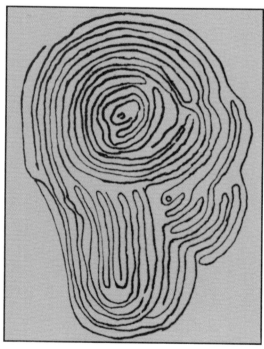

with him. Then, helped by Ariadne, they escaped to the harbour and sailed for home.

Such is the story of the Cretan labyrinth – but what was its purpose? According to the legendary narrative, the Cretan labyrinth was built simply to house the Minotaur. The existence of the monstrous creature, half man, half bull, wounded the pride of King Minos, for it was the offspring of his own Queen, Pasiphae. She had conceived a passion for, and mated with, a bull – again, with the help of the ingenious Daedalus, who built for Pasiphae a wooden cow, hidden in which she mated with the bull. Outraged, Minos had the labyrinth built to hide the Minotaur, the result of his wife's scandalous love affair.

There are, of course, some glaring absurdities in the labyrinth legend: since the victims from Athens were publicly rounded up as fodder for the Minotaur, the story that the labyrinth was built as an elaborate way of hiding the monster hardly seems to make any sense. And the narrative of the Cretan labyrinth may be concealing a deeper meaning. For a curiously similar maze tradition from South Africa seems to hint at some more universal significance: a popular Zulu game, played for hours at a time and often while smoking cannabis, is to draw a maze on the ground and to take turns at finding the 'king's hut' marked in the centre without hitting a dead end. Sometimes the game is played with toy armies in the shape of bulls' heads that have to march through the labyrinth to reach an adversary's starting point. Strangely enough, we find in this game, played thousands of miles south of Crete, the same disparate elements that appear in the Minoan legend – kingship, a bull's head and conflict in a labyrinth. We can hardly explain the Zulu myth in terms of King Minos's marital problems – clearly we are dealing

Below left: an Athenian vase of the sixth century BC showing Theseus killing the Minotaur, the bull-headed monster that was said to have been imprisoned in a vast maze, the labyrinth on Crete, by Minos, king of the island. According to legend, the Cretan labyrinth was copied from an original in Egypt, where a 'divine' bull (below: the emblem of the god Ptah-Seker-Asari) was ritually killed in place of the sacred pharaoh as a sacrifice for the state. The same disparate elements – the bull, kingship and struggle in a labyrinth – appear in a Zulu game from South Africa. A maze (below far left) is drawn, and toy armies of miniature bulls' heads are marched through it towards a 'king's hut' marked in the centre

where we may find a common origin for the Cretan and African labyrinths.

Ancient Greek writers actually stated that Daedalus had borrowed his 'invention' of the labyrinth from an original in northern Egypt. Little survives of it today except for a few fragmentary brick courses, but we are lucky enough to have an eyewitness description of its former splendour from the Greek traveller Herodotus, who visited Egypt in the fifth century BC. Somewhat overawed, he commented that 'it must have cost more in money and labour than all the walls and public work of the Greeks put together.' This enormous complex, built by Pharaoh Amenemhet around 1900 BC, consisted of some 3000 rooms, half of which were underground:

The upper rooms I saw with my own eyes and it is hard to believe they are the work of men; the numerous winding passages through the various courts were an endless wonder to me. I passed from small apartments to spacious halls, and from these to magnificent courts almost without end.

As for its purpose, Herodotus claimed the labyrinth was constructed as a meeting place

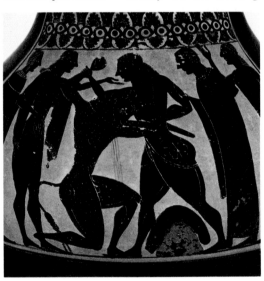

with rituals with much broader significance.

The deeper meanings of the labyrinth myth can be elucidated with the help of archaeology. Excavations at the Cretan capital of Knossos at the beginning of the 20th century uncovered evidence of a bull cult practised in a maze-like palace of hundreds of corridors, cloisters and chambers. Scenes on brightly coloured frescoes, dating from around 1400 BC, depict the famous 'bull dance' in which acrobats seized the animal's horns and somersaulted over its back. Tokens of bull worship, such as ceremonial horns, together with other Cretan myths linking the dynasty of Minos with bulls, strongly suggest that the vitality of the Minoan kings, like that of the pharaohs of ancient Egypt, was identified with a bull or bull-god. Thus the search for the source of the 'maze urge' appears to lead us to Egypt,

and burial ground for the Egyptian kings. This second, funerary, aspect seems to have been most important – there is archaeological evidence from as long ago as 3000 BC of labyrinths associated with royal tombs. Maze patterns on seals left in graves, convoluted architectural designs surrounding royal tombs and clues preserved in religious texts have been pieced together by Egyptologists to tell a story that may explain the Cretan and Zulu labyrinth traditions. In Egypt, as in many other ancient cultures (see page 1400), the sacred king seems to have been ritually 'killed' as a sacrifice for the state. The sacrifice was, however, only token – a 'divine' bull was substituted for the king in the culmination of several days of ritual dance, drama and combat performed in a labyrinth complex. A similar cult must lie behind the Cretan myth. The Minotaur – the 'bull of Minos' – would have been the representative of the kingship and power of Minos; and Theseus, by killing the bull and taking the king's daughter, was clearly claiming the throne.

In the opinion of ancient historian C. N. Deedes, who studied the evolution of the maze from ancient Egypt to medieval Europe, the plan and meaning of the labyrinth clearly originated in Egypt, where it was the scene of the religious dramas involved in 'killing' the god-king in the shape of a bull. Many other scholars would concur. But although this theory may explain why bull, king and labyrinth occur together in both Crete and Egypt, it does not really explain the importance and meaning of the labyrinth shape itself – or why the same

A labyrinth carved on a rock face in Rocky Valley, near Tintagel, Cornwall. Identical examples of this, perhaps the most widespread of all the basic maze patterns, are found on ancient coins from Knossos, as a sacred symbol among the Hopi Indians, and as a Manas-Chakra, a religious emblem, in Rajasthan, India

design is found all over the world.

While many archaeologists of the old-fashioned school that believed that all civilisations diffused from ancient Egypt might be content with the idea that the maze pattern and labyrinth cults were derived from Amenemhet's labyrinth, the sheer volume of evidence of an independent maze tradition in Europe suggests that this is not the whole truth. The Egyptian labyrinths were always composed of straight lines, and the abstract mazes on seals were usually made up of square fret patterns. Cretan coins from classical times often depict labyrinths, but while some seem to be of the Egyptian fretwork kind, the maze usually shown is of a quite different construction – the square or rounded spiral design of European tradition, never found in Egypt.

Troy mazes

The spiralling maze – the basic maze of Europe – consists of a series of interlocking concentric bands, often seven in number, with a straight line of exit running from the centre to the base. This is the form taken by practically all the ancient mazes of Europe, including all those known to have been centres of folk activity – festivals, dancing, games – presumably since prehistoric times. As late as the 19th century these mazes were being cut from turf by farmers and peasants in Scotland, Wales and Ireland. They are known locally as 'Troytowns' – for reasons that remain obscure. Spiral maze sites with names apparently derived from the word 'Troy' are found all over Europe – in Wales, England, Italy, Germany, Sweden, Norway and Russia. The Scandinavian examples are usually built from rounded stones set into the ground and are often found by the coast; they are perhaps connected with the megalithic cultures of prehistoric Europe.

These megalithic cultures, it is now widely accepted, developed independently of influence from the ancient Near East and Egypt, and radiocarbon dates now show that many of our oldest megalithic henges and chambered tombs date from between 5000 and 3500 BC, *before* the first flowering of Egyptian civilisation. Since there is absolutely nothing Egyptian about the Troy mazes – and every reason to see them as a part of our megalithic heritage, like Stonehenge or Avebury – any idea of an Egyptian origin must be abandoned. This reasoning is amply confirmed by the spiral symbols, some of them approaching the spiral labyrinth shapes of the later Troy mazes, found carved on the earliest megalithic monuments of Europe. Most of these spiral shapes, strangely enough, are found at tomb sites, such as the magnificent chambered tomb of Newgrange, Ireland, the walls of which are spattered with spiral carvings.

Here, in the maze-like spirals of the megalithic tombs and the labyrinthine structures of Egyptian royal tombs, we find that

Left: a turf maze – untended but still just discernible – at Alkborough, Humberside, and a spiral detail (below) from a kerbstone in the Newgrange passage grave in County Meath, Ireland. The same spiral motif appears in the Nazcan desert lines (bottom) in Peru

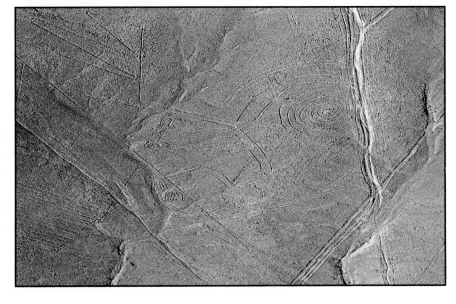

two independent aspects of the maze puzzle meet – and that what they have in common is human mortality. What did Theseus find and conquer in the Cretan labyrinth? One obvious answer is death. So was the labyrinth, first and foremost, a symbol of the underworld? Perhaps it was: another Greek myth shows Theseus to be one of the few heroes of the ancient world to have visited Hades and returned. The point that Theseus returned is important. The Egyptian 'killing' of the pharaoh-god, incarnate as a bull, in a labyrinthine structure representing the prison-like underworld, was a ritual meant to ensure the revitalisation rather than destruction of the king's power. Like the god Osiris, he would descend into the land of the dead (at least by proxy, in the form of a bull), only to be resurrected.

From the ancient perspective, the maze was an excellent symbol of the nether world. Once in it, ordinary mortals would be trapped and die; but the initiated could return from the depths and conquer death. The basic maze of Europe and Crete may have been a map of the underworld, but it was essentially a spiral that turned back upon itself, symbolising a return from whatever lay at the centre – even if the way was difficult and hidden. In pre-Christian times, the maze spiral appears to have been used as a symbol of resurrection. But whatever its symbolism, one question remains: why was the maze shape chosen, over again, as a symbol of the meeting of life and death?

A visit to Troytown

Mazes all over Europe, of a curiously similar design, bear the name 'Troy'. Is there a connection with the classical city – or is the link to be found still further back in history? PETER JAMES examines this intriguing aspect of the mystery of the labyrinth

THE NAME OF TROY usually conjures up romantic images of the 10 years' struggle between the Greeks and Trojans over the infamously beautiful Helen. This was the Troy immortalised in the epic poetry of Homer. Yet, strangely, the defeated city also seems to have been commemorated in the names of dozens of places scattered over the map of Europe. Often called 'Troytowns', these places are generally not human settlements but mazes, marked out on the ground with stones or lines of turf that, as far as we can judge, may be remnants of a tradition dating back to the megalithic cultures of prehistoric Europe. But why were they built, and what possible connection can the mazes of rural Europe have with the Troy of classical legend?

The fragments of traditional lore still associated with the British and continental 'Troytowns' are sparse and tantalising. We have records of the seasonal cutting of so-called 'walls of Troy' from pieces of turf by Welsh shepherds in the 18th century, but no indication of why this was done. In some parts of Britain there was certainly a custom of running the maze; for example, it was said locally at Breamore in Hampshire that one person could run from the 'Mizmaze' there to Gallows Hill some half a mile (800 metres) away and back again in the time that it took another runner to complete the circuit of the maze. The 'Shepherds' Ring' or 'Shepherds' Race' at Boughton Green, Northamptonshire, was once the site of a popular midsummer fair in which the main event was the custom of 'treading' the maze, which was presumably a race of some kind. Other mazes are situated near abbeys – but which is older, the abbey or the maze? The abbey mazes are thought to have had a purely devotional function, providing the monks with a secluded path through which to meander during their meditations.

Few of these local traditions have any real substance to them. Rather, the memories that have survived concerning the 'Troytowns' are relics that merely hint of old customs and beliefs without providing any concrete insights. The well-known 18th-century antiquarian William Stukeley commented scathingly: 'The lovers of antiquity, particularly of the inferior class, always speak of 'em with great pleasure as if there was something extraordinary in the thing, tho' they cannot tell what.'

A clue to the original customs performed at the mazes, as well as the Troy association, seems to come from the *Aeneid* by the Roman poet Virgil, who was active in the first century BC. According to legend, the foundations of the later Rome were laid by the fugitive Trojan prince Aeneas, and Rome was the spiritual successor to Troy. A curious passage in the *Aeneid* describes how the hero's son Ascanius led a ceremonial dance of the Trojan youths, in which the weaving, spiralling movements were said to represent the twists and turns of the Cretan labyrinth. This *Troia* or 'Troy game' was performed

Right: stages of development in one of the commonest maze patterns, found in exactly the same form throughout the world. It has been proposed that the shape may be in some way archetypal – a suggestion borne out by an experience related by Geoffrey Russell. One night in 1944 he awoke from sleep with a compulsion to note on paper a design of which he had just dreamed. Over 20 years later he realised the design was the basic maze pattern

The basic maze pattern, in varying degrees of complexity, repeats itself: the turf maze at Troy Farm, Somerton, Oxfordshire (above); the 'City of Troy' turf maze in Brandsby cum Stearsby parish in North Yorkshire (right); and the Troy maze on St Agnes, Scilly Isles (above right), in 1885, with the deserted wreck of the *Earl of Lonsdale* behind it. The recurrence of the name 'Troy' is striking – but can it really indicate a link with the classical city of Troy?

that the more ancient civilisations of Troy itself had enough influence to stamp its name and customs on prehistoric Europe, seems hopelessly far-fetched, and there is no evidence to support it.

Perhaps, then, the association with Troy is mistaken, becoming linked with the spiral-shaped mazes of Europe after knowledge of Homer's epics had been spread through Europe by the Romans. But why should the name Troy have been chosen for mazes? Troy, unlike Knossos (see page 1639), was never the site of a famous labyrinth. And can we seriously argue that shepherds and peasants throughout Europe were so well-versed in the classics that they were impelled to commemorate the name of Troy by attaching it to their traditional maze sites?

The only possible solution of the problem is that the association with Troy is as old as the mazes themselves and that there is no connection with the famous Homeric city. This conclusion has been reached by most linguists who have tackled the 'Troytown' problem. The reality seems to be that the

Above left: an Etruscan terracotta wine-jar from around 600 BC, found in Tragliatella, Italy. It shows a warrior on horseback trailing behind him an unmistakable maze shape identical to the 'Troytown' maze designs that are to be found throughout Europe. In the outside layer of the maze stands the word TRUIA. All the clues seem to point to a link between mazes and the city of Troy – but experts believe that the word comes from an ancient Indo-European root meaning 'turning', 'winding' or 'spiralling'

annually at Rome, and evidently became a religious ritual of great importance. As described by the classical scholar Jackson Knight 'the Troia must have been intended to create a magical field of exclusive force, an abstract defensive entanglement.' One illustration of the ritual, on an Etruscan vase dating from around 600 BC, shows a line of warriors, some on horseback and some on foot, trailing behind them an unmistakable maze shape identical to the 'Troytown' labyrinths of Europe. In the last fold of the spiralling maze stands the word TRUIA.

It is easy to infer from all this that the ancient 'Troytowns' were built as centres for the Roman spiralling dance that commemorated the ancestral city of Troy, but such a picture would yield little sense. How could the Romans have spread the 'Troy' maze shape when the oldest spiral and maze patterns are thousands of years older than the Roman Empire? The alternative hypothesis,

names are derived from words in Indo-European languages meaning 'to turn' – such as the Latin *troare* the the Celtic root *-tro*. Thus the maze known in Wales as 'Gaer Droia' does not signify the 'Castle of Troy', but the 'Castle of Turnings', or 'Turning Castle', an apt enough description of the spiral ground maze. The Roman *Troia* ritual, likewise, may have been named after the spiralling motions of the magical dance, and the connection with Troy may simply be an erudite mistake on the part of the Romans themselves.

Thus the theory that mazes have anything to do with the city of Troy proves to be as much a dead end as the idea that all mazes were derived from an ancient Egyptian labyrinth (see page 1639). It would seem more likely that the maze design arose independently in several different areas. This conclusion seems unavoidable in view of the geographical extent of the basic spiral maze pattern, which is far more widespread than is generally recognised in academic texts concerning the architectural development of the labyrinth. The same maze shape occurs not only on the classical Cretan coins showing the labyrinth of Minos, but also occurs as a sacred symbol in ancient Rajasthan, India, and even in the New World with the Hopi Indians and among the patterns included in the Nazca desert drawings of Peru (see page 2002).

Attempts have been made to understand the recurrence of the basic maze pattern in terms of psychological archetypes of the kind envisaged by Carl Jung (see page 1580). An experience related by Geoffrey Russell certainly suggests that the maze design can drift into the human unconscious in a most unexpected way. One day in 1944 he awoke from a dream with the compulsive urge to commit a certain pattern to paper. Nearly two decades later he realised that the drawing, which he had filed in his papers, was identical in design to ancient mazes from both Tintagel in Cornwall and a pattern that appears on the coins of ancient Crete.

Seventh heaven

A unifying theme that lies behind all the ancient mazes and labyrinths is their use as a symbol of the nether world, death and resurrection (see page 1641). Even in ancient Babylonia, where there were no labyrinths as such, similar ideas seem to have lain behind the use of the spiral shape. The original Tower of Babel, the Etemenanki of Babylon, was a seven-tier mass of brickwork with a spiral stairway. Its upper half – the seven visible tiers – was thought to symbolise the stages of the upper world of heaven. (Today we still talk of 'seventh heaven', unwittingly following Babylonian tradition.) The subterranean half of Etemenanki (actually largely imaginary) was supposed to mirror the upper part and extend down to the bowels of the underworld, in a seven-level spiral structure similar to the model world above.

Mazes have, as often as not, seven sets of curves around a central point. If the labyrinth is indeed a symbol of death and resurrection, this recurrence of the number seven forms a striking parallel to the seven-layered underworld of Babylonian thought. Similarly, in an Old Welsh poem *The spoils of Annwm*, telling of a raid by King Arthur and his warriors on a fairyland or underworld, the refrain stresses the fact that only seven men returned. The link with maze mythology is assured by the name given to this otherworld – Caer Sidi or 'Spiral Castle', curiously similar to Caer Droia or 'Turning Castle'. Writer Geoffrey Ashe made a brave attempt to explain the persistent elements behind all these traditions – spiral and circle, maze, underworld and the number seven – by proposing a novel theory in which the 'ancient wisdom' behind the old myths is derived from an original centre of mysticism

Right: the Rollright circle of standing stones in Oxfordshire. Members of the Dragon Project (below) have found spiral 'lines of force' along the surfaces of the stones; and Charles Brooker, in a report published in *New Scientist* in January 1983, told of an experiment in which he had used a gaussmeter to confirm the existence of 'lines of force' spiralling outwards from the centre (below right), sensed by a dowser

in the Altai mountains of central Asia. But Ashe's concept of a repository of abstract occult knowledge in prehistoric times does not explain anything; Ashe finds nothing more significant behind the awe in which the number seven is held than a suggested association with the constellation of Pleiades. Something more potent and vital, surely, must have lain behind the 'maze urge'. Ashe himself perhaps points the way when he describes the seven-fold maze as 'an association of "charged" centrality with hard or roundabout access'. Could the circular design of many of the mazes, suggestive of the spiral, have been symbolic of an actual force sensed by ancient Man?

The idea that maze building involved ancient sensitivity to an unknown form of energy was put forward in the 1960s by Guy

Underwood, a dowser whose extensive field work included all the major prehistoric monuments of Britain. Underwood claimed he could detect a lingering energy field rippling through the Earth's surface. This geodetic force channelled itself through underground streams, and prehistoric Man chose to place his sacred sites at their confluences (see page 1697). With regard to the maze lore of the ancient world, Underwood's crucial claim was that the mysterious geodetic force often formed spiral shapes under standing stones and stone rings that, through some natural law, twisted into multiples of seven coils.

Underwood's work was idiosyncratic, to say the least, and the word of one dowser alone is, of course, insufficient reason to consider the maze problem solved. But Underwood's claims are backed by dozens of other dowsers for whom the tingling sensations produced by an invisible force at megalithic sites are commonplace. The force, as magnetometer experiments have shown, appears to be part of the Earth's magnetic field. In 1979 an extraordinary, and successful, experiment was carried out on a standing stone by writer Francis Hitching, mathematics professor John Taylor and Bill Lewis, one of Britain's most capable dowsers

(see page 1707). Lewis's claim that he could detect a band of force spiralling up the stone in seven coils was apparently confirmed by the readings of a gaussmeter, which registered anomalously high magnetic strengths at the points where Lewis had marked the stone.

Early in 1983 *New Scientist* carried a report of some even more startling results achieved by engineer Charles Brooker at the Rollright Stones in Oxfordshire. Using a magnetometer, Brooker found distinct fluctuations in the geomagnetic field within the stone circle and was surprised to find that a local dowser also 'reported tingling sensations exactly where the recording magnetometer produced blips on the chart'. Brooker then conducted a more detailed survey and discovered that the 'magnetic pattern inside the stone circle forms a seven ring spiral, broadening as it moves outward until it leaves the circle. . . .' Brooker's conclusion – though he remains baffled by the implications – is that the stone circles were deliberately set up as 'magnetic refuges – Stone Age Faraday cages'. Here we find the idea of containment or protection that is so conspicuous in the maze symbol.

Maze urge

The idea that the ancients were aware of a force as subtle as the Earth's magnetic field seems bizarre from a 20th-century perspective. Yet Brooker's discovery – and there is no good reason to doubt it – of a seven-ring magnetic field at Rollright provides the first neat explanation for the 'maze urge', tying together the spiral shape, the underworld connotations (perhaps derived from the magnetic forces inside the Earth), the standing stones and the ubiquitous number seven. No other force or idea has been suggested that makes such coherent sense of all the strands in the maze puzzle. We are obliged to consider the idea that some understanding of the Earth's magnetic field lay behind the maze cult and, more generally, the ancient fascination with spirals of seven coils.

Were the spiralling maze-like dances such as the *Troia* performed and the spiral and circular structures built simply to imitate geomagnetic eddies – or, as appears to be the case at Rollright, to contain and control them? What significance did the geomagnetic field have to the ancients, that it evoked such important symbols of life and death? What precisely the ancients knew, or how they used or hoped to use geomagnetic forces is, for the present, unfathomable. The spiral forms manifested by the Earth's field are only now being rediscovered with the aid of magnetometers and the pioneering work of scientists like Brooker. The ancient maze patterns, as well as being eloquent symbols of ancient cosmology and ritual, may well be evidence of an older and more intimate acquaintance than our own with the magnetic forces inherent in the Earth.

0 metres 5
0 yards 5

North Mag True

Below: the 'Shepherd's Ring' maze at Boughton Green, Northamptonshire, once the site of a midsummer fair in which the main event was 'treading' the maze – presumably some kind of race. The inside of the maze is spiral in shape, the outer parts taking the form of concentric circles. Not all mazes are, strictly speaking, spiral; however, scientific research such as Booker's suggests that they are all built to imitate, or perhaps to control, the local geomagnetic field

Further reading
Adrian Fisher, *Labyrinth: solving the riddle of the maze*, Crown 1990
W. H. Matthews, *Mazes and labyrinths*, Dover 1970
Jill Purce, *The mystic spiral*, Peter Smith 1983

Bizarre dreams of a gallows that would not work haunted both the convicted man and his executioner in the Victorian Babbacombe murder case. FRANK SMYTH relates the strange story of the man who could not be hanged

James Berry, the hangman who failed to execute John Lee. In the 19th century most hangmen worked as freelances, receiving their commissions from local county sheriffs, who were the officers charged with carrying out the death sentence. Berry worked as an executioner from 1884 to 1892 and during that time executed 134 men and women

called them 'dreams of things that never will be, and which is (*sic*) impossible.'

What distressed him most about these dreams was that they concerned the failure of his equipment. In the worst one, he stood on the gallows desperately working the lever that released the trapdoor for the fatal drop – but the trap stayed shut.

By the strangest of coincidences, the dream that so shook Berry gave sublime confidence to a man named John Lee, who was to dream it too.

In the late autumn of 1884, Berry came across the name John Lee in the columns of his local newspaper. Lee had been accused of killing Miss Emma Ann Whitehead Keyse, a former maid of honour as well as a friend to Queen Victoria. She was found battered to death, her oil-soaked clothing on fire, in her dining room on the night of 15 November 1884. Among her servants at The Glen, the house where she lived in Babbacombe in Devon, were 19-year-old John Lee, her footman, and his half-sister, Elizabeth Harris, the cook. It was Elizabeth Harris who gave the alarm and was the principal witness at the Exeter Assizes the next month.

Lee, the court was told, was a convicted petty thief who had been hired by the kindly rich woman at a wage of four shillings a week. Lee had come under suspicion of theft again and, though Emma Keyse had given him another chance, she had docked his wages by half. On the night of the murder, Elizabeth

Third time lucky

ON THE NIGHT BEFORE he became a public hangman, James Berry began to suffer from bad dreams. This upset him the more because, as he repeatedly asserted, his waking conscience was clear. The stocky, 32-year-old Yorkshireman was the son of a woollen worker who had a profound belief in Methodism and law and order. Berry inherited these beliefs, and so chose the police force as his first career.

During his 10 years as a constable in the West Riding, Berry had become friendly with William Marwood, executioner to the City of London and County of Middlesex, and had learned most of the tricks of the trade from him. When the old man died in September 1883, Berry, having left the police force, applied for the post. He did not get it. Indeed, he did not receive his first hanging commission until March 1884: he was to hang two men at Calton Prison, Edinburgh, for a fee of 20 guineas (£21), a second-class return rail ticket from his home in Bradford, Yorkshire, and his board and lodging. As he lay waiting for the dawn of that first assignment, the dreams began.

Berry later refused to use the word 'nightmare' to describe his unsettling visions. He

The scene of the murder at Babbacombe, Devon, shown in a contemporary engraving (right) and in a modern photograph (far right). Miss Keyse, the murdered mistress of the villa known as The Glen, was an austere, wealthy and God-fearing woman who regarded her servants as children for whom she was responsible

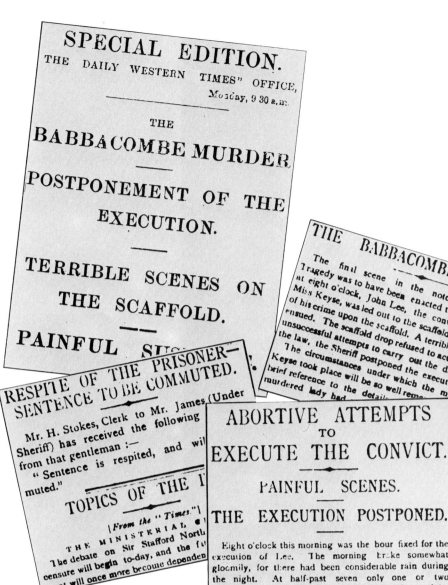

SPECIAL EDITION.

THE "DAILY WESTERN TIMES" OFFICE,
Monday, 9 30 a.m.

THE

BABBACOMBE MURDER

POSTPONEMENT OF THE
EXECUTION.

TERRIBLE SCENES ON
THE SCAFFOLD.

PAINFUL SUS...

RESPITE OF THE PRISONER—
SENTENCE TO BE COMMUTED.

Mr. H. Stokes, Clerk to Mr. James (Under Sheriff) has received the following from that gentleman :—
"Sentence is respited, and wil muted."

TOPICS OF THE T...

[From the "Times."]
THE MINISTERIAL ...
The debate on Sir Stafford North censure will begin to-day, and the fu ment will once more become dependen

THE BABBACOMBE MURDER.

The final scene in the notorious Babbacombe Tragedy was to have been enacted this morning, when, at eight o'clock, John Lee, the convicted murderer of Miss Keyse, was led out to the scaffold to pay the penalty of his crime upon the scaffold. A terrible scene, however, ensued. The scaffold drop refused to act, and after three unsuccessful attempts to carry out the dread sentence of the law, the Sheriff postponed the execution.

The circumstances under which the murder of Miss Keyse took place will be so well reme... brief reference to the detai... murdered lady had ... that only a ... usary. The ... t a house

ABORTIVE ATTEMPTS
TO
EXECUTE THE CONVICT.

PAINFUL SCENES.

THE EXECUTION POSTPONED.

Eight o'clock this morning was the hour fixed for the execution of Lee. The morning broke somewhat gloomily, for there had been considerable rain during the night. At half-past seven only one or two loiterers were to be observed in the neighbourhood of the

faint at the horrible sight. When he faced the village constable he said tearfully: 'I have lost my best friend.'

During the police investigation, a great deal of circumstantial evidence built up against Lee. His clothing was bloodstained and hairs like those of his employer were found on it; the knife and chopper he had used were bloodstained too. The maid he had caught in a faint found bloodstains on her nightdress where he had touched her. And a can of lamp oil, which his half-sister said should have been full, was found empty in his pantry. The very proximity of the pantry

Left: headlines from the local press carrying news of the abortive execution – and granting of respite – on 23 February 1885. Later the same week the *Devon Evening Express* published a letter written by Lee to his family before his 'execution' in which he said, 'They have not told six words truth, that is, the servants and that lovely step-sister who carries her character with her'

to the murder scene told against him.

On the other hand, Lee had made no attempt to escape, though he probably had ample time before the alarm was raised. He had helped to carry his mistress's body, which might well account for the bloodstains and hairs found on his own clothing. Some of the stains could easily have been Lee's own, since he had gashed his hand while smashing the window to let out smoke; those on the maid's nightdress and on the knife and chopper were almost certainly his. And, although the chopper may have been used in the murder, equally it may not have been.

Lee repeatedly swore his innocence, but the prosecution claimed he had a motive: he had killed his employer because she had cut

Harris said, she had awoken in her smoke-filled room, made her way to the dining room and found the body.

Her mistress's head had been battered in and her body doused in lamp oil and ignited in an apparent attempt to hide the crime. According to the cook's testimony, Lee had emerged from his pantry adjoining the dining room, smashed a window to let out the smoke and cut away burning wood and fabrics with a knife and chopper. He had steadied one of the maids, who had become

his paltry wages in half. In vain the defence pointed out that two shillings were better than none, and that Lee and the whole household were thrown out of work by Emma Keyse's death. Nevertheless the jury found Lee guilty. Asked if he had anything to say before sentence was passed, Lee drew himself upright in the dock and said calmly: 'I am innocent. The Lord will never permit me to be executed.'

Later there were murmurings that Lee's half-sister, whose evidence against him was so important, had been seeing a lover. In the prim Emma Keyse's household, this would have been a far worse offence than petty theft, and instant dismissal would probably have been Elizabeth Harris's lot. Perhaps, the rumours went, she had been discovered with her lover by her employer, and he had struck out in panic – leaving Elizabeth Harris to eradicate the crime by lighting the fire. Whatever the truth, such conjecture came too late to help Lee.

James Berry was nearing the end of his first full year as an executioner and, with about a dozen successful hangings to his credit, he felt that he might be called upon in the Lee case. And in the first week of February he received an official commission from Henry M. James, under sheriff of Devonshire, to hang John Lee at Exeter jail for the murder of Emma Ann Whitehead Keyse. The sentence was to be carried out at 8 a.m. on Monday 23 February 1885. Berry arrived at Exeter two days before.

Machinery of death

On the night before the execution, Berry pointed out what he considered to be short-comings in the scaffold's machinery of death. He told the prison governor that the leaves of the oak trapdoor were too light; that spring clips should be set in the walls of the pit beneath to catch the doors as they fell open; that the iron strips edging the doors were too thin and that the bolts holding the trap shut were badly adjusted. The governor explained that the scaffold had been moved and re-erected by a gang of convicts, but had been used without any problems a few months before. Using a sandbag weighing the same as Lee, Berry tested the lever several times, and each time the trapdoor dropped perfectly.

Later that night, Lee had a final interview with the prison governor and the chaplain. The governor told him that there was no possibility of a reprieve. Lee merely shrugged, reasserted his innocence and added mysteriously: 'Elizabeth Harris could say the word which could clear me, if she would.' Both men noted Lee's coolness.

On the morning of the execution, Berry was disturbed to learn about Lee's dream of the night before: his own uneasy vision from another angle. For Lee had dreamed that he was standing on the gallows with the noose around his neck – and the trapdoor did not

fall when the hangman pulled the lever. Lee had laughed when he told his dream, saying: 'You see, I shan't be hanged today. You will never hang me. You wait and see.'

When Berry entered the condemned cell at 7.56 a.m., Lee rose from his bunk to meet him, rather pale but calm – as Berry put it later, 'the coolest customer I ever handled'. Berry, Lee, the governor and four warders set out across the prison yard, preceded by the chaplain reading the service. At the door of the shed housing the scaffold, they were met by the under sheriff and the prison surgeon. Ten newspaper reporters watched from positions by the shed windows. According to some of their reports, as Lee entered the shed a white dove alighted on the roof and then flew over the prison walls.

The grim party ascended the steps of the gallows. Berry led Lee to the centre of the trap, strapped his legs together below the knee, fixed the noose around his neck and placed the white hood over his head. The chaplain faced him. The hangman then stepped back, kicked out the restraining pin and pulled the lever. The rattle of the bolts being drawn was heard – but the trap failed to fall.

It was the moment that both Berry and Lee had lived before in their dreams. For a few seconds Berry gaped at the fully drawn lever under his hand, and then he moved forward and stamped on the trapdoors. They remained firmly closed. Two warders joined him, thumping on the traps with their heavy boots.

Six minutes elapsed before Berry –

Below: a modern artist's impression of the scaffold in Exeter jail (left), where John Lee's execution was to take place. The gallows was contained in an old coach shed in the prison yard. A heavy beam had been let into the brickwork at either end of the shed and an iron eye bolt set into the centre of the beam to take the rope. Directly under this a platform had been built with a double-leaved trapdoor in its centre. The trap was held shut by two iron bolts running underneath it; these were withdrawn when a lever on the platform (normally held in the safe position by a metal pin) was drawn back. The key words used by the hangman were 'straps, noose, hood, pin, lever, drop' and if all went smoothly the whole thing could be over in 12 seconds from the moment the condemned man stepped onto the trap

'clearly shaken', as the reports said – took off the hood and noose from Lee, who was 'ashen, but not whiter than some of the witnesses'. He was led off while Berry tested the trap with the sandbag again: it worked perfectly.

Lee was brought back, and this time Berry yanked the lever back with such force that it bent under his weight. But the doors remained firm under Lee's feet. For the next 20 minutes, Berry, the carpenter and the prison engineer worked on the scaffold and tested it repeatedly. They greased the bolts, planed the doors, and were finally satisfied.

Back came Lee and the chaplain. As the latter recalled: 'The lever was pulled again and again. A great noise was heard, which sounded like the falling of the drop. But to my horror, when I turned my eyes to the scaffold, I saw the poor convict standing upon the drop as I had seen him twice before. I refused to stay any longer.' In fact the

Above: a contemporary engraving of a public execution, a macabre relic of medieval England that persisted until 1868. After that time executions were carried out within the prison, with only official witnesses present

chaplain buckled at the knees and was caught by a warder, then led off the gallows with Lee. Everyone was in a tremulous state and some of the warders were in tears. But John Lee kept his composure.

A messenger was sent to London to report to the Home Secretary. Meanwhile, Lee was asked if there was anything he would like and he said that he could eat another 'last' breakfast. He ate the huge repast ordered for Berry, who had lost his appetite completely.

That evening a telegram arrived from the Home Secretary granting Lee a respite, and his sentence was subsequently commuted to life imprisonment. Berry too began a life sentence of a kind: not only did his dream of the jammed trapdoor recur more frequently, but he had to face constant questions about the Lee affair from everyone.

A lucky escape?

The most plausible explanation for the jammed trapdoor was not put forward until 40 years later, when most of the principals were dead. This theory was that a fault in the construction of the platform had caused the problem: a plank of wood, set edge on to the trapdoors, had been warped and therefore arched upwards in the middle. When the chaplain stood on it opposite Lee to read the prayers, the plank straightened out and jammed under the hinged side of the trap. When the sandbag was used for testing, the chaplain was absent and the trap worked.

But how could the plank withstand the violent stamping of three men? And if it were the true explanation, Lee's escape would be even more remarkable: for if he had not been moved at exactly the same time as the chaplain, the chances are that the trap mechanism would have worked.

Lee served 20 years in prison. Shortly after he came out in 1905 he married a woman who had apparently waited for him, and the couple went to the United States. There he died in 1933. He declared his innocence to the end of his life, and insisted that divine intervention had saved him.

As for Berry, the fiasco at Exeter had one personal satisfaction: he was invited to collaborate with Lieutenant-Colonel Alten Beamish, Royal Engineers, who was attached to the surveyor's department of the Home Office, in designing a 'standard' gallows. Their design was fitted in British prisons until the abolition of the death penalty for murder in the late 1960s.

Long before his own death in 1913, however, Berry had turned strongly against capital punishment. But though he had turned to religion with renewed fervour, he spurned the theory of divine intervention for Lee's miraculous escape from the gallows. For, he would ask, why should God intervene for Lee and not for the many other almost certainly innocent victims among the 134 men and women he had hanged in eight years as a public executioner?

Left: Buddha teaches his disciples. The teachings of many Eastern religions have an essentially non-intellectual character highly at odds with the analytical approach prevalent in the West. But modern neurological research has found that we all possess two brains – one intuitive and non-intellectual, the other rational and analytical. At what cost has the West suppressed the intuitive brain – or the East the rational?

In two minds

Science has revealed that the human brain is split in two – that, quite literally, we all have two independent brains. BRIAN BAXTER describes the different roles of our two minds – and explores the far-reaching implications of this extraordinary discovery

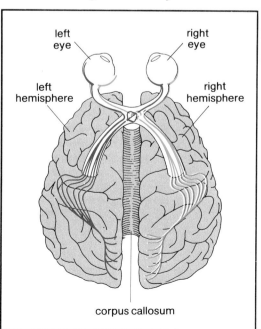

left eye

right eye

left hemisphere

right hemisphere

corpus callosum

ONE OF THE GREATEST ACHIEVEMENTS of the famous French mathematician Henri Poincaré (1854–1912) was the resolution of a difficult mathematical problem concerning what he called 'Fuchsian functions'. He says in his memoirs that he studied the problem diligently and logically for some time but failed to get a suitable answer. In the midst of intensive mathematical work on the problem, he took a short break to go on a geological excursion, where the excitement of the travel made him forget all about mathematics. So, with his mind full of geology rather than Fuchsian functions, he waited for the bus that was to take him on a field visit. The bus arrived – and suddenly, as he boarded it, the solution to his problem came to him in a kind of intuitive, unthinking flash. He was so confident that he had got the right answer that he did not bother to verify his intuitive insight until he had returned from the excursion. His insight, which turned out to be absolutely correct, had succeeded where logic had failed.

There are many instances in history of 'flashes of insight' – many of them occurring in dreams (see page 780) – suddenly providing a person who is worrying over some problem or other with the correct solution. What is especially interesting is that these insights often occur when the person concerned is not *consciously* thinking about the problem. It is as if, by 'letting go' and

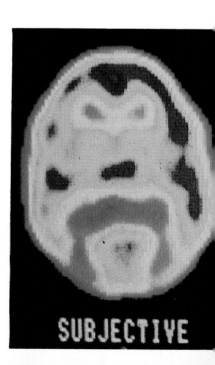

SUBJECTIVE

Mysterious powers that lie hidden in our right brain may prove to be the origin of a whole range of experiences that defy rational explanation. Among them are the abilities that we call psychic – for there are indications that psychic activity is left-brain activity.

Water diviners, for instance, often dowse in a relaxed, almost trance-like state in which the left brain does not assert its dominance and the right brain can act freely. It is possible that the right brain recognises the presence of water and causes the arm muscles to contract involuntarily, making the dowsing rod move. The involvement of the right brain in psychic abilities may explain,

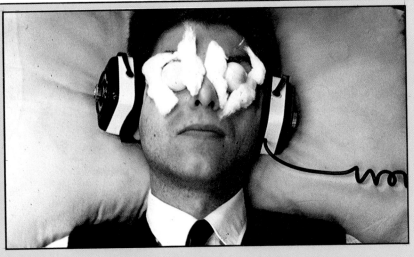

Sinister purposes

An 18th-century water diviner (left) and the subject of a Ganzfeld telepathy test at the University of Cambridge (above). Are both dowsing and telepathy controlled by the right brain?

too, why phenomena like metal bending, telepathy and clairvoyance are so notoriously difficult to reproduce in the laboratory: the scientific environment of the laboratory may repress psychic abilities by accentuating the dominance of the left brain at the expense of the right brain.

There is another startling possibility. Perhaps telepathy – apparently an elusive ability that surfaces only fitfully – is actually simply the way our right brains speak to each other. To restore the balance between left and right brains might be to restore an ability latent in everyone to communicate by telepathy.

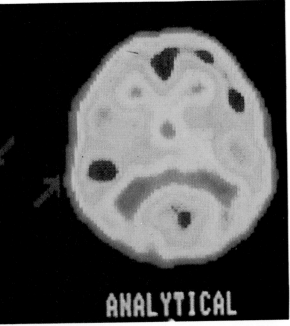

ANALYTICAL

Far left: a section through the human brain. The brain is made up of two distinct halves linked by a 'bridge' of around 200 million nerve fibres called the *corpus callosum*. The left hemisphere controls most of the right-hand side of the body, while the right hemisphere controls most of the left-hand side. The two hemispheres have different cognitive functions: broadly, the analytical functions occur in the 'left brain' while the intuitive functions occur in the 'right brain'. These brain scans (left) were taken while the subject was listening to music. In the scan on the left he is reacting intuitively and subjectively – and the neural activity is predominantly in the right brain. In the scan on the right he is listening more analytically – and the main neural activity has shifted to the left hemisphere of the brain

allowing itself to wander away from strictly logical thinking, the brain can provide the answers through intuitive insight.

Does Poincaré's experience, and others like it, mean that the brain can work in two distinct ways – either under our conscious control, thinking logically in a systematic, step-by-step way, or intuitively, without our conscious control?

The answer, according to a growing number of physiologists and psychologists, appears to be 'yes'. That is, our brain does seem to operate both logically and intuitively – and will oscillate between these two distinct forms of behaviour according to circumstances.

Work carried out by anatomists and neurophysiologists, who study the brain and its functions, supports these bold claims. Anatomically, we know that the human body is roughly *bilaterally symmetrical*. It is possible to draw an imaginary line through the middle of a person bisecting the nose and ending between the feet and, with a few rather important exceptions – such as the heart – the right side of the body is a mirror image of the left. On a general anatomical level, this holds true for the brain. Looked at from above, the brain is made up of two cerebral hemispheres. Joining these two hemispheres is a bridge of about 200 million nerve fibres called the *corpus callosum*. This structure is one of several *commissures* or bundles of nerve fibres linking equivalent centres on the two sides of the brain. Now, although each hemisphere of the brain appears to be the approximate mirror image of the other, this is not the case: when the hemispheres are examined more closely, profound differences emerge between the functions of the left and right sides.

There are, of course, other instances of seemingly symmetrical parts of our body that, although they mirror each other anatomically, are actually rather different functionally. The most obvious example is our hands: 90 per cent of people write using their right hand. Right-handed individuals are termed 'right-hand dominant'. In these people, the left hand is termed the 'minor' hand. The 10 per cent of people who write with their left hand are thus called 'left-hand dominant'.

The two hemispheres of the brain also show this 'dominant-minor' distinction, but in this case the *left* side of the brain is usually the dominant side (for 96 to 98 per cent of the population) with the right hemisphere taking the 'minor' role.

It may seem curious at first that, although the *left* hemisphere of the brain is dominant, it is the *right* hand, in most people, that is dominant. But there is a straightforward anatomical explanation: in the hind-brain (the rearmost part of the brain, continuous with the upper end of the spinal cord) many bundles of nerve fibres 'decussate' – cross over – from right to left, and vice versa. This decussation of fibres is responsible for the fact that the left side of the brain generally controls the right side of the body, and vice versa. So the dominant left hemisphere of the brain controls the dominant right hand.

The roots of dexterity

But what does it mean to say that the left hemisphere of the brain is dominant? Dominance in a hand is quite clear. It is stronger, more dextrous – the word itself comes from the Latin *dexter*, meaning the right side – and, for most people, the hand they write with. The brain, however, encased in its hard skull, is much more of an enigma. Perhaps not surprisingly, it was not until 1844 that it was proposed – by A. L. Wigan, in his book *The duality of mind* – that the fact that the brain has two hemispheres might mean that people have two separate minds. This idea – which was then extremely controversial – was suggested to Wigan by a post-mortem examination he carried out on a man with no history of mental illness, whose brain turned out to have only one hemisphere. The fact that half his brain was missing had apparently had no noticeable effect during his life.

This was the first recorded instance of extreme one-hemisphere dominance. Although more recent anatomical evidence

has been less dramatic, neurophysiologists probing the brain have found many examples in which one hemisphere dominates the other in specific ranges of functions.

One important method of examining the functions of the two sides of the brain is 'split-brain' research. Splitting the brain means carrying out a commissurotomy – that is, cutting the corpus callosum which, as we have seen, is a thick bundle of nerve fibres connecting the two halves of the brain. Originally, this rather drastic-sounding treatment was carried out, in the early 1960s, by Joseph Bogen of California to ease the pain of sufferers of extreme fits of epilepsy. By cutting the corpus callosum and the anterior commissure, another bunch of nerve fibres joining the two hemispheres of the brain, epileptic seizures were kept from spreading from one side to the other. The patients who underwent this surgery stopped having fits and in every respect appeared quite normal.

This fact was a source of puzzlement to neurophysiologists, because they could not understand why this major surgery apparently had no negative effects on the patients. Perhaps A. L. Wigan was right: perhaps after all, humans did have two separate minds, and cutting the connecting links simply enhanced their independence.

However, it was not until R. W. Sperry and his colleagues at the California Institute of Technology started studying 'split-brain' effects in cats and monkeys and then extended their research to 'split-brain' humans that some curious anomalies in behaviour emerged. Sperry and his fellow researchers had reasoned that cutting the human corpus callosum meant that the speech and writing

Above: a 17th-century engraving showing magicians in concert. Western society regards magic as *sinister* – from the Latin for left-sided – perhaps because it apparently has no rational foundation

Below: the sacred boat of the Egyptian goddess Isis sails through the night. Processions in honour of Isis were led by priests bearing the image of a left hand

Right: a portrait by Jaco Bar of Fra Luca Pacioli, one of the great Renaissance geometers. In the Western tradition, the analytical has always been favoured at the expense of the intuitive. But intuition sometimes plays a part in the most analytical thought processes. The famous 19th-century French mathematician Henri Poincaré (below) made an important mathematical discovery apparently almost by accident: it came to him in a flash of intuition while he was not consciously using his left brain to think of the problem

areas located in the dominant left hemisphere were no longer in contact with the right hemisphere that controlled the left side of the body. Therefore, they argued, if an object were presented in the left-hand side of the field of vision (which was perceived by the right hemisphere of the subject's brain) the 'split-brain' patients would be able to see the object, but neither explain what it was, nor write about it – these functions being a left-brain activity.

Sperry and his team set up a series of

simple experiments to explore these ideas. In one such experiment a split-brain patient sat on one side of a screen. Behind the screen, out of his view, was a collection of small, simple objects such as a hammer, a knife, a nut, a bolt, and so on. The name of one object was flashed for one tenth of a second onto the screen in such a way that it was recognised only by the right hemisphere. When the patient was asked to name the object he failed, but if he felt behind the screen with his *left* hand, he selected the correct object.

Many other experiments on this theme have been carried out, together with investigations of brain activity using electro-encephalographs to compare the neural activity in the two hemispheres when the subject is carrying out a number of varied tasks.

The left brain controls speech, writing and numerical abilities; its mode of thought is analytical, logical, and rational; it proceeds by rigorous step-by-step analysis of the problems it is set. The right hemisphere, on

the other hand, controls the ability to visualise in three dimensions, 'sense of direction' and musical ability; it is perceptual, intuitive, methaphorical, imaginative, and discerns things as wholes or in terms of patterns rather than analysing them logically in the manner of the left hemisphere.

The reason why, for most people, the left hemisphere of the brain appears to be dominant is that its abilities in the verbal, analytical and logical areas are those that are the most highly regarded in Western culture.

The mathematician is trained so that his left-brain functions are developed to a high degree, whereas the value of his right brain can go unnoticed until the left brain relaxes its hold over the thought processes. Poincaré's insights came to him in a flash – demonstrating that the processes of his right brain were largely unconscious.

There are the artists, sculptors, mystics and people who 'drop out' of the system and counter this left-brain domination by trying to assert the value of right-brain activity – but they still remain, in general, a barely tolerated minority on the fringes of our society. Nonetheless, their presence may indicate that they are the vanguard of a new form of consciousness – a consciousness that embraces both right-brain and left-brain thought and behaviour.

This new form of consciousness will have a difficult struggle if it is to counter the powerful forces that favour left-brain dominance. Bearing in mind that the *left* brain controls the *right* side of the body we would

expect that, under the regime of the old consciousness, *right*-sidedness would be favoured, while the *left* side would have a flavour of disrepute about it.

The evidence confirms this: for instance the Bible (Matthew 25:33) indicates that God 'shall set the sheep on his right hand, but the goats on his left'. The goats are not only placed on the left: they are ultimately destined to be thrown to the Devil.

Light and dark

In the Greek tradition of Pythagoras – a patriarchal tradition – the right side was associated with the light and the Sun, the straight, the good and the male, whereas, the left corresponded to the dark and the Moon, the crooked, the evil and the female. And in ancient Egypt – a matriarchal society – the Isis cult honoured the female Isis rather than the male Osiris; night was revered rather than day, and the Isis processions were led by priests holding an image of the left hand.

Western society, with its patriarchal, male-dominated view of the world, inherited from the Greeks, has suppressed the matriarchal view of the Egyptians – and there seems little alternative but to conclude that this is because a rival order constitutes a threat to the dominance of the right side.

It is perhaps significant that Western society sees as *sinister* – from the Latin for left-sided – such activities as magic and mysticism, because there appears to be no rational logic behind them. But activities such as transcendental meditation, yoga, faith healing, parapsychology, divining and achieving altered states of consciousness through the use of drugs all defy left-brain logic, yet are practised by large numbers of people. The growth in the pursuit of these 'sinister' activities has arisen, it seems, because increasing numbers of people are rebelling against the alienation, depersonalisation and rationalisation imposed by Western technological existence, and are

Above: a medieval wall painting from St Thomas's church, Salisbury, England, showing the Last Judgement. The souls who are to go to heaven are sitting at God's right hand; those who are doomed to perdition are on his left

Right: a Tarot card designed for Aleister Crowley by Frieda Harris, with the interlocking symbols of *yin* and *yang* – the female and male principles, whose integration represents the whole of existence. *Yin* and *yang* also broadly delineate the characteristics of the right and left brains. Some psychologists believe that only with the restoration of the balance between left and right brain will balanced mentality emerge

seeking to let their right brains come alive, thereby restoring the balance between left and right brains. The right brain can be seen to be reasserting itself in all aspects of life, ranging from the increasing willingness to take paranormal occurrences seriously to the interest in Zen and other Eastern mystical 'religions'.

If this rebellion by the right brain is to generate a new consciousness of life, it is important to keep a sense of perspective. What is necessary is not left- or right-brain *dominance*, but harmony between the two hemispheres of the brain. This harmony can arise only through an open dialogue between the halves of the brain, each contributing its own strengths and abilities. To this end, we may be able to train ourselves to use our right brains more consciously through, for example, biofeedback (see page 1462), giving time – from school age onwards – to 'right-brain' activities and training ourselves to realise when to 'let go' or forget a problem so that the right brain can help to resolve it. We may also be able to learn from the Chinese, who have long held the view that all existence is represented by the integration of opposites called *yin*, the female principle, and *yang*, the male principle – opposites that also, broadly, delineate the contrast between the right and left brains. The philosophers of ancient China, it seems, were wiser than we are: they knew – centuries before Western neurophysiologists began to discover the same truth – that without this active union of opposites we are but half-brained.

Tom Lethbridge is a major figure in the world of the paranormal, but, as COLIN WILSON explains, he took many years of painstaking academic and practical research to reach his important conclusions

NO ONE WHO IS interested in the paranormal can afford to ignore Tom Lethbridge, yet when he died in a nursing home in Devon in 1971, his name was hardly known to the general public. Today, many of his admirers believe that he is the single most important name in the history of psychical research. His ideas on dowsing, life after death, ghosts, poltergeists, magic, second-sight, precognition, the nature of time, cover a wider field than those of any other psychical researcher. Moreover, they fit together into the most exciting and comprehensive theory of the 'occult' ever advanced.

These ideas were expressed in a series of small books published in the last 10 years of his life. The odd thing is that Lethbridge took no interest in psychic matters until he retired to Devon in his mid fifties. He was trained as an archaeologist and a historian, and spent most of his adult life in Cambridge as the Keeper of Anglo-Saxon Antiquities at the University Museum. But even in that respectable setting he was a maverick, and in 1957 he left Cambridge in disgust at the

Above: Tom and Mina Lethbridge were keen – and accomplished – dowsers

Below: Ladram Bay, Devon, where people felt a strong urge to jump off the cliffs

hostile reception of one of his books on archaeology. Together with his wife Mina, he moved into Hole House, an old Tudor mansion on the south coast of Devon. He meant to spend his retirement reading and digging for bits of broken pottery. In fact, the most amazing period of his eventful life was about to begin.

The person who was most responsible for this change of direction was an old 'witch' who lived next door. This white haired little old lady assured Lethbridge that she could put mild spells on people who annoyed her, and that she was able to leave her body at night and wander around the district – an ability known as 'astral projection'. Lethbridge was naturally sceptical – until something convinced him.

The witch explained to him one day how she managed to put off unwanted visitors. What she did was to draw a five pointed star – a pentagram – in her head, and then visualise it across the path of the unwanted visitor – for example, on the front gate.

Shortly afterwards, Tom was lying in bed, idly drawing pentagrams in his head, and imagining them around their beds. In the middle of the night, Mina woke up with a creepy feeling that there was somebody else in the room. At the foot of the bed, she could see a faint glow of light, which slowly faded

A seeker after truth

as she watched it. The next day, the witch came to see them. When she told them that she had 'visited' their bedroom on the previous night, and found the beds surrounded by triangles of fire, Tom's scepticism began to evaporate. Mina politely requested the old witch to stay out of their bedroom at night.

Three years later, the old lady died in peculiar circumstances. She was quarrelling with a neighbouring farmer, and told Lethbridge that she intended to put a spell on the man's cattle. By this time, Lethbridge knew enough about the 'occult' to take her seriously, and he warned her about the dangers of black magic – how it could rebound on to the witch. But the old lady ignored his advice. One morning, she was found dead in her bed in circumstances that made the police suspect murder. And the cattle of two nearby farms suddenly got foot and mouth disease. However, the farmer she wanted to 'ill wish' remained unaffected. Lethbridge was convinced that the spell had gone wrong and 'bounced back'.

The invisible world

But the old lady's death resulted – indirectly – in one of his most important insights. Passing the witch's cottage, he experienced a 'nasty feeling', a suffocating sense of depression. With a scientist's curiosity, he walked around the cottage, and noticed an interesting thing. He could step *into* the depression and then out of it again, just as if it was some kind of invisible wall.

The depression reminded Lethbridge of something that had happened when he was a teenager. He and his mother had gone for a walk in the Great Wood near Wokingham. It was a lovely morning; yet quite suddenly, both of them experienced 'a horrible feeling of gloom and depression, which crept upon us like a blanket of fog over the surface of the sea'. They hurried away, agreeing that it was something terrible and inexplicable. A few days later, the corpse of a suicide was found a few yards from the spot where they had been standing, hidden by some bushes.

About a year after the death of the witch, another strange experience gave Tom the clue he was looking for. On a damp January afternoon, he and Mina drove down to Ladram Bay to collect seaweed for her garden. As Lethbridge stepped on to the beach, he once again experienced the feeling of gloom and fear, like a blanket of fog descending upon him. Mina wandered off along the beach while Tom filled the sacks with seaweed. Suddenly she came hurrying back, saying: 'Let's go. I can't stand this place a minute longer. There's something frightful here.'

The next day, they mentioned what had happened to Mina's brother. He said he also had experienced the same kind of thing in a field near Avebury, in Wiltshire. The word 'field' made something connect in Tom's brain – he remembered that field telephones

Above: Hole Mill and Hole House in Devon. Hole Mill was the home of Lethbridge's neighbour, a 'witch' or 'wise woman' whose strange powers convinced Lethbridge that the world of the paranormal was worth investigating. Hole House became the Lethbridges' home after Tom left Cambridge in disgust at the reception of one of his books. Here he was to develop his theories on psychic phenomena until his death in 1971

often short-circuit in warm, muggy weather. 'What was the weather like?' he asked. 'Warm and damp,' said the brother.

An idea was taking shape. *Water . . .* could that be the key? It had been warm and damp in the Great Wood. It had been warm and damp on Ladram beach. The following weekend, they set out for Ladram Bay a second time. Again, as they stepped on to the beach, both walked into the same bank of depression – or 'ghoul' as Lethbridge called it. Mina led Tom to the far end of the beach, to the place she had been sitting when she had been overwhelmed by the strange feeling. Here it was so strong that it made them feel giddy – Lethbridge described it as the feeling you get when you have a high temperature and are full of drugs. On either side of them were two small streams.

Mina wandered off to look at the scenery from the top of the cliff. Suddenly, she walked into the depression again. Moreover, she had an odd feeling, as if someone – or something – was urging her to jump over. She went and fetched Tom, who agreed that the spot was just as sinister as the place down on the seashore below.

Now he needed only one more piece of the jigsaw puzzle, and he found it – but only years later. Nine years after the first known experiences of depression were felt on those cliffs a man did commit suicide there. Lethbridge wondered whether the 'ghoul' was a feeling so intense that it had become timeless and imprinted itself on the area, casting its baleful shadow on those who stood there.

Whether from the past or from the future the feelings of despair were 'recorded' on the surroundings – but how?

The key, Lethbridge believed, was water. As an archaeologist, he had always been mildly interested in dowsing and water-divining. The dowser walks along with a forked hazel twig held in his hands, and when he stands above running water, the muscles in his hands and arms convulse and the twig bends either up or down. How does it work? Professor Y. Rocard of the Sorbonne discovered that underground water produces changes in the earth's magnetic field, and this is what the dowser's muscles respond to. The water does this because it has a field of its own, which interacts with the earth's field.

Significantly, magnetic fields are the means by which sound is recorded on tape covered with iron oxide. Suppose the magnetic field of running water can also record strong emotions – which, after all, are basically electrical activities in the human brain and body? Such fields could well be strongest in damp and muggy weather.

Magnetic emotions

This would also explain why the banks of depression seem to form a kind of invisible wall. Anyone who has ever tried bringing a magnet closer and closer to an iron nail will know that the nail is suddenly 'seized' by the magnet as it enters the force field. Presumably the magnetic field of water has the same property. And if it can 'tape record' powerful emotions, then you would feel them quite suddenly, as you stepped into the field. Both Tom and Mina noticed that the ghoul on Ladram beach came to an end quite abruptly

And what about 'ghosts' – that is, things actually seen, rather than just sensed? Here again, Lethbridge was convinced that his electrical theory fitted the facts. In 1922 – when he was an undergraduate at Cambridge – he had seen a ghost in the rooms of a friend. He was just about to leave, late at night, when the door opened and a man wearing a top hat came in. Assuming he was a college porter who had come to give his friend a message, Lethbridge said goodnight, and went out. The man did not reply. The next morning, Lethbridge saw his friend, and asked casually about the identity of the man in the top hat. His friend flatly denied that anyone had come in. And when Lethbridge brooded on it, he realised that the man had not worn a porter's uniform. He wore hunting kit. Then why had he not recognised the red coat? Because it wasn't red; it was grey – a dull grey, like a black and white *photograph*. Lethbridge realised that he had seen a ghost. Moreover, his friend's rooms overlooked the river, so there was a damp atmosphere.

Tom had seen a ghost in the witch's garden, in the year before she died. He had been sitting on the hillside, looking down at the witch's house, when he noticed two women in the yard. One was the witch; the other was a tall old lady dressed in rather old-fashioned grey clothes. Later, he saw the witch and asked her about her visitor. The witch looked puzzled; then, when Lethbridge described the figure, said, 'Ah, you've seen my ghost.'

This happened in 1959, before Lethbridge had his important insight on Ladram beach. So it never entered his head that the ghost was a 'tape recording'. His first

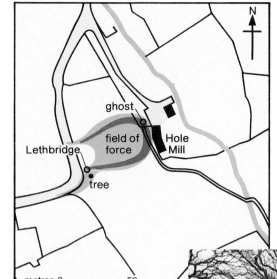

Left: map showing the position of the ghost at Hole Mill in relation to the underground stream and its field of force. Lethbridge plotted the area 'blind' with his hazel twig. Later excavation showed this plot to be correct in every detail

Right: the 'witch's' house, Hole Mill, as seen from Hole House. This was the spot where Lethbridge saw the ghost of an old lady and experienced a curious tingling sensation when he stood over an underground stream. He later discovered that the two experiences were connected

Below: the Reverend Bishop Leonidas Polk, who intrigued Professor Joseph Buchanan in the 1840s by being able to detect brass in the dark simply by touching it with his fingers

thought was that the old lady in grey might be some kind of thought projection – in other words, a kind of television picture, caused by someone else *thinking* about the ghost, and somehow transferring the thought into his own mind. Then it struck him that ghosts are supposed to reappear on anniversaries. So he and Mina decided they would go to the same spot at the same time the following year, and see what happened.

In fact, nothing happened. They stood quietly at the same spot, on a fine, warm morning, but the old lady failed to reappear. However, both of them noticed a kind of electrical tingling feeling in the atmosphere. There was a tiny underground stream running down the lane – under a drain cover – and they felt the tingling most strongly when they stood on top of it. Tom would only realise the significance of that tingling feeling after his experience on Ladram beach. And then he decided to explore the stream and see where it led. The result confirmed his suspicions. The stream turned at right angles quite close to the witch's house. And it was directly above this stream that he had seen the old lady in grey. He had been connected to the spot by the magnetic field of the flowing water. But the witch, standing a few yards away from the underground stream, had seen nothing.

So Lethbridge had been quite mistaken to believe that his 'old lady' was some kind of television picture projected by someone else's mind, or a ghost that would return exactly a year later. It was almost certainly just another 'tape recording' – a kind of videotape recording this time – but in black and white, just like the huntsman he had seen in his friend's rooms at Cambridge.

It would be very satisfying to be able to add that he decided to investigate the apparitions, and found that a huntsman had died of apoplexy in the room in Cambridge, or that the old lady had drowned in the underground stream. No such neat, satisfactory solutions can be provided. And neither is it necessary. The huntsman had probably been a previous inhabitant of the rooms; the old lady had probably lived most of her life in Hole Mill – the witch's house. (From her clothes, Lethbridge thought she dated back to before the First World War.) But there is no earthly reason why the 'force field' of water should record only unpleasant emotions. The old lady might have been unusually happy or excited when she was 'photographed' on the field. Or perhaps she passed over the spot so often that her image finally became indelibly imprinted there.

How much evidence is there for the Lethbridge theory of ghosts and ghouls? Well, to begin with, it is worth noting that his 'tape recording' theory was by no means new. In America in the 1840s, a professor named Joseph Rhodes Buchanan was intrigued when a certain Bishop Polk told him that he could

A diagram showing the 'psyche-field' around a tree, plotted with a hazel twig. The shaded area shows the limits of the force field that can be 'picked up' by a dowser

A Hawaiian volcano erupting. In the mid 19th century William Denton gave a piece of volcanic rock to a sensitive who 'saw' a volcano exploding. This was one of the first serious experiments into psychometry – or object reading – and its results had far-reaching implications for dowsing

detect brass in the dark by touching it with his fingers; it produced an unpleasant taste in his mouth. Buchanan tested him and found it was true. He discovered that certain of his students also had the same curious ability. In fact, some of them could even detect different substances when they were wrapped up in brown paper. Buchanan decided that the nerves produce some kind of force field – he called it the 'nerve aura' – which streams out of the finger ends, and which operates like an extra sense.

A strange talent

What really puzzled him was that some of his sensitives could hold a sealed letter, and describe the person who had written it, and whether the writer was sad or happy at the time. Buchanan explained this by suggesting that all substances give off emanations (another name for a force field) on which human emotions can be recorded. He had stumbled on Lethbridge's theory just about 100 years before Lethbridge.

Buchanan's friend William Denton, a professor of geology, took the theory even further. He tried wrapping a piece of Hawaiian volcanic rock in paper and handing it to a sensitive, who immediately saw in his mind an island in the midst of blue seas, and an exploding volcano. When handed a pebble of glacial limestone, the sensitive saw it frozen in deep ice. A fragment of meteor produced a picture of the depths of space, with glittering stars. Denton was so excited by all this that he believed he had discovered a new – or forgotten – human faculty, and that one day we shall be able to look back into the past just as easily as we can now look at the stars (which may have died millions of years ago) through a telescope.

Buchanan and Denton called this strange faculty *psychometry*, and for a few years it caused considerable excitement in the scientific world. Then, with the coming of Darwin, T. H. Huxley and the rest, a more sceptical climate prevailed, and it was forgotten. Even so, Sir Oliver Lodge, the notable scientist who dared to be interested in psychical research, wrote in 1908:

> Take, for example, a haunted house . . . wherein some one room is the scene of a ghostly representation of some long past tragedy. On a psychometric hypothesis, the original tragedy has been literally *photographed* on its material surroundings, nay, even on the ether itself, by reason of the intensity of emotion felt by those who enacted it.

It may seem, then, that Lethbridge's discovery was not so remarkable after all. That would be a mistake. For it was only a part of a far more comprehensive and more important theory of the paranormal.

EYEWITNESS: Personal encounters with the strange, extraordinary and sometimes terrifying mysteries of the vast unknown – *The Unexplained*.

Dear Sir,
On reading your article about Tom Lethbridge, I was surprised – and rather reassured – to learn that other people too have had strange experiences with force fields. Last year I and a few other people visited a friend who lives in the Clapham Wood area and we decided to go for a walk in the wood. At first it seemed a rather nice place, not at all hostile; but soon we all experienced a cold sensation as we passed through the area we now know is called The Chestnuts. It seemed as if some strange force were turning the air cold and still. Then I heard an odd rustling sound through the undergrowth and I drew this to the attention of my friends as quietly as I could. We tried to find the source of the noise, but couldn't see anything. When the sound stopped suddenly, I moved forward and kicked at the undergrowth, but there was nothing there. Then the noise began again. Eventually, as we moved out of the area, the cold feeling disappeared, and we quickly left the wood; the place seemed to come alive again as we did so.

I still don't know what it was that made the sounds, but I am sure it was not an animal as we would have seen it. And it could not have been my imagination as all of us felt and heard the same things.

Yours faithfully,

J. Perry

London

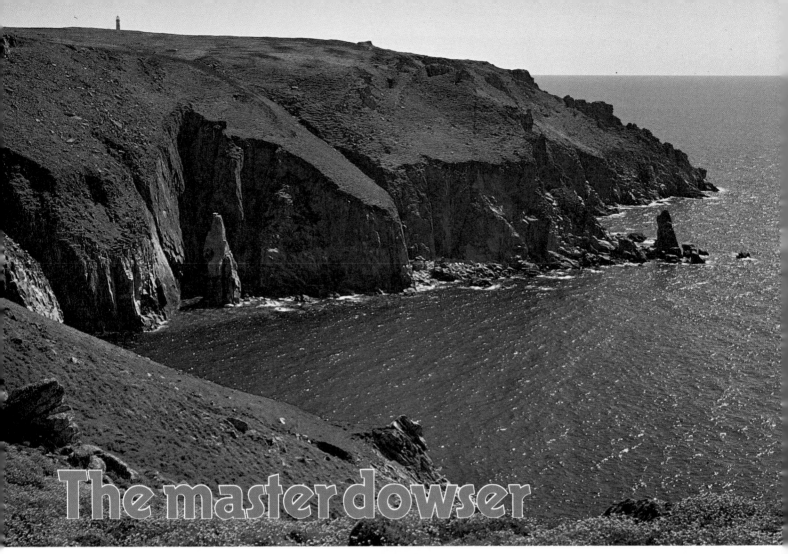

The master dowser

During his career as an archaeologist Tom Lethbridge discovered dowsing – 'picking up' electrical fields of objects and reacting to them. But this, as COLIN WILSON explains, was only the beginning of an important series of experiments

ALTHOUGH TOM LETHBRIDGE had no interest in ghosts or 'ghouls' before he retired to Devon, he had always been fascinated by dowsing.

It all started in the early 1930s, when he and another archaeologist were looking for Viking graves on the island of Lundy in the Bristol Channel. They located the graves, then, having time on their hands while they waited for the boat back to the mainland, they decided to try some experiments with dowsing. Hidden under the soil of Lundy Island are seams of volcanic rock that pass up through the slate. Lethbridge decided to see if he could locate these. So he cut himself a hazel twig, allowed his friend to blindfold him, and was then led along the cliff path, the forked hazel twig held tightly in his hands. (The twig has to be held with the forks bent slightly apart, so it has a certain amount of 'spring'.) Every time he passed over a volcanic seam, the hazel fork twisted violently in his hands. His friend had an extra-sensitive

Above: Tom Lethbridge, the archaeologist who became a master dowser

Top: the island of Lundy in the Bristol Channel, where Lethbridge conducted his first experiment into dowsing. Using a forked hazel twig, he and a colleague dowsed for volcanic seams. The hazel twig located the seams by twisting violently when held over them

magnetometer, so he was able to verify that Lethbridge had accurately located every single one of the volcanic seams.

To Lethbridge, that seemed logical enough. Like running water, a volcanic seam has a faint magnetic field. Presumably he was somehow able to pick up these fields through the hazel twig, which reacted like a sensitive instrument. In one of his earlier books he wrote: 'Most people can dowse, if they know how to do it. If they cannot do it, there is probably some fault in the electrical system of their bodies.'

The garden of Lethbridge's house in Devon was full of interesting archaeological remains – some of them dating to Roman times. And, soon after moving in, Lethbridge remembered an experiment he had seen performed in the University Museum of Archaeology and Ethnology in Cambridge. Someone had asserted that a pendulum can tell whether a skull is male or female, and demonstrated this by dangling one over an ancient skull. The pendulum swung back and forth, which meant – apparently – that it was a man's skull. If it had swung round in a circle, the skull would have been female. Midwives sometimes use the same method to determine the sex of an unborn baby, dangling a wedding ring on a piece of thread over the stomach of the pregnant woman.

But how can such a method possibly work? It sounds completely absurd. Male and female skulls do not have electrical fields; and even if they did, there is no reason why one of them should make a pendulum swing back and forth, and the other make it swing in a circle.

With characteristic thoroughness, Lethbridge set out to test it for himself. His first question was: if a pendulum can somehow respond to different substances, then how does it do it? A pendulum is, after all, just a weight fixed to the end of a piece of string. It must be the unconscious mind – or possibly the muscles – of the dowser that respond. But respond to what? The answer seemed to be: to some kind of vibration. In which case, it seems a fair assumption that different lengths of the pendulum respond to different vibrations.

It was the most fruitful assumption he ever made. And he set out to test it by putting a wooden bob on the end of a long piece of string, and then winding the string round a

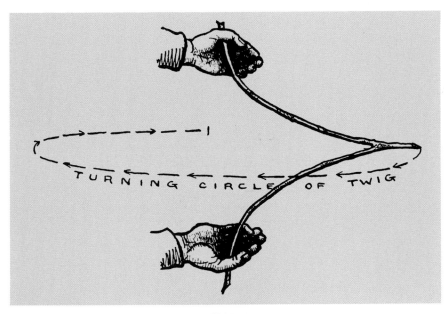

Above: the characteristic movement of a forked hazel twig when actively dowsing. Its usual – though not invariable – reaction when held over a subterranean stream, for example, is to turn in a circle from right to left

Left: dowsing demonstrated, showing the power of the hazel twig as it pulls downwards when reacting to the presence of underground water

pencil, so he could lengthen or shorten the pendulum at will. Next, he put a piece of silver on the ground, held the pendulum over it, and then carefully began to lengthen the string. And, when he had unwound about 2 feet (60 centimetres), the pendulum suddenly began to go into a circular swing. Lethbridge measured his string. It was precisely 22 inches. (Lethbridge believed one could dowse successfully only using Imperial measurements. Feet and inches, he said, were 'natural' measurements based on the human body, whereas metric measurements were 'unnatural'. So pendulum 'rates' will be given in inches only.)

The pendulum reacts

Next, he went out into the courtyard of Hole House – which dates back to Tudor times – and walked around with his pendulum. At one place, it went into a circular swing. Lethbridge dug down carefully, and eventually located a small piece of Rhineland stoneware pottery. He tried his pendulum over it; it went into a powerful circular swing. That puzzled him greatly, until he tried his 22-inch pendulum over a piece of lead, and it also went into a circular swing. Apparently, 22 inches is the 'rate' for both silver and lead. And Rhineland pottery in the 17th century was glazed with lead.

Now very excited, Lethbridge kept the pendulum at the same length and walked round the courtyard until it went again into a circular swing. He dug down, and found a bit of lead from an Elizabethan window. So he proved that the pendulum was accurate. He tried holding the pendulum over a copper pot, and found that it reacted at $30\frac{1}{2}$ inches. He walked around the courtyard until the pendulum responded, and this time, dug up a tiny copper tube. It was very small, so evidently the pendulum was extremely sensitive.

Convinced that he had made a major discovery, Lethbridge spent days testing all kinds of different substances with his pendulum and discovered, to his delight, that every one of them had its own 'rate': glass, sulphur, iron, slate, amber – even alcohol, garlic and apples. When he held it over a bottle of Australian Burgundy, the pendulum responded at 14, 20, $25\frac{1}{2}$ and 32 inches, which Lethbridge proved to be the 'rates' for glass, vegetable matter (the label), alcohol and iron.

He even tested a truffle – that delicious fungus that is used in *foie gras*. The pendulum responded at 17 inches. Trying to locate any buried truffles, Lethbridge stood with his pendulum in one hand, while pointing his other hand around in a slow semi-circle. When the 17-inch pendulum began to swing, he drew a straight line in the direction he was pointing. Then he went and stood several yards away, and repeated the experiment. Where the two lines crossed, he dug down with a trowel. He located a tiny, dark

object, the size of a pea, and sent it to the Science Museum in London for identification. Incredibly, it turned out to be a rare variety of truffle.

There were still a number of minor mysteries – such as how to distinguish between lead and silver, when both react at 22 inches, or between truffles and beech wood, both of which respond to a 17-inch pendulum. Further experimentation solved that one. The number of times the pendulum gyrated was equally important. For lead, it gyrates 16 times, then goes back to its normal back-and-forth motion; for silver it gyrates 22 times. It looked as if nature had devised a simple and

Above: the corner of the courtyard at the Lethbridge home, Hole House in Devon, where dowsing revealed a number of buried objects

Below: how dowsing with a pendulum works
A. dowser's psyche-field
B. static field of object
C. pendulum – where A meets B it begins to move in a circle
D. how the pendulum length is controlled by dowser

foolproof code for identifying any substance.

And not just substances. The pendulum also responded to colours – the natural colours of flowers, for example: 22 inches for grey, 29 for yellow, 30 for green, and so on. Lethbridge found himself wondering whether the pendulum would respond to thoughts and emotions as well as substances. A simple, two-part experiment convinced him that this was so. During his last excavations near Cambridge, Lethbridge had collected a number of sling-stones from an Iron Age fort. He tried his pendulum over them, and found that they reacted at 24 inches and also at 40. He fetched a bucketful of stones from the beach and tried the pendulum over those. They failed to react at either 'rate'. Now he divided the stones into two piles, and told his wife Mina to throw half of them at a wall, while he threw the rest. He tried the pendulum again. All Mina's stones now reacted at 29 inches (the 'rate' for females), while those he had thrown reacted at 24 – like the Iron Age stones. So it looked as if the Iron Age stones had been thrown by males. But what about their reaction to a 40-inch pendulum? Could it, he wondered, be the rate for anger or death? Lethbridge set the pendulum at 40 inches and thought about something that made him angry; immediately, the pendulum began to gyrate. So it looked as if 40 was indeed the rate for anger. He later ascertained that it was also the rate for death, cold and blackness.

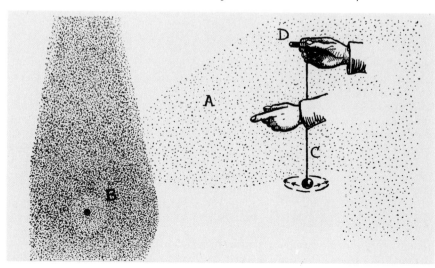

Now all this, admittedly, seems absurd. Yet Lethbridge repeated the experiments dozen of times, and each time he got the same result. The pendulum responded to ideas – like evolution, pride, life, danger and deceit – just as readily as to substances. Moreover Mina got the same results. And, through his experience of psychometry, Lethbridge realised that there is nothing very odd in a pendulum responding to ideas. If a 'sensitive' can hold an unopened letter, and somehow feel the emotions of the person who wrote it, then it seems reasonable to assume that human beings possess some 'sense' that registers these things just as our eyes register colours and shapes – a sixth sense perhaps? In fact, you could say that a pendulum is merely an aid to psychometry. A psychometrist – or sensitive – can pick up these vibrations directly; non-sensitive people, like Lethbridge, can only feel them indirectly through the pendulum.

After months of experiment with the pendulum, Lethbridge constructed tables of the various 'rates'; and it became clear that 40 inches was some kind of limit. Every single substance that he tested fell between zero and 40 inches. And at this point he discovered something rather odd. Sulphur reacts to a 7-inch pendulum. If he extended the pendulum to 47 inches – 40 plus 7 – it would still react to a heap of sulphur. But not when directly over the heap. It only reacted a little

to one side. The same was true of everything else he tried beyond 40 – the pendulum reacted, but a little to one side.

Forty inches is also the 'rate' for death. Was it possible, Lethbridge wondered, that when the pendulum registers beyond 40 inches, it registers a world beyond death – another dimension? He remembered an experience of being at the dentist, under anaesthetic, and finding himself outside his body – hovering up in the air, and slightly to the left – just like the 'displacement' reaction of the pendulum to the heap of sulphur.

He noticed another odd thing. Below 40 inches, there is no 'rate' for the concept of time; the pendulum simply will not respond. But when he lengthened the pendulum to 60 inches, he got a strong reaction for time. He

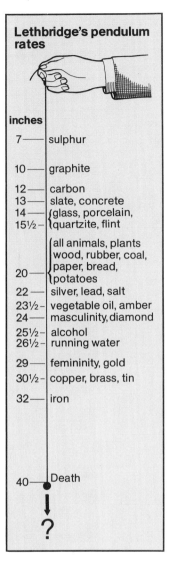

Lethbridge's pendulum rates

inches	
7	sulphur
10	graphite
12	carbon
13	slate, concrete
14	glass, porcelain,
15½	quartzite, flint
20	all animals, plants wood, rubber, coal, paper, bread, potatoes
22	silver, lead, salt
23½	vegetable oil, amber
24	masculinity, diamond
25½	alcohol
26½	running water
29	femininity, gold
30½	copper, brass, tin
32	iron
40	Death

?

Above: table of pendulum 'rates' as discovered by Tom Lethbridge in the course of his experiments. Through trial and error he came to realise that the pendulum reacted consistently at certain lengths to specific substances, qualities and even abstract ideas

Left and right: mended pots that had been found in fragments in the courtyard and orchard of Hole House solely through dowsing. Lethbridge dowsed them to find their ages, finally coming up with the dates he scratched on the bottoms. Lethbridge achieved a high degree of accuracy – his dates for certain standing stones, for example, were later proved to be correct by carbon dating. As he said 'It may seem absurd, but it delivers the goods'

reasoned that because 'our world' – that is, the world that registers below 40 – is in time, there is no reaction to the idea of time itself – just as you could not appreciate the speed of a river if you were drifting down at the same speed as the current. But there is a reaction to the idea of time in this 'world beyond death'. Moreover, Lethbridge found that if he lengthened the pendulum beyond 80, he got the same result all over again – as if there is yet another world – or dimension – beyond that one. And this 'third world' also has a reaction for time. But when Lethbridge lengthened the pendulum beyond 120 inches he discovered that the 'world' beyond that also had no reaction for time.

Secrets of the 'other you'

Tom Lethbridge's own explanation of this strange 'power of the pendulum' is that there is a part of the human mind – the unconscious, perhaps – that knows the answers to all questions. Unfortunately, it cannot convey these answers to the 'everyday you', the busy, conscious self that spends its time coping with practical problems. But this 'other you' *can* convey its messages via the dowsing rod or pendulum, by the simple expedient of controlling the muscles.

Lethbridge had started as a cheerfully sceptical investigator trying to understand nature's hidden codes for conveying information. His researches led him into strange,

bewildering realms where all his normal ideas seemed to be turned upside down. He compared himself to a man walking on ice, when it suddenly collapses and he finds himself floundering in freezing water. Of this sudden immersion in new ideas he said: 'From living a normal life in a three-dimensional world, I seem to have suddenly fallen through into one where there are more dimensions. The three-dimensional life goes on as usual; but one has to adjust one's thinking to the other.' He did more than adjust his thinking; he set out boldly to explore the fourth dimension – and came to highly significant conclusions.

Gateway to other worlds

Tom Lethbridge progressed from finding hidden objects through dowsing to exploring the timeless world beyond death. COLIN WILSON concludes his series on the man called the 'Einstein of the paranormal'

IN 1962, FIVE YEARS AFTER his move to Devon, Tom Lethbridge's ideas on ghosts, 'ghouls', pendulums and dowsing rods began to crystallise into a coherent theory, which he outlined in a book called *Ghost and divining rod*. This appeared in 1963, and it aroused more interest than anything he had published so far. It deserved to be so popular, for its central theory was original, exciting and well-argued.

He suggested that nature generates fields of static electricity in certain places, particularly near running water. These 'fields' are capable of picking up and recording the thoughts and feelings of human beings and other living creatures. But human beings are also surrounded by a mild electrical field, as the researches of Harold Burr of Yale University in the United States revealed in the 1930s. So if someone goes into a room where a murder has taken place and experiences a distinctly unpleasant feeling, all that is happening is that the emotions associated with the crime (such as fear, pain and horror) are being transferred to the visitor's electrical field, in accordance with the laws of electricity. If we are feeling full of energy, excitement, misery or anger, the emotional transference may flow the other way, and our feelings will be recorded on the field.

But if human emotions can be imprinted in some way on the 'field' of running water, and picked up by a dowser, then this world we are living in is a far more strange and

Above: Tom Lethbridge cataloguing some archaeological finds

Below: Saddell Abbey, Strathclyde, Scotland – a place of curiously strong and varied atmospheres: menacing in the castle, melancholy in the abbey ruins and peaceful at the wishing well. Lethbridge believed that 'atmospheres' are powerful emotions 'recorded' in the electrical field of water

complex place than most people give it credit for. To begin with, we must be surrounded by hidden information – in the form of these 'tape recordings' – that might become accessible to all of us if we could master the art of using the dowser's pendulum.

It looks – says Lethbridge – as if human beings possess 'psyche-fields' as well as bodies. The body is simply a piece of apparatus for collecting impressions, which are then stored in the psyche-field. But in that case, there would seem to be a part of us that seeks the information. Presumably this is what religious people call the spirit. And since the information it can acquire through the pendulum may come from the remote past, or from some place on the other side of the world, then this spirit must be outside the limits of space and time.

It was this last idea that excited Lethbridge so much. His experiments with the pendulum seemed to indicate that there are other worlds beyond this one, perhaps worlds in other dimensions. Presumably we cannot see them – although they co-exist with our world – because our bodies are rather crude machines for picking up low-level vibrations. But the psyche-field – or perhaps the spirit – seems to have access to these other invisible worlds.

It also seems to have access to other times and other places. In May 1964, a BBC camera

other times. He used to keep a notebook and pencil by his bed, and jot down his dreams the moment he woke up. He was convinced that we all dream about the future – probably every night of our lives – but that we forget it almost as soon as we wake up.

Lethbridge decided that if he wanted to study this mystery of dreams, he should keep a dream notebook. It was soon filled with his own vivid and idiosyncratic observations.

He became convinced that Dunne was correct in believing that we all dream of future events, but that most of these are so trivial – or so brief – that we fail to remember them. One night, he woke up dreaming about the face of a man that seemed to be looking at him out of a mirror. He was doing something with his hands, which seemed to be moving in the area of his chin. Lethbridge thought he might be shaving.

The next day, Lethbridge was driving slowly along a narrow lane; a car came round the corner, and at the wheel was the man he had seen in his dream. His face was framed by the windscreen – which Lethbridge had mistaken for a mirror – and his hands were moving in the area of his chin, on top of the steering wheel. Lethbridge was certain that he had never seen the man before.

He also noted that some of his dreams seemed to go backwards. He once dreamed of a furry snake-like object coming into his bedroom; but all the furniture in the room was reversed, as in a mirror. The snake-like object he recognised as the tail of their Siamese cat, walking backwards. A friend also told him about two 'backward dreams' she had had recently: in one, she saw a couple she knew walk backwards out of their door and drive their car backwards down a lane. In another, she saw some men walking backwards carrying a coffin, and one of them uttered the baffling sentence: 'Burnt be to

team went to Hole House to record an interview with Lethbridge about dowsing. A young cameraman looked so dazed and startled as he got out of the car that Lethbridge asked him: 'Have you been here before?' The cameraman shook his head. 'No. But I've dreamed about it.' He asked if he could look behind the house. Pointing to a wall that Lethbridge had knocked down and rebuilt, he said: 'It wasn't like that years ago. There used to be buildings against it.' That was true – but not in Lethbridge's time. In the herb garden, the cameraman said: 'There used to be buildings there, but they were pulled down.' In his dream a voice had said, 'Now we shall be able to see the sea.' Again, it was true – but many years before, at the turn of the century. Now a row of trees blotted out the view of the sea.

The cameraman had never been in the area before, and he had no friends or relatives there who might have told him about it. Yet on five occasions he had dreamed about Hole House – as it was before he was born.

Lethbridge had always been interested in dreams, ever since he read J. W. Dunne's *An experiment with time* in the 1930s. Dunne was an aeronautics engineer, and around the turn of the century he had a number of impressive dreams of the future – for example, he dreamed accurately about the forthcoming eruption of the volcano, Mount Pelée, on Martinique. Dunne had suggested that time is like a tape or a film, which may get twisted or tangled, so that we can catch glimpses of

Above: diagram illustrating Lethbridge's theory about the creation of the world-wide belief in nymphs:
1. Aroused youth, pausing within the static field of a stream (A), vividly creates the image of a girl bathing (C) in his own static field (B). The image leaks into the weaker field (A) where it is 'recorded'.
2. Perhaps years later a passing youth with a weak psyche-field (D) comes into contact with (A) from which the image of the girl (C) leaks into his field (D). He thinks he has witnessed a supernatural being when he has really only seen the recording of a thoughtform

Right: eruption of the volcanic Mount Pelée, Martinique. J. W. Dunne, author of *An experiment with time*, had dreamed accurately of the event some time before it happened. This and other dreams convinced him that we dream regularly of future events but do not always remember these dreams

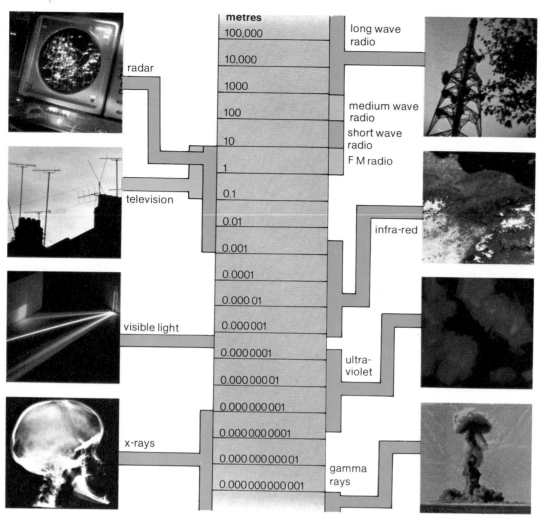

metres

100,000	long wave radio
10,000	
1000	
100	medium wave radio
10	short wave radio
1	F M radio
0.1	
0.01	
0.001	infra-red
0.0001	
0.000 01	
0.000001	
0.0000001	ultra-violet
0.000 000 01	
0.000 000 001	
0.000 0000001	
0.000 000 000 01	gamma rays
0.000 000 000 001	

radar

television

visible light

x-rays

Left: the spectrum of electromagnetic (EM) vibrations. EM waves consist of electric and magnetic fields vibrating with a definite frequency, corresponding to a particular wavelength. In order of increasing frequency and decreasing wavelength, the EM spectrum consists of: very long wave radio, used for communication with submarines; long, medium and short wave radio (used for AM broadcasting); FM radio, television and radar; infra-red (heat) radiation, which is recorded in the Earth photographs taken by survey satellites; visible light; ultraviolet light, which, while invisible, stimulates fluorescence in some materials; X-rays; and high-energy gamma rays, which occur in fallout and in cosmic rays. The progressive discovery of these waves has inspired speculations concerning unknown 'vibrations' making up our own and higher worlds

enough good woods any.' On waking up, she wrote down the sentence, read it backwards, and realised that it actually said: 'Any wood's good enough to be burnt.'

But why, Lethbridge asked, should time sometimes go backwards in dreams? The clue was provided by his pendulum, which informed him that the energy vibrations of the next level – the world beyond ours – are four times as fast as those of our world. Lethbridge speculated that during sleep, a part of us passes through this world to a higher world still. Coming back from sleep, we pass through it once again to enter our own much slower world of vibrations. The effect is like a fast train passing a slower one; although the slow train is moving forward, it appears to be going backwards.

More impressive examples of precognitive dreams came from his correspondents. One woman dreamed of the collapse of a building as the side was blown out and heard a voice say: 'Collapsed like a pack of cards.' A month later a gas explosion blew out the side of a block of flats called Ronan Point in East London, and a newspaper report used the phrase· 'Collapsed like a pack of cards'. Another correspondent described a dream in which he saw a square-looking Edwardian house with many chimneys being burnt down; a few days later, Tom saw a house of

The ruined London tower block, Ronan Point. A gas explosion ripped through the building causing death and devastation. One woman dreamed precognitively of the disaster, hearing the very words of the subsequent newspaper headline 'Collapsed like a pack of cards' spoken clearly

this description being burnt down on a television newsreel.

The more he studied these puzzles, the more convinced Lethbridge became that the key to all of them is the concept of *vibrations*. Our bodies seem to be machines tuned to pick up certain vibrations. Our eyes will only register energy whose wavelength is between that of red and violet light. Shorter or longer wavelengths are invisible to us. Modern physics tells us that at the sub-atomic level matter is in a state of constant vibration.

Worlds beyond worlds

According to Lethbridge's pendulum, the 'world' beyond our world – the world that can be detected by a pendulum of more than 40 inches – consists of vibrations that are four times as fast as ours. It is all around us yet we are unable to see it, because it is beyond the range of our senses. All the objects in our world extend into this other world. Our personalities also extend into it, but we are not aware of this, because our 'everyday self' has no communication with that 'other self'. But the other self can answer questions by means of the pendulum. When Tom and Mina Lethbridge visited a circle of standing stones called the Merry Maidens, near Penzance in Cornwall, Lethbridge held a pendulum over one of the uprights and asked how old it was. As he did so, he placed one hand on the stone, and experienced something like a mild electric shock. The pendulum began to gyrate like an aeroplane propellor, and went on swinging in a wide circle for several minutes – Lethbridge counted 451 turns. Arbitrarily allowing 10 years for each turn, Lethbridge calculated that the circle dated back to 2540 BC – a result that sounds highly consistent with carbon 14 dating of other megalithic monuments like Stonehenge. His 'higher self' – outside time – had answered his question.

In 1971 Lethbridge was engaged in writing his book on dreams – *The power of the pendulum* – when he became ill and had to be taken into hospital. He was a huge man, and his enormous weight placed a strain on his heart. He died on 30 September, leaving his last book unrevised. He was 70 years old, and his life's work was by no means complete. Yet even in its unfinished state, it is one of the

Further reading
Tom Graves, *Elements of pendulum dowsing*, Tempest Brookline 1989
Tom Graves, *Dowser's workbook*, Sterling 1990
T. C. Lethbridge, *The power of the pendulum*, Viking Penguin 1991
Colin Wilson, *Mysteries*, Putnam Publishing Group 1980

The ancient circle of standing stones known as the Merry Maidens near Penzance, Cornwall. While dowsing over the stones Lethbridge experienced a mild electric shock as if the stones were some kind of battery. But, persisting with his pendulum, he was able to dowse for the age of the stones. Later, more sophisticated techniques – such as carbon 14 dating – were used to date the Merry Maidens and Lethbridge's dating was confirmed

most important and exciting contributions to parapsychology in this century.

Lethbridge's insistence on rediscovering the ancient art of dowsing also underlined his emphasis on understanding the differences between primitive and modern Man. The ancient peoples – going back to our cavemen ancestors – believed that the Universe is magical and that Earth is a living creature. They were probably natural dowsers – as the aborigines of Australia still are – and responded naturally to the forces of the earth. Their standing stones were, according to Lethbridge, intended to mark places where the earth force was most powerful and perhaps to harness it in some way now forgotten.

Modern Man has suppressed – or lost – that instinctive, intuitive contact with the forces of the Universe. He is too busy keeping together his precious civilisation. Yet he still potentially possesses that ancient power of dowsing, and could easily develop it if he really wanted to. Lethbridge set out to develop his own powers, and to explore them scientifically, and soon came to the conclusion that the dowsing rod and the pendulum are incredibly accurate. By making use of some unknown part of the mind – the unconscious or 'superconscious' – they can provide information that is inaccessible to our ordinary senses, and can tell us about realms of reality beyond the 'everyday' world of physical matter.

Lethbridge was not a spiritualist. He never paid much attention to the question of life after death or the existence of a 'spirit world'. But by pursuing his researches into these subjects with a tough-minded logic, he concluded that there are other realms of reality beyond our world, and that there are forms of energy that we do not even begin to understand. Magic, spiritualism and occultism are merely our crude attempts to understand this vast realm of hidden energies, just as alchemy was Man's earliest attempt to understand the mysteries of atomic physics.

As to the meaning of all this, Lethbridge preserves the caution of an academic. Yet in his last years he became increasingly convinced that there is a meaning in human existence, and that it is tied up with the concept of our personal evolution. For some reason, we are being *driven* to evolve.

EYEWITNESS: Personal encounters with the strange, extraordinary and sometimes terrifying mysteries of the vast unknown – *The Unexplained*.

Dear Sir,

As an astrologer, I am working on a technique of prediction which seems to work to the extent that my life is almost like a journey in an observation car – you can see ahead, but it is hard to recognise or interpret what you see.

Whether it is because I am so absorbed in the idea of seeing ahead I don't know, but I would like to report three dreams I have had:

1) A strange coastal town. A road sloped down towards the sea, another road rose up at an angle to the other road. I walked up this second road, looking into the windows of houses (all had plants in the windows). There was some kind of pier, or scaffolded construction, below. There had been a disaster and people were being brought in from the sea, but I never saw this, only heard about it as I walked through. I knew that nobody I knew was involved and I felt no anxiety at all.

Two mornings later I awoke to the radio news about the oil-rig disaster off Stavanger; I wondered if I had dreamed of it – it being the nearest point on land to which the victims could have been taken. But I have yet to see if Stavanger tallies with my dream.

2) A previous dream had involved the same curious lack of anxiety or any strong emotion on my part. I had been looking on, while flames leaped around – especially in an area that seemed to be near a lift-shaft, on an upper floor of a large building. People were unable to escape from that particular area.

Three days after this dream the news of the Woolworth's fire in Manchester arrested my attention. I wondered if I had a preview of it, if I was having one of these dreams many people claim to have had before big disasters. In each case, the reports on the radio made me feel that it was my dreams that were being referred to!

I then decided that the next time I had such a dream I would announce it to other people immediately.

3) On the night of Saturday, 15 November 1980, I dreamed that I was walking by a sandy beach. I think a river ran into the sea. There were images of crumbled, collapsed buildings. 'We are now afraid of gas,' said my (unidentified) companion. 'Well,' I replied, 'I don't see any evidence of anyone being hurt – just empty, broken buildings.'

'Well, that's all you would see, isn't it?' said my companion.

While I was still asleep I was wondering at the nature of what I was 'seeing' and decided to announce the dream to my family – all before I woke up. (I know this is not unusual, but it is hard to remain asleep once you realise you're dreaming!) So I woke up and described the dream to my husband and family. The Italian earthquake disaster happened just over a week later. (The comment in my dream 'we are now afraid of gas' seemed to me to link it with reports about the problems of the aftermath of the Italian earthquake.)

I monitor all my dreams, but these three had a certain quality that I should recognise again, I know they have become part of my life now.

Yours faithfully,

Penelope Baird London SW17

Right: Alphonse-Louis Constant, better known as the magical writer Eliphas Levi, as a young man. Constantly searching for a cause, Levi had devoted himself to the Church, then to revolutionary politics, but it was only when he met the exiled Polish mystic J. M. Hoene-Wronski (below) that he found his life's work – to become the world's foremost ritual magician

Laying down the lore

Modern students of the occult often cite the 19th-century French writer Eliphas Levi as an authority. But, as FRANCIS KING points out, Levi's own background in magic was far from the scholarly work it was deemed to be

AT THE PRESENT day every great city of the Western world has a Polish community, men and women exiled from their homeland because of their opposition to the Polish government and its Russian masters. The situation was similar throughout much of the 19th century. Numbers of these exiles lived in Paris: some took refuge in political plotting, others in mystical dreams, seeing Poland as the 'Messiah nation', a sacrificial victim whose sufferings would redeem the rest of Europe.

Among these latter was J.M. Hoene-Wronski (1776–1853), perhaps the oddest dreamer of them all, the first occult teacher to inspire the French writer who called himself Eliphas Levi. Wronski was originally a soldier by profession, but abandoned the military life for philosophy and science and made his way to France, where he supported himself by taking mathematical pupils. By 1810 he had come to believe that he had 'discovered the Absolute' – in other words, that he had come, through reason, to a perfect understanding of the nature of ultimate reality and truth. He expressed this supposed 'understanding' in mathematical formulae that proved incomprehensible not only to laymen but to other mathematicians. Nevertheless, so convinced was he of his own genius that he visited London in order to petition Parliament for grants and subsidies. Here he made such a nuisance of himself that one distinguished mathematician, a member of the scientific committee known as the Board of Longitude, opined that 'in the interests of social order one must hope that Wronski will one night go to bed and not wake up again the next day.' This gentleman's distaste for Wronski would probably have been even stronger if he had realised that the Polish savant was an occultist and mystic, a student of such strange subjects as gnosticism and qabalism, who believed that by means of mystical processes ordinary human beings could attain God-like powers.

In 1850 Wronski met Alphonse-Louis Constant (1810–1875), better known as Eliphas Levi, a hack journalist who had once trained for the priesthood but had lost his faith, dabbled in revolutionary politics and become disillusioned, and was looking for a new set of beliefs that would give meaning to a purposeless existence. To Levi – to use the name he adopted – Wronski expounded his doctrine of the Absolute, his belief that Poland was 'the Christ of Europe', his interpretations of the *qabalah* and other mystical systems, and his belief that, through the practice of ritual magic, men could attain semi-divinity.

Levi was captivated. He threw himself into the study of all the 'occult sciences', from alchemy to cartomancy, from magic to astrology. He rifled the libraries of Paris for esoteric books and manuscripts, reading them voraciously, and spent many hours with obscure soothsayers, diviners, magicians and self-appointed prophets, hoping to extract wisdom from his long and often pointless conversations with them. He came to believe that the ancient texts of alchemy and magic were written in a symbolic code, and that if he could only break this code he would learn the ultimate secrets of the Universe and become the custodian of spiritual

Below: Levi undertakes the supreme magical rite – the 'evocation to visible appearance' of the 1st-century sage, Apollonius of Tyana. After lengthy and peculiar preparations Levi evoked Apollonius three times on consecutive days in order to ask the spirit profound questions on the nature of the Universe. Apparently the apparition complied, but unfortunately Levi did not record the conversations

truths beside which the discoveries and interpretations of Wronski would pale into insignificance.

In 1853 Wronski died, mourned – but not deeply regretted – by Levi, who by this time believed that he had already surpassed his former master and was well on the way to receiving some great spiritual revelation. A year later, in 1854, he decided that his researches were sufficiently advanced for him to carry out an occult experiment – the 'evocation to visible appearance' of the spirit of Apollonius of Tyana, a philosopher and wonder-worker of the first century.

Levi recorded that he prefaced this rite by three weeks of preparation and purification – eating only vegetables, avoiding other people, and carrying on imaginary conversations with the long dead sage.

The preparations over, Levi, clad in white vestments and wearing on his head a wreath of vervain entwined with a golden chain, began the ceremony by lighting charcoal fires in two copper chafing dishes. On these he burned various types of incense, their heavy smoke designed to provide the material from which the spirit of the philosopher could build himself a 'body'. Levi began to read the words of the ritual he was employing. Then, as he stated:

The smoke spread . . . floating above the altar . . . I heaped more fuel and

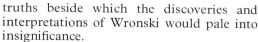

With due ceremony

Eliphas Levi, who was born in 1810, grew up and spent his adult life in a period characterised by an all-pervading romanticism – which often degenerated into a frantic search for the merely picturesque, or the abnormal.

By the time Levi was 30 the Romantic movement dominated the cultural life of France – and Levi was ensnared by it, being a man with a desperate need to believe; he could not face the world without holding up some ideological banner inscribed with 'the truth'. The nature of this 'truth' changed as Levi grew older; as an adolescent he found it in romanticised Catholicism, as a young man in an equally romanticised revolutionary Socialism, and for his last 20 years or so in a grossly distorted, 'picturesque' interpretation of the occult tradition of the Western world.

This was shaped by Levi's wide reading, uncritical acceptance of the assertions of unscholarly historians, and his remarkable capacity for self-deception (shared by the later occultist Aleister Crowley (see page 625), who believed he was the reincarnation of Levi, whom he eclipsed in learning).

Levi's written statements regarding

perfume upon the chafing dishes. . . I beheld distinctly before the altar, the figure of a man of more than normal size. . . . Three times, with closed eyes, I invoked Apollonius. When I again looked there was a man in front of me, wrapped from head to foot in a shroud. . . . I experienced an abnormally cold sensation, and when I endeavoured to question the phantom I could not utter a syllable. I . . . pointed my magic sword at the figure, mentally commanding it to obey me. . . . The form became vague and suddenly vanished. I ordered it to return and presently felt, as it were, a breath close by me; something touched the hand with which I was holding the sword, and immediately my forearm became numb. I guessed that the sword displeased the spirit, and I placed its point downward, close by me, within the circle. . . . I experienced such a weakness in all my limbs, and a fainting sensation came so quickly over me, that I sat down, whereupon I fell into a profound lethargy accompanied by dreams of which I had only a confused recollection when I recovered consciousness. . . .

The spirit of Apollonius did not speak to Levi, but the answers to the two questions he had intended to ask it, one on behalf of a friend, one on his own account, came into his mind. The reply to the friend, who had asked about someone's health, was 'Death'; the answer to his own (unrecorded) question was similarly gloomy.

Very secret secrets

Over the next few days Levi twice more evoked Apollonius. Each time, claimed Levi, the sage appeared and gave profound philosophical answers to Levi's equally profound questions. Unfortunately the exact wording, of neither the questions propounded nor the answers received, was recorded, so it is impossible to estimate the truth of Levi's claim that Apollonius revealed secrets 'which might change, in a short time, the foundations and laws of society at large, if they became generally known'.

If the secrets were, indeed, as astonishing as Levi claimed it is rather remarkable that he proceeded to warn others against carrying out similar occult experiments. He wrote:

. . . I regard the practice as destructive and dangerous. . . . I commend the greatest caution to those who propose devoting themselves to similar experiences; their result is intense exhaustion, and frequently a shock sufficient to occasion illness.

Not many months after his raising of the

the many surviving printed and manuscript *grimoires* – medieval and Renaissance textbooks of ritual magic (see page 2459) – typified his whole attitude. When he quoted from these works he did so selectively and inaccurately, picking out (and heavily amending) passages that were sufficiently romantic to read as though extracted from a particularly lurid Gothic novel. If no passages in any extant grimoire were sufficiently dramatic to suit his purposes he did not scruple to invent them.

Take, for example, Levi's description of the processes involved in 'infernal evocations' – the raising of the denizens of hell to visible appearance. The sorcerer begins, said Levi, with 15 days of a curious dietary observance – getting totally drunk every five days on wine in which hemp and poppy have been infused and which has been strained through a cloth 'woven by a prostitute'. The actual evocation should be carried out in a haunted graveyard or 'the vaults of an abandoned convent' – both, significantly enough, popular settings for Gothic novels. Among the essential requirements for the ceremony were, claimed Levi, such items as 'the head of a black cat which had fed on human flesh for five days, four nails from the coffin of an executed criminal, and the horns of a goat that had experienced sexual intercourse with a young girl' (shown in a magical design, the Goetic circle, left). All this is very melodramatic, but almost none of it was actually derived from the grimoires that were its supposed sources.

Levi's imagination made his books very readable – but valueless as serious studies of the occult tradition.

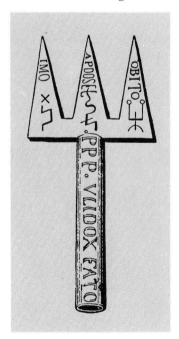

Above: Levi's version of the 'trident of Paracelsus' to which he attributed extraordinary qabalistic significance. However his misreading of the ancient texts had led him astray – Paracelsus merely regarded the trident as a device to cure sexual impotence brought about by witchcraft

Left: Levi's design for the Great Seal of Solomon, sometimes known as the Double Triangle of Solomon. This shows the magician's acknowledgement of the duality of all things – with the good shown above and the evil below – and also the belief that each man reflects the Universe (the 'macrocosm') in himself (the 'microcosm'); thus fulfilling the laws of heaven as expressed in the magical formula 'As above, so below'

ghost of Apollonius to visible appearance Levi published a book entitled *The dogma of high magic*. In this and its sequel, *The ritual of high magic*, published two years later, Levi presented what he claimed to be an accurate account of the theory and practice of alchemy, ceremonial magic, divination and the other 'occult sciences'. In reality these treatises are often grossly inaccurate where matters of fact are concerned. Many of his definitive statements are, quite simply, erroneous. Some of these errors were probably the result of carelessness in the use of manuscripts and other primary sources – Levi was a widely, but not deeply, read man – others can be attributed to deliberate distortion for no other purpose than the production of exciting reading. A particularly gross example is provided by Levi's account of 'the Trident of Paracelsus', a three-pronged fork inscribed with various mystic symbols. Levi asserted that the three prongs represented both the Christian Trinity of Father, Son and Holy Ghost and the alchemical elements (principles) of salt, sulphur and mercury. The trident expressed, Levi added:

> . . . the synthesis of the Trinity in Unity. . . . Paracelsus ascribed to it all the virtues which cabbalistic Hebrews attribute to the Name of Jehovah and the thaumaturgic [magical] properties of ABRACADABRA, used by the hierophants of Alexandria.

All this is unmitigated rubbish. Paracelsus certainly wrote of this trident; equally certainly he did not attribute to it all the virtues of 'the Name of Jehovah' – he regarded it as a device to be used for the cure of sexual impotence brought about by witchcraft. According to Paracelsus those inflicted in

this way should make a trident from an old horseshoe 'on the Day of Venus and in the Hour of Saturn', inscribe it with various occult symbols, and conceal it in the bed of a running stream. 'By this means,' wrote Paracelsus, 'thou shalt be delivered in nine days and the person that has brought this mischief upon thee shall get something himself in that place [the genitals].' All this is very interesting, no doubt – but it is a long way from Levi's 'synthesis of the Trinity in Unity' and 'the thaumaturgic properties of Abracadabra'.

Designs upon the Tarot

On occasion Levi did more than distort the facts – he invented them to suit his purpose. Thus, for example, he wanted to prove that the Tarot cards (see page 740) were known to, and employed by, occultists of the 16th and 17th centuries. He therefore specifically stated that there were references to the Tarot in the writings of such men as Abbot Trithemius, the 16th century scholar, and Knorr von Rosenroth, the 17th century qabalist. In truth there are no such references.

Inaccuracies of this sort flawed all the literary work of Levi; anyone who looks for reliable accounts of the history of Western occultism and the techniques employed by its devotees must seek elsewhere than in the writings of the French magician.

Nevertheless, Levi's *theories* as to how magic supposedly works cannot be neglected. For not only are they interesting in their own right, but they have inspired whole generations of occultists, including H.P. Blavatsky (see page 377) and the magician

Aleister Crowley (see page 625).

As far as Levi was concerned three fundamental theories – which he called 'dogmas' – explained all allegedly supernatural phenomena, from miraculous healings apparently induced by holy relics to the table-turning of Spiritualist mediums.

The first of these theories is the 'dogma of correspondence', an idea of great antiquity. According to this the soul of a human being is a microcosm, a little universe that properly reflects in miniature the macrocosm, the great universe in which we live. Every factor in the universe has its counterpart in the soul and, by means of traditional occult practices, the magician can change the world outside himself by changing the little world inside.

The link between the inner and outer worlds is the 'astral light', an invisible but all pervading substance whose existence forms the basis of the second of Levi's dogmas. According to Levi this astral (literally 'starry') light has a close relationship to matter, each physical object having an astral twin that is, in a sense, primary – to the mage the world of matter reflects the astral world rather than vice versa. By manipulating the astral light it is possible, said Levi, for the occultist to influence both the physical universe (to tip tables or heal the sick, for example) and the feelings and modes of consciousness of other living beings.

This manipulation can be achieved by the trained human imagination and will; Levi's third fundamental theory is that will and imagination are real natural forces, capable – when properly harnessed – of producing even more spectacular effects than those produced by, say, electricity.

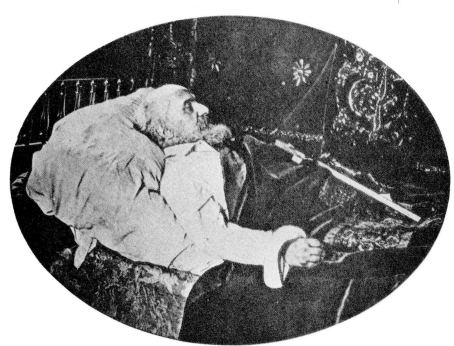

During his lifetime Levi's theories attracted little attention. His books sold only moderately, and he eked out a scanty living by taking 'occult pupils'. And many of his contemporaries regarded him as no more than a charlatan.

Yet he had his disciples, men and women who believed that they had learned much of value from his writings. And there are those in the late 20th century who think the same – Levi's influence has proved an abiding one. In a sense the ghost of Apollonius, raised by Levi well over a century ago, is still with us today – casting a long shadow.

Above: Levi on his deathbed in 1875. Many modern occultists still regard him as one of the world's greatest authorities on the theory and practice of ritual magic, holding in special esteem his writings on the symbolism of the Tarot cards, some of which he designed himself, such as the '14th Key of the Tarot', the card of Temperance from the 22 cards of the Greater Trumps (left). Other occultists have used it as the inspiration for their own cards, such as those designed by the early leader of the Golden Dawn, S. L. MacGregor Mathers (far left) and the modern designer Miranda Payne's pack (right)

Defying the law of gravity

The power to overcome the force of gravity may be the product of long training, or may occur spontaneously, amazing levitator and onlookers alike. LYNN PICKNETT **surveys some famous cases of this extraordinary talent**

THREE NOTABLE MEMBERS of London society witnessed, on 16 December 1868, an incident so extraordinary that it is still the focus of controversy. Viscount Adare, the Master of Lindsay and Captain Wynne saw the famous medium Daniel Dunglas Home rise into the air and float out of one window in a large house in fashionable London and then float in at another – over 80 feet (24 metres) from the ground it is claimed. D. D. Home became known primarily for his levitations, of himself and of objects – on one occasion a grand piano – but he was not alone in having this 'impossible' ability to defy the law of gravity.

St Joseph of Copertino (1603–1663) flew into the air every time he was emotionally excited. Being of an excitable nature, he often made levitations, and they were well witnessed. A simple peasant – some say he was actually feeble-minded – this boy from Apulia, Italy, spent his youth trying to achieve religious ecstasy by such means as self-flagellation, starvation and wearing hair-shirts. He became a Franciscan at the age of 22, and then his religious fervour 'took off' quite literally.

St Joseph and his 'giddiness'

Joseph became something of an embarrassment to his superiors. During Mass one Sunday he rose into the air and flew onto the altar in the midst of the candles; he was quite badly burned as a result.

For 35 years Joseph was excluded from all public services because of his disconcerting habits, but still tales of his levitations spread. While walking with a Benedictine monk in the monastery gardens he suddenly flew up into an olive tree. Unfortunately he couldn't fly back down, so his fellow-monks had to fetch a ladder.

A surgeon, at least two cardinals and one Pope (Urban VIII), among many others, witnessed Joseph's extraordinary spells of weightlessness – which he called 'my giddi-nesses'. He spent his entire life in a state of prayer, and the Church concluded the levitations must be the work of God.

Another levitating saint was St Teresa of Avila, who died in 1582. This remarkable mystic experienced the same feelings as many people feel during the common 'flying dreams'. She described how she felt about her levitations:

It seemed to me, when I tried to make some resistance, as if a great force

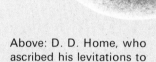

Above: D. D. Home, who ascribed his levitations to the work of spirits

Above right: Home floats into the air with no visible means of support

Below: St Joseph of Copertino owed his canonisation to his ability to levitate

beneath my feet lifted me up. . . . I confess that it threw me into great fear, very great indeed at first; for in seeing one's body thus lifted up from the earth, though the spirit draws it upwards after itself (and that with great sweetness, if unresisted) the senses are not lost; at least I was so much myself as able to see that I was being lifted up. After the rapture was over, I have to say my body seemed frequently to be buoyant, as if all weight had departed from it, so much so that now and then I scarce knew my feet touched the ground.

So insistent were her levitations that she begged the sisters to hold her down when she felt an 'attack' coming on, but often there was no time for preventive measures – she simply rose off the floor until the weightlessness passed.

Most levitators are believers in one particular system, be it Christianity, Hindu mysticism, ancient Egyptian mysteries or Spiritualism. It was to this last category that D. D. Home belonged.

Born in Scotland and brought up in America, Home was a puny, artistic child. At the age of 13 he had a vision of a friend, Edwin. Home announced to his aunt's family

that it must mean that Edwin had been dead for three days. This was proved to be true. Home's career as a medium had begun – but it was not until he was 19 that he was to defy the law of gravity.

Ward Cheney, a prosperous silk-manufacturer, held a seance at his home in Connecticut in August 1852. D. D. Home was there to provide the usual 'spiritualist' manifestations – table-turning, rappings, floating trumpets and mysterious lights.

Home was quite capable of keeping the guests entertained in this fashion but something happened, completely unannounced, that made his name overnight. He floated up into the air until his head was touching the ceiling. Among the guests was the sceptical reporter, F. L. Burr, editor of the *Hartford Times*. He wrote of this bizarre and unexpected incident:

Suddenly, without any expectation on the part of the company, Home was taken up into the air. I had hold of his hand at the time and I felt his feet – they were lifted a foot [30 centimetres] from the floor. He palpitated from head to foot with the contending emotions of joy and fear which choked his utterances. Again and again he was taken from the floor, and the third time he was carried to the ceiling of the apartment, with which his hands and feet came into gentle contact.

Home's career advanced rapidly; he was lionised in seance parlour and royal court alike. He came back to Europe to inspire adoration and scepticism (Robert Browning's

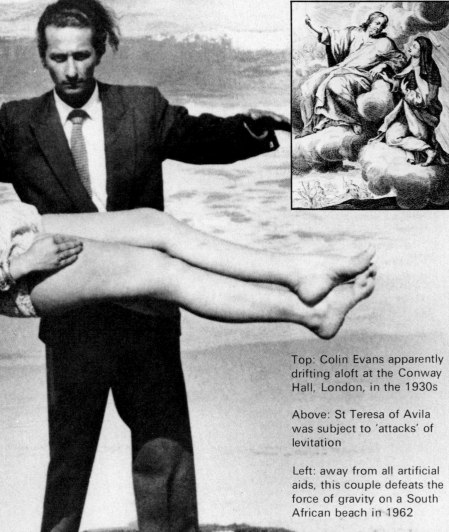

Top: Colin Evans apparently drifting aloft at the Conway Hall, London, in the 1930s

Above: St Teresa of Avila was subject to 'attacks' of levitation

Left: away from all artificial aids, this couple defeats the force of gravity on a South African beach in 1962

satirical poem 'Mr Sludge' was based on his own biased view of the medium). Wherever he went there were bizarre phenomena – winds howled in still rooms, apports of fresh flowers fell from the ceiling, doors opened and shut, fireballs zigzagged around the room – and Home levitated.

The famous occasion already mentioned when he floated out of one window and in through another, is still the subject of heated debate, particularly since the incident was documented by respectable witnesses. One of them, the Master of Lindsay (later the Earl of Crawford) wrote:

I was sitting with Mr Home and Lord Adare and a cousin of his [Captain Wynne]. During the sitting Mr Home went into a trance and in that state was carried out of the window in the room next to where we were, and was brought in at our window. The distance between the windows was about seven feet six inches [2.3 metres], and there was not the slightest foothold between them, nor was there more than a 12-inch [30-centimetre] projection to each window, which served as a ledge to put flowers on. We heard the window in the next room lift up, and almost immediately after we saw Home floating in the air outside our window. The moon was shining full into the room; my back was to the light, and I saw the shadow on the wall of the windowsill, and Home's feet about six inches [15 centimetres] above it. He remained in this position for a few seconds, then raised the window and glided into the room feet foremost and sat down.

Sceptics such as Frank Podmore or, more recently, John Sladek, have tried to disprove

Top: the classic stage levitation. The girl, Marva Ganzel, is first hypnotised into a cataleptic trance while balanced on two swords. When one is taken away, she somehow remains suspended in mid-air

Above: Frank Podmore, who suggested that D. D. Home's most famous levitation was merely an hallucination

Right: accounts of levitation and other manifestations of the seance room did not impress *Punch*, which in 1863 published this lampoon, showing that some surprises, at least, could be administered by all too explicable means

this levitation, although neither of them was among the witnesses. Sladek attempts to discredit the three who were present by comparing the details of their stories – such as how high the balconies were from the street, or indeed, whether there were any balconies at all.

Podmore, on the other hand, is more subtle in his scepticism. He mentions the fact that a few days before the levitation, and in front of the same witnesses, Home had opened the window and stood on the ledge outside. He had pointedly drawn their attention to himself standing on the narrow ledge some considerable distance from the ground. Podmore remarked drily 'the medium had thus, as it were, furnished a rough sketch of the picture which he aimed at producing.' On another occasion Home suddenly announced 'I'm rising, I'm rising', before proceeding to levitate in front of several witnesses.

Podmore implied that Home's levitations were nothing more than hallucinations produced by his hypnotic suggestion, rather in the same manner that the Indian rope trick is said to be a mass hallucination, the secret being in the magician's patter.

But even in the face of extreme hostility, Home remained a successful levitator for over 40 years. Among his witnesses were Emperor Napoleon III, John Ruskin and Bulwer Lytton – and many hundreds more, not all of whom were as inconsistent in their testimonies as Adare, Wynne and Lindsay. Moreover during that long span of time and mostly in broad daylight, Home was never proved to be a fraud. And despite Podmore's accusations Home never went out of his way to build up an atmosphere heavy with suggestibility. In fact, he was one of the few

Ridicule has long been poured on the notion that people can free themselves from the force of gravity: this cartoon (left), entitled 'The Day's Folly', was published by Sergent in 1783. But Alexandra David-Neel (below) came back from 14 years in Tibet with no doubt that adepts could achieve weightlessness

mediums who actively eschewed 'atmosphere' – he preferred a normal or bright light to darkness and encouraged the sitters to chat normally rather than 'hold hands and concentrate'.

Although in his mature years Home could levitate at will, he apparently also levitated without being aware of it. On one occasion, when his host drew his attention to the fact that he was hovering above the cushions of his armchair, Home seemed most surprised.

Stage illusionists frequently pride themselves on their *pièce de résistance*; putting their assistant into a 'trance', balancing her on the points of two swords – then removing the swords so that she hangs in the air without apparent support. Sometimes she is 'hypnotised' and seen to rise further into the air – still without visible means of support. One of two things must be happening: either she does not rise into the air at all (that is, we

all suffer a mass hallucination) or she rises aided by machinery invisible to us.

Of course, Home and other spiritualists would also attribute their feats of apportation or levitation to 'machinery invisible to us' – but in their case the machinery would be the agency of spirits. To the end of his life, Home maintained that he could only fly through the air because he was lifted up by the spirits, who thus demonstrated their existence. But he described a typical levitation as follows:

I feel no hands supporting me, and, since the first time, I have never felt fear; though, should I have fallen from the ceiling of some rooms in which I have been raised, I could not have escaped serious injury. I am generally lifted up perpendicularly; my arms frequently become rigid, and are drawn above my head, as if I were grasping the unseen power which slowly raises me from the floor.

The gravity enigma

And yet we do not refer in this spiritualistic way to the 'unseen power' that keeps us *on* the floor. Every schoolboy knows about Newton and his discovery of the law of gravity. But psychical research points to the relative ease with which certain sensitives can turn this law on its head.

In her book *Mystère et magique en Tibet* (1931), Madame Alexandra David-Neel, the French explorer who spent 14 years in and around Tibet, told how she came upon a naked man, weighed down with heavy chains. His companion explained to her that his mystical training had made his body so light that, unless he wore iron chains, he would float away.

It would seem that gravity does not necessarily have the hold on us we have been taught it has. Sir William Crookes, the renowned scientist and psychical researcher, had this to say about D. D. Home:

The phenomena I am prepared to attest are so extraordinary, and so directly oppose the most firmly-rooted articles of scientific belief – amongst others, the ubiquity and invariable action of the force of gravitation – that, even now, on recalling the details of what I have witnessed, there is an antagonism in my mind between *reason*, which pronounces it to be scientifically impossible, and the consciousness that my senses, both of touch and sight, are not lying witnesses.

So we conclude that in some *special* cases – such as saints or particularly gifted mediums – levitation exists. But there is a growing body of thought that puts forward the idea that anyone can do it, providing he or she has the right training – students of transcendental meditation claim to do it all the time.

The art of levitation

It is claimed that many ancient peoples knew the secrets of levitation. But it is not, apparently, a lost art: some people today claim to be able to attain weightlessness at will. LYNN PICKNETT investigates

A UNIQUE SERIES of photographs appeared in the magazine *Illustrated London News* on 6 June 1936. They showed the successive stages in the levitation of an Indian *yogi*, Subbayah Pullavar – thus proving that, whatever else it was, this phenomenon was not a hypnotic illusion.

A European witness of the event, P. Y. Plunkett, sets the scene:

> The time was about 12.30 p.m. and the sun directly above us so that shadows played no part in the performance. . . . Standing quietly by was Subbayah Pullavar, the performer, with long hair, a drooping moustache and a wild look in his eye. He salaamed to us and stood chatting for a while. He had been practising this particular branch of yoga for nearly 20 years (as had past generations of his family). We asked permission to take photographs of the performance and he gave it willingly. . . .

Plunkett gathered together about 150 witnesses while the performer began his ritual preparations. Water was poured around the tent in which the act of levitation was to take place; leather-soled shoes were banned inside the circle, and the performer entered

Photographs taken of a levitation performance carried out by an Indian yogi, Subbayah Pullavar, before a large number of witnesses. The photographs were taken by the Englishman P. Y. Plunkett and a friend, and published in the *Illustrated London News* of 6 June 1936. The first photograph (below) shows the yogi before levitation, lying inside a tent. He is grasping a cloth-wrapped stick, which he continues to hold throughout the performance. The tent is then closed (right) for some minutes during the mysterious act of levitation itself

the tent alone. Some minutes later helpers removed the tent and there, inside the circle, was the fakir, floating on the air.

Plunkett and another witness came forward to investigate: the fakir was suspended in the air about a yard from the ground. Although he held on to a cloth-covered stick, this seemed to be for purposes of balance only – not for support. Plunkett and his friend examined the space around and under Subbayah Pullavar, and found it innocent of any strings or other 'invisible' apparatus. The yogi was in a trance and many witnesses believed that he had indisputably levitated,

As the levitation performance continues, the curtains of the tent are drawn back and the yogi appears, floating in mid-air (top). Plunkett and his friend examined the space beneath and around the yogi, but were unable to find any evidence of strings or other supporting apparatus. Although some sceptics have claimed that the yogi was, in fact, not levitating but merely in a cataleptic trance, the relaxed position of the hand on the post suggests that the body of the yogi was indeed very nearly weightless during the performance. After levitation (above right) the yogi's body was so stiff that five men could not bend his limbs

although it has been suggested that he had, in fact, merely passed into a cataleptic trance. The famous photographs were taken from various angles during the four minutes of the performance, and then the tent was re-erected around the fakir. Evidently the 'descent' was something very private, but Plunkett managed to witness it through the thin tent walls:

> After about a minute he appeared to sway and then very slowly began to descend, still in a horizontal position. He took about five minutes to move from the top of the stick to the ground, a distance of about three feet [1 metre] . . . When Subbayah was back on the ground his assistants carried him over to where we were sitting and asked if we would try to bend his limbs. Even with assistance we were unable to do so.

The yogi was rubbed and splashed with cold water for a further five minutes before he came out of his trance and regained full use of his limbs.

The swaying motion and horizontal position that Plunkett witnessed seem to be essential to true levitation. Students of transcendental meditation (TM) are taught, under the supervision of the Maharishi Mahesh Yogi at his headquarters in Switzerland, to levitate. One student described this 'impossible' achievement:

> People would rock gently, then more and more, and then start lifting off in to the air. You should really be in a lotus position to do it – you can hurt yourself landing if you've got a dangling undercarriage. To begin with it's like the Wright brothers' first flight – you come down with a bump. That's why we have to sit on foam rubber cushions. Then you learn to control it better, and it becomes totally exhilarating.

So can *anyone* induce levitation? The TM

Right: the Transcendental Meditation movement claims that this photograph shows students levitating. It is alleged that, under the supervision of tutors, the students achieve weightlessness through meditation

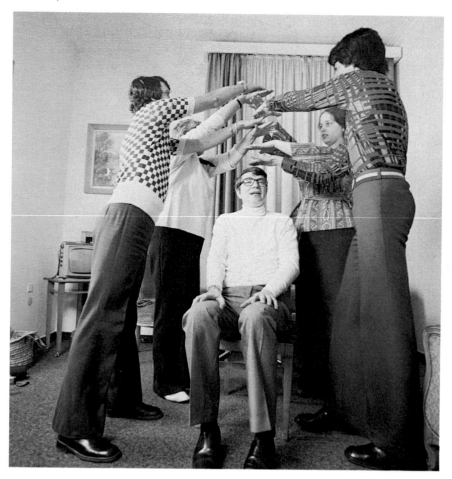

dowser's rod, intervenes to achieve the miracle of nullifying the force of gravity.

It seems that religious fervour may have something to do with the phenomenon; there are many reports of levitation by both Christian and Buddhist monks. In 1902 Aleister Crowley met his compatriot Alan Bennett, who had become a Buddhist monk, at his monastery in Burma in 1902; he, too, had become so weightless that he was 'blown about like a leaf'.

Alexandra David-Neel, the French explorer of the early 20th century, describes witnessing an extraordinary kind of long-distance running by a Tibetan lama: 'The man did not run. He seemed to lift himself from the ground proceeding by leaps. It looked as if he had been endowed with the elasticity of a ball and rebounded each time his feet touched the ground. His steps had the regularity of a pendulum.' The lama is said to have run hundreds of miles using this strange form of locomotion, keeping his eyes fixed on some far-distant goal.

The famous Russian ballet dancer Nijinsky, too, had the extraordinary ability of appearing to be almost weightless. He would jump up high and fall as lightly – and slowly – as thistledown in what was known as the 'slow vault'.

Like many inexplicable phenomena, levitation seems to be singularly useless. The distance covered is rarely more than a few

students believe they can, after a stringent mental training; the disciplines, both spiritual and physical, of the yogis seem to prepare them to defy gravity. It is fairly easy to induce a state of semi-weightlessness, as this account of a fat publican – a perfectly ordinary person – being raised in the air as a party trick shows.

The fat man sat on a chair and four people, including his small daughter, demonstrated the impossibility of lifting him with their index fingers only, placed in his armpits and the crooks of his knees. They then removed their fingers and put their hands in a pile on top of his head, taking care to interleave their hands so that no one person's two hands were touching. The four concentrated deeply for about 15 seconds; then someone gave a signal, and quickly they replaced their fingers in armpits and knees – and the fat publican floated into the air.

Sceptics might point to the intervention of non-spiritual spirits, bearing in mind the location of the event, but the phenomenon has been witnessed hundreds of times in pubs, homes, and school-yards. If it works – and one must assume it does – then how is it possible?

The sudden burst of concentration of four people with a single, 'impossible' target could, some people believe, unlock the hidden magic of the human will. Or it has been suggested that a little-known natural force, perhaps the same one that guides the

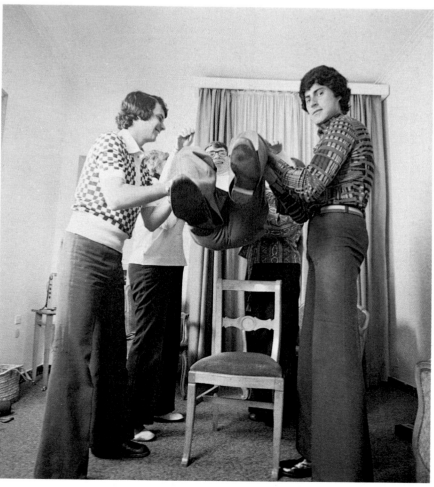

Left: an aerial view of the white horse at Uffington in Oxfordshire. The terrain on which it is carved is so hilly that its true shape can only really be appreciated from the air – a fact that has led some to speculate that the people who carved it were able to levitate and inspect their work from above

Opposite page: Uri Geller and some friends conduct a levitation session with Colin Wilson as subject. First (top) the experimenters place their hands on top of the subject's head, in such a way that no one person's two hands are touching. Then, on a command from Geller, they remove their hands from the subject's head and place their index fingers under his arms and knees. The subject immediately rises into the air (bottom)

feet or, at the most, the height of a room – useful only for dusting or decorating the home. But some people believe that the ancients could levitate quite easily, and did so to design certain enormous earthworks that can be appreciated only from the air, such as some of the white horses of the chalk downland in England and the desert patterns in Peru.

The limitations of modern levitation need not have applied to the ancients – perhaps they had developed the art to a high degree and could soar into the sky at will. Like other psychic faculties, it appears that levitation is an art, once almost lost, that is now being re-learned by determined students. Perhaps one day, modern levitators will be able to 'fly' as the ancient Druids supposedly could.

The reported 'flights' of the ancients suggest to some researchers that they were out-of-the-body experiences (see pages 2149 and 2152) or astral travel, rather than transportation. Certainly, many accounts of levitation or flying read like lucid dreams – and dreams of flying are very common experiences. Some dreamers wake up convinced they *can* fly; fortunately, the sights and sounds of the real world generally bring them to their senses before they can experiment.

With a few exceptions, it seems that one can levitate only after long periods of training and discipline: in this way, the body is mysteriously 'given permission' to defy the law of gravity. Perhaps there is a law of levitation with a secret formula – an 'Open, Sesame' – which the initiate uses before rising off the ground.

This theory would explain the unusual cases of spontaneous or random levitation that fascinated Charles Fort. One such case was 12-year-old Henry Jones from Shepton Mallet who, during the year 1657, was observed on several occasions to rise into the air. Once he was able to put his hands flat against the ceiling, and on another occasion he took off and sailed 30 yards (27 metres) over the garden wall. The phenomenon lasted only a year – but this was long enough for the rumour to spread that he was 'bewitched'.

Certainly levitation is a rare phenomenon, but when considered with other accounts of equally rare and bizarre human attributes, such as incombustibility, elongation and superhuman strength, it must be taken seriously. Mothers who lift cars off their trapped children, firewalkers (see page 1093) and sleepwalkers who perform 'impossible' feats pose profound questions about the nature of Man's physical and psychical potential. Perhaps we are intended to be able to defy gravity at will. Until we understand the nature of the phenomenon it must remain one of Man's mysterious hidden powers.

D. D. Home: flight from reality?

The pinnacle of D. D. Home's career came when he was seen to float out of one window and in through another. But, asks LYNN PICKNETT, could this famous incident have been his one act of calculated fraud?

ONE OF THE MOST controversial events in the history of paranormal phenomena involved the most famous Victorian medium, Daniel Dunglas Home, who had never been detected in fraudulent activity during any of his 1500 recorded seances. This particular event, so special yet to many so suspicious, was Home's alleged levitation out of one window – some considerable distance from the ground – and back in through another. There were three witnesses to this bizarre incident: Lord Adare, his cousin Captain Charles Wynne, and the Master of Lindsay – all prominent and reputable members of London society. Yet the curious thing is that

Above: an artist's impression of Home levitating. Although his psychic talents included incombustibility, bodily elongation and the manifestation of apports, he was primarily famous for his spectacular levitations

those are the only details about this event that are known with any certainty. The classic – some would say credulous – account is given on page 1674. The results of more penetrating and objective modern research are given space here.

On 13 December 1868 those three gentlemen met for a seance with Home in an apartment in the central London area. Even their accounts of where the incident took place differed. Lord Adare said 5 Buckingham Gate, Kensington; he also said in another account that it took place at Ashley Place, Westminster. Lindsay, however, favoured Victoria Street, Westminster.

Author, sceptic and debunker of the paranormal John Sladek lists other discrepancies among the witnesses' various statements in his book *The New Apocrypha*:

There was a ledge 4 inches [10 centimetres] wide below the windows (Adare); a ledge 1½ inches [4 centimetres] wide (Lindsay); no foothold at all (Lindsay); balconies 7 feet [2 metres] apart (Adare); no balconies at all (Lindsay). The windows were 85 feet [25 metres] from the street (Lindsay); 70 feet [21 metres] (Lindsay); 80 feet [24 metres] (Home); on the third floor (Adare); on the first floor (Adare). It was dark (Adare); there was bright moonlight (Lindsay). Home was asleep in one room and the witnesses went into the next (Adare); Home left the witnesses in one room and went himself into the next (Adare).

In the footsteps of D. D. Home

Significantly, Captain Wynne's only recorded statement on the matter simply says: 'Home went out of one window and came in at another.' The word 'levitation' is conspicuous by its absence.

However, discrediting the witnesses by quoting the discrepancies in their statements does not necessarily imply the incident never took place. Nor have the conflicting addresses given proved too much of an obstacle in tracing the scene of the phenomenon. Archie Jarman, in his meticulously researched article published in *Alpha* magazine in October 1980, described how he managed to track down the house in question, using as his first reference *one* letter – written to Sir Francis Burnand by Lord Adare.

In this letter Adare states that the event took place at Ashley House, but gave it the wrong address, saying it was in Victoria Street. Archie Jarman noted:

The two rooms at Ashley House were connected by folding doors . . . The sash-windows opened onto stone balconies about 15 inches [38 centimetres] wide and running the width of the windows. Lord Lindsay later recorded that the balconies were 7 feet 5 inches [2 metres 13 centimetres] apart and it was this gap that Home was supposed to have crossed by means of levitation.

An important clue given by Adare was that there was a 6-inch [15-centimetre] recess in the main wall of the building between the windows.

Jarman walked the length of Victoria Street hoping to find a faded inscription on one of the older buildings that would reveal the real 'Ashley House', but he found nothing helpful and no one who knew of its existence. But he did find an 'Ashley Place' close to the precincts of Westminster Cathedral and one of its few remaining older buildings looked promising. This was 1–10 Ashley Place. The caretaker told Jarman of the building's chequered history since its construction in 1845; of the minor repairs carried out after a bomb had exploded close to it in 1944, and that the suites – residential in Home's time – were now offices. But more significant was the fact that it used to be called 'Ashley House' before the GPO changed it to 'Ashley Place' in 1930 for some reason of their own.

Teetering on the ledge

As Jarman says, 'seeing as Home had been flying high' he took the lift to the top floor, which was occupied by a firm of architects. Surprisingly, perhaps, Mr Perry, one of the executives of the firm, did not think Mr Jarman a crank in his search for the suite where D.D. Home 'flew'. Indeed, he was most helpful. He showed Jarman that two of his rooms were, in fact, connected by folding doors as described in Adare's account.

Mr Perry and Archie Jarman measured the distance between the balconies – 7 feet 5 inches (2 metres 13 centimetres), confirming Lindsay's description and the 6-inch (15-centimetre) recess mentioned by Adare was also present. The drop to the ground was 45 feet (13.5 metres) – not quite the 80 feet (24 metres) claimed by Home, but still a long way to fall.

Jarman noticed an architectural feature not mentioned in any of the witnesses' accounts – a flat cornice, or ledge, about 5 inches (13 centimetres) wide, ran just below the balconies. Perhaps, after all, the irreproachable Home had edged his way along this narrow foothold from window to window, simply fulfilling Captain Wynne's baldly descriptive statement.

However, Mr Jarman was nothing if not courageous. With some help from the caretaker, and taking sensible precautions, he tried to make his own way along the ledge but soon gave up. It was impossible to cross between the balconies on that ledge.

Another explanation that occurred to Archie Jarman was that Home had perhaps walked a tightrope between the balconies, having previously strung a rope or cord between them and attached it to the old-fashioned pivot-bolt of the blinds, which would have protruded beyond the windows. Intrepidly, Jarman proposed to try this death-defying feat himself but the landlords

Right: Daniel Dunglas Home (1833–1886) was undoubtedly the most famous medium of all time. He claimed to be the love-child of a Scottish peer but was brought up modestly in the United States by an aunt

Above: Home was often the butt of cartoonists. His spectacular feats brought him wealth and fame; but critics accused him of being a fraud and a gold-digger and his close friendship with Lord Adare was whispered to be 'unnatural'. The press made the most of Home's legal adoption by a rich old lady, and the fact that he fled from her when her attentions became more than motherly

Further reading
T. H. Hall, *New light on old ghosts*, Duckworth 1965
D. H. Rawcliffe, *Occult and supernatural phenomena*, Dover 1987
Steve Richards, *Levitation*, Borgo Press 1986
John Sladek, *The New Apocrypha*, Granada Publishing 1978

refused to sanction such a dangerous 'reconstruction'. However, it seems likely that Home could have faked his *pièce de résistance* by some artificial means such as tightrope-walking, or even swinging, Tarzan-like, between balconies.

Jarman's suspicions had been aroused by two unusual conditions surrounding the 'levitation' on the evening of 13 December 1868. One was Home's insistence that he *would* 'levitate' out of a specific window and back in through another. Yet this was the very medium who often remarked that he had no control over the 'spirits' who, he believed, raised him up. So why put them to the test with 45 feet (13.5 metres) of thin air and a stony pavement beneath him?

Jarman draws our attention to a second suspicious factor. Before his exit from the window Home made the three witnesses promise not to move from their chairs until he re-emerged. When he reappeared he thanked them for their co-operation in this matter. But if they had rushed to the window what would they have seen, what would their presence have ruined? The powers of the spirits? Home's concentration as he walked the tightrope or swung from balcony to balcony? Home's entire reputation once and for all? We shall never know, for like the noble English gentlemen they were, they kept their promise and remained seated, well away from the window. They saw him go out of one window and come in through another. That is all they saw.

And yet hundreds of people had witnessed Home levitate in drawing rooms in America and all over Europe. There was no doubt in their minds that the levitations they witnessed were totally genuine, inexplicable phenomena. It would be very sad if Home's only deliberate cheating was on the occasion of his most famous 'triumph'.

The ley line puzzle

Is the network of straight lines that joins the sacred megalithic sites of Europe merely a relic of a system of ancient pathways? Or is it an indication that the technology of primitive Man was far more advanced than we suppose? ANNA PAVORD investigates

LOOKING OUT OVER THE COUNTRYSIDE at Blackwardine one June day in 1921 Alfred Watkins, a respectable Herefordshire brewer, had a startling vision – which he later described as 'a flood of ancestral memory'. What he saw was a totally new pattern in the familiar countryside in front of him – a complex network of straight lines linking burial mounds, hilltops, ancient churches and crossroads to make 'a fairy chain, stretched from mountain peak to mountain peak, as far as the eye could reach, and paid out until it touched the high places of the earth at a number of ridges, banks and knowls.'

Watkins, who had his reputation in a small town to consider, did not at first tell anyone about his discovery. He sat down with maps

and rulers and began carefully checking for evidence that would back up his inspired vision. Time and again, he found that the lines on his maps passed through the same *kinds* of places – all ancient, and all of some significance to Man.

It was Watkins who coined the term *ley* to describe these lines. Others call them scemb lines, geomantic corridors, or simply alignments – but all who believe in their existence agree on the features that can be taken as their primary markers.

Stone circles – of which there are about 900 in Britain – are important markers, as are stone rows, such as the one on Stall Moor that marches for 2 miles (3 kilometres) across Dartmoor, linking a stone circle with a

Above: Alfred Watkins, the Herefordshire brewer who discovered that many of the megalithic sites of ancient Britain are aligned. It was he who coined the word 'ley' for these alignments – because many of the places on them have names ending in 'ley', 'lay', 'lee', 'lea' or 'leigh'

Left: monolith in the churchyard at Rudstone, Humberside. At 25 feet 6 inches (7.7 metres), it is the tallest standing stone in Britain. A ley runs through the stone itself – but not through the adjacent Norman church

Barrows – man-made mounds dating from prehistoric times – are regarded as primary ley markers. It can be difficult to tell them apart from natural hillocks – many of them are no more than 18 inches (50 centimetres) high. But one feature generally indicates a genuine barrow: in fields that are otherwise grazed, or ploughed by farmers, barrows are often left intact, as is the case with the Stoney Littleton long barrow in Avon (left). Long barrows are among the oldest in Britain, many of them dating from Neolithic times. They are often asymmetrical, with one end higher than the other. The commonest mounds in Britain are round barrows. They are often grouped like those at Winterbourne Stoke in Dorset (below)

important ley markers, often indicating the starting point of a ley.

Castles and early churches often appear on leys, because many of them are built on the sites of more ancient buildings or earthworks – castles, for instance, were generally built on hills because this gave the defenders a good view of the countryside and a strong defensive position. The hill itself was often a prehistoric earthwork. Excavations at Worcester, Penworham and Warrington have brought to light pre-Norman artefacts in the mounds of each of these castles.

There is a great deal of evidence to show how churches replaced and supplanted pagan shrines on the same sites. Pope Gregory, writing at the end of the sixth century AD, complained that 'The English nation, placed in an obscure corner of the world, has hitherto been wholly taken up with the adoration of wood and stones,' but concluded that 'It is not well to make people of an obstinate turn grow better by leaps, but rather by slow steps.' The missionary Augustine was advised not to destroy the old shrines and temples, but to modify them, sprinkle them with holy water, incorporating the healing qualities of the pagan wells, and

prehistoric cairn on Green Hill. Other standing stones are also possible ley markers, but not all of them are shown on the Ordnance Survey maps. It is difficult to miss a stone like the Rudston monolith, which towers 25 feet (7.5 metres) high in a churchyard near Bridlington, Humberside, or the Devil's arrows near Boroughbridge, North Yorkshire, but other stones are much smaller and more difficult to find, sometimes hidden in hedges or converted into churchyard crosses.

Patterns in the landscape

Cairns, tumuli, prehistoric camps and mounds form another group of ley markers. The oldest of these are the Neolithic long barrows, mounds of earth or of chalk that can be several hundred feet long and 100 feet (30 metres) wide. One feature that makes them easily recognisable is that one end is generally higher than the other. Round barrows are the commonest sort of mound – there are about 20,000 of them in Britain; sometimes they are clustered together, like the collection close to the A35 road at Winterbourne Abbas in Dorset, sometimes solitary.

Circular moats count as ley points, for they have often developed from ditches round tumuli. Square moats are often much later developments and cannot really be counted as 'safe' primary ley markers. Ponds sometimes fall on leys, as the light reflected from the surface of the water provides a clear landmark. Ponds and fords are not generally considered to be primary markers, but can act as points of confirmation of leys. Holy wells, such as St Ambrew's Well at Crantock, near Newquay in Cornwall, and St Hilda's Well at Hinderwell in North Yorkshire, are

continues by way of a moat and an old church at Marston Magna to finish at Ansford Church, just north of Castle Cary.

Despite the evidence, there are many people who do not believe in the existence of these strange patterns and alignments. Statisticians discount the existence of leys by saying that, in an island as small, as varied and as densely populated as Britain, straight lines drawn in any direction on Ordnance Survey maps are bound to run through ancient sites, holy wells, tumuli and other features that ley hunters consider significant. Mathematicians prepared formulae and tested them on a computer in an attempt to prove that ley lines occur simply by chance. Unfortunately for the statisticians, however, their formulae turned out to be enemies rather than allies. Their analysis showed that the chance factor was only one in 200 for a six-point ley – that is, for six significant and generally accepted ley markers to fall exactly in a straight line not more than 30 miles (50 kilometres) long. For a seven-point ley, the random element soars to one in 1000. These results were obtained from formulae that were, if anything, loaded *against* the ley concept, for many alignments feature six or more points in a length of perhaps only 10 or 12 miles (12 or 15 kilometres).

Rifle-barrel accuracy

A completely separate and detailed computer analysis was prepared to test some work that John Michell published in *The old stones of Land's End*. Michell had surveyed 53 sites in Cornwall, using only those that were known to be prehistoric. He found 22 leys between them, 'of rifle-barrel accuracy', with the sites visible from one to the next and forming precise alignments up to 6 miles (10 kilometres) long. The computer analysis verified all but two of Michell's alignments – and

to convert the local people slowly. This is why many churches stand on top of ancient man-made hills, such as Brent Tor on Dartmoor, or inside henge monuments, like the ruins of the strange church at Knowlton in Dorset, a 12th-century building that stands centrally in a huge prehistoric religious enclosure, a quarter of a mile (350 metres) from the village, surrounded on all sides by other enclosures and burial mounds.

A typical ley includes a number of key features. The 8-mile (13-kilometre) alignment between Warmwell and Winterbourne Steepleton in Dorset involves seven markers; two of them are churches, three tumuli. Another Dorset ley runs from the lookout point at West Bay, Bridport, right up to the prehistoric fort of Castle Cary in Somerset. This alignment, on a compass bearing 21° east of north, passes through the holy well of St Andrew's in Bridport, over the summits of Mangerton Hill and Hackthorn Hill to a group of standing stones on Toller Down. The line takes in the church at Corscombe and a settlement of Saxon times, and skims the moat surrounding the island site on which stand the 13th-century buildings of Court Farm. It then passes through the site of an abbey grange and then over the remains of a Roman building. A mile (1.5 kilometres) further on is the church of Halstock, whose parish boundaries are recorded in a charter of AD 847; the name means 'holy place'. At roughly 2-mile (3-kilometre) intervals, moving northwards, come the churches of Sutton Bingham and Barwick, then a crossing over the river Yeo at Yeovil. The ley

Above: the holy well of St Ambrew at Crantock, Cornwall. Holy wells often mark the ends of leys

Below: the ruined church at Knowlton, Dorset, which stands at the centre of a huge earthen circle. Churches were often built on sacred megalithic sites – and often act as ley markers

at Grovely Castle. The distance between the two was 6 miles (10 kilometres). He then found that Old Sarum, another prehistoric hilltop site where Salisbury's first cathedral had been built, also lay exactly 6 miles (10 kilometres) from Stonehenge, and that the same distance separated Old Sarum from Grovely Castle. The three points make a perfect equilateral triangle, too perfect to have occurred by chance. It was the first hint of megalithic Man's obsession with patterns and numbers, which he worked out in the countryside in which he lived.

Further research showed that the alignments stretched beyond the original triangle. Northwards, the line leads over Tan Hill Beacon to Cirencester; south-west, it passes through the rampant hill-figure of the Cerne Abbas giant in Dorset to end at the tree-topped beacon behind Puncknowle on the coast. The Old Sarum line, extended to the south, runs right through the present site of Salisbury Cathedral to end at the prehistoric monument of Clearbury Rings. Did the men who rebuilt the cathedral in 1220, two miles (3 kilometres) away from Old Sarum, choose this new site by chance? It seems not.

Inconceivable precision

Another bombshell for the archaeologists came in 1967 from the research of Alexander Thom, Professor Emeritus of Engineering Science at Oxford. Thom surveyed more than 600 megalithic sites in Britain and France and concluded that prehistoric Man had laid them out, with astonishingly precise engineering skill, in an astronomical alignment. Thom also discovered a basic unit of measurement, the megalithic yard of 2 feet $8\frac{5}{8}$ inches (83 centimetres).

These discoveries forced many people to revise their ideas. The eminent archaeologist Professor Atkinson wrote:

> It is important that non-archaeologists should understand how disturbing to archaeologists are the implications of Thom's work, because they do not fit the conceptual model of the prehistory of Europe which has been current during the whole of the present century and even now is beginning to crumble at the edges. . . . In terms of this model, it is almost inconceivable that mere barbarians on the remote north-west fringes of the continent should display a knowledge of mathematics and its applications hardly inferior if at all, to that of Egypt at about the same date, or that of Mesopotamia considerably later.

Professor Thom's meticulous research had established beyond doubt that early Man had constructed his monuments with precision and forethought. But what was it that inspired him to do so?

added 29 more leys he had not identified!

Professional archaeologists form another group that looks on the idea of a ley system linking Britain's ancient sites in some meaningful grid as totally absurd. They have shown not only a complete lack of interest in, but a positive hostility to, the notion. Professor Glyn Daniels, editor of *Antiquity*, the mouthpiece of the profession, has refused to accept advertisements for the monthly journal *The Ley Hunter*. The question of leys, when brought up in interviews with archaeologists, elicits the sort of response that the flat-earthers must have given to the first brave person who began to think of the world as a sphere.

Yet it was an exceedingly reputable scholar, Sir Norman Lockyer, the Astronomer Royal who, at the beginning of the century, first rediscovered an important alignment centring on Stonehenge. Lockyer found that the principal axis on which Stonehenge is aligned – the angle of the midsummer sunrise – joined with the Neolithic settlement

Above: the Iron-Age hill fort of Old Sarum in alignment with Salisbury Cathedral and another hill fort, Clearbury Ring. These sites form part of the important Old Sarum ley, which also passes through Stonehenge

Earth, energy and intuition

from instead of towards the earth.

The problem is that we look at the past with the eyes of the present, with minds trammelled by generations of conditioning. It is possible that the ley system will never make sense to us until we can free ourselves from historical preconceptions and look upon the whole idea with fresh eyes.

Alfred Watkins regarded leys in a completely matter-of-fact way, although there are hints that he suspected a more mystical aspect might exist. The alignments were there, he was sure, but he took them to be ancient trackways, with mounds, standing stones and hill notches acting as sighting marks along the way. He did a great deal of research into place-names and constructed a complicated theory based on trade routes for certain important commodities: salt, clay, tin, gold. 'Salt' place-names are very common (Salford, Sale, Saltash), but Watkins conjectured that 'white' place-names also marked ancient salt routes, and traced many leys of this kind. One in the Black Mountains passes through Whitfield House, White House, White Stone, Whitwick Manor and White House at Suckley.

There were limitations to the theory of ancient trackways, as Watkins was the first to admit. A chapter of his book *The old straight track* is headed 'Obscurities and objections'. In it Watkins forestalls his critics – and there

When he discovered the ley system, Alfred Watkins assumed that the alignments were old trading routes. But modern research suggests that they are channels for some mysterious power, as ANNA PAVORD explains

IT IS DIFFICULT – for archaeologists exceedingly difficult – to accept that the life of megalithic Man was not, as was long thought, short and uncultured, that he seemed to have access not only to sophisticated mathematical knowledge, but also to a much more arcane knowledge that is now lost to us. It irritates our sense of superiority to think that perhaps he knew something that we do not. It brings into question our reliance on the whole concept of progress; it raises a niggling suspicion that perhaps we are travelling in the wrong direction, away

Above: Men-an-tol, the Stone of the Hole, which stands at one end of a Cornish ley. Like many ley megaliths, it is traditionally a healing stone: scrofulous children, as well as people suffering from rickets and cricks in the neck, were allegedly cured by being passed three times through the central hole, and then dragged round the stone

were many – by asking why leys climb precipices when an easier route exists close by. Why do they cross the deep part of a river when a shallow reach or ford exists a little way upstream? Why do tracks sometimes run closely parallel like tramlines? What can be made of the odd confusions of burial mounds found in certain places such as the Dorset downs and Salisbury plain? The number and close proximity of these mounds far exceed what would be needed for sighting points on leys.

The places of the paths

Another chapter, 'Bible record', suggests that Watkins, despite his apparent rejection of the mystical aspect that dominates the present conception of leys, had a suspicion that trackways might not provide the complete answer, though tracks might have evolved from an earlier system laid down for a different purpose. He quotes more than 30 Bible references that he believed alluded to the ley system. From Proverbs 8:1–2 he takes the following quotation: 'Doth not wisdom cry? and understanding put forth her voice? She standeth in the top of high places, by the way in the places of the paths.'

The modern idea of the ley system is bound up with the concept of an earth force,

Above: photographs of markers on the Offa Street ley in Hereford, published by Alfred Watkins, discoverer of the ley system, in his book *The old straight track* (1925). The ley runs through St Peter's Church (left) and Hereford Cathedral (right) along Offa Street, and aligns with a small pond and a circular wooded knoll

Left: Bradgate ley in Leicestershire, showing three of the aligning points. The ley runs through two churches and a crossroads before reaching a standing stone (foreground) in a field just outside the village of Anstey. One meaning of the name 'Anstey' is 'narrow path'. The ley next passes through the 14th-century church of St Mary and runs up an ancient track on Old John Hill to end at a notch in the hillside – visible across half Leicestershire

of a pulsing, vibrant form of primal energy. Many contemporary writers on the subject believe that megalithic Man understood and practised a form of geomancy, and that he harnessed the earth force, and was able to channel it along ley lines to use it for psychic purposes that we no longer understand. Barrows, henges, earthworks, standing stones, stone circles form the tangible legacy of these lines of power. They were all elements of a great communication grid, megalithic 'radio masts' beaming energy in specific directions. The major receiving stations were the great ritual centres of Avebury, Glastonbury and Stonehenge. These 'temples' were built where the forces of the earth were concentrated most powerfully, and where ritual in some way harnessed the force and utilised it for the benefit of the community.

The concept of 'earth energy' presupposes an earth that is itself a living being permeated with a strange force – a force that waxes and wanes, possibly under the influence of the Moon or other planets. The force seems to have polarity. It can be defined as either 'positive' or 'negative', but cannot be classified simply as a magnetic or as an electrical force. The strangest and most important thing about it is that it seems to

Tracking down leys

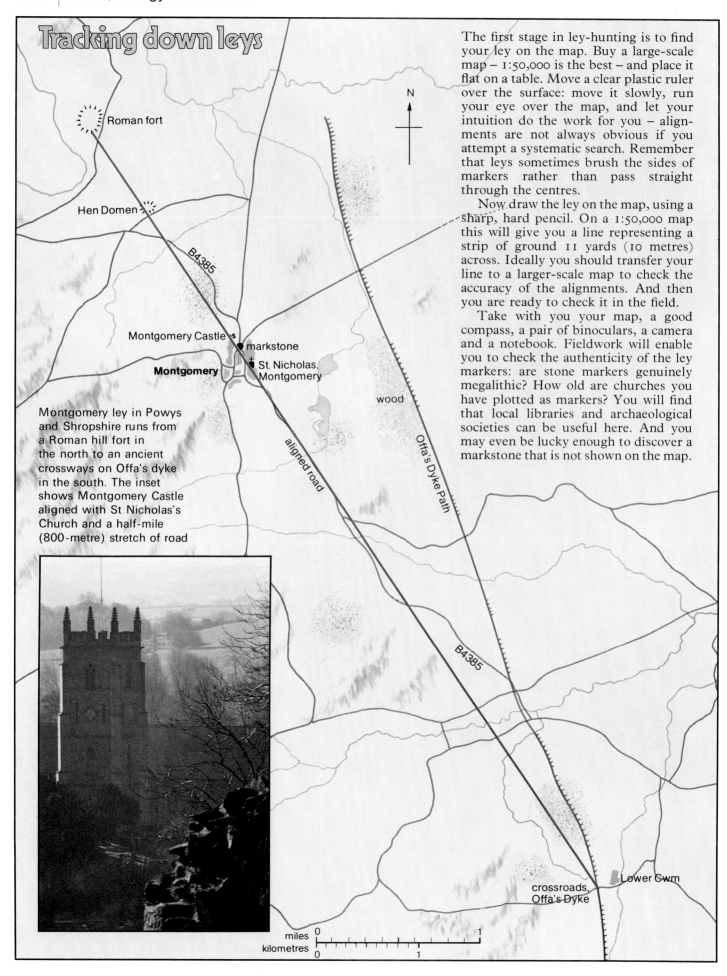

Roman fort

Hen Domen

B4385

Montgomery Castle

markstone

Montgomery

St. Nicholas, Montgomery

wood

aligned road

Offa's Dyke Path

B4385

Lower Cwm

crossroads, Offa's Dyke

N

Montgomery ley in Powys and Shropshire runs from a Roman hill fort in the north to an ancient crossways on Offa's dyke in the south. The inset shows Montgomery Castle aligned with St Nicholas's Church and a half-mile (800-metre) stretch of road

miles 0 1
kilometres 0 1

The first stage in ley-hunting is to find your ley on the map. Buy a large-scale map – 1:50,000 is the best – and place it flat on a table. Move a clear plastic ruler over the surface: move it slowly, run your eye over the map, and let your intuition do the work for you – alignments are not always obvious if you attempt a systematic search. Remember that leys sometimes brush the sides of markers rather than pass straight through the centres.

Now draw the ley on the map, using a sharp, hard pencil. On a 1:50,000 map this will give you a line representing a strip of ground 11 yards (10 metres) across. Ideally you should transfer your line to a larger-scale map to check the accuracy of the alignments. And then you are ready to check it in the field.

Take with you your map, a good compass, a pair of binoculars, a camera and a notebook. Fieldwork will enable you to check the authenticity of the ley markers: are stone markers genuinely megalithic? How old are churches you have plotted as markers? You will find that local libraries and archaeological societies can be useful here. And you may even be lucky enough to discover a markstone that is not shown on the map.

interact in some way with the human mind and, through it, affects the working of the body as well.

Hundreds of ancient sites throughout Britain are renowned in folklore for their healing properties. Despite centuries of propaganda from the Church, the myths survive, and the practices too. In Cornwall, the power of the great holed stone Men-an-tol has cured rickets in children. Wells, long before they were dubbed 'holy', were used ritually for many different illnesses. Certain standing stones and stone circles, invoked in a particular way, ensured the fertility both of crops and of women.

Anthropologists have noted how medicine men of the Sioux Indian tribe used a particular megalith, Standing Rock in South Dakota, by pressing their spines up against the stone to reactivate their psychic powers. A rock cleft in a wall of the fortress city of Sacsahraman in the Andes was used by warriors in a similar fashion. Before battle, each warrior would thrust his fist into the crevice, which was shaped like a serpent standing on its tail, and so receive, he believed, supernatural strength and courage. It seems that the force was not entirely imaginary, for a compass placed inside the cleft records a magnetic anomaly powerful enough to make the needle swing violently.

With his rod or pendulum, the dowser plays an important part in our rediscovery of the ley system, for he acts as a conductor of the earth force, in either its positive or its negative form. He also provides a useful link between the practical and mystical sides of the subject. The starting point for the practical ley hunter is the map, on which he notes possible ley markers. Then, with ruler and pencil, he tries to sort the markers out into meaningful alignments, which are checked in the field. The mystical ley hunter relies instead on the 'feelings' that he receives from certain sites. His is an intuitive rather than a quantitative approach.

Tracing the secret energy

The dowser can follow clues provided by either method and come up with corroborative evidence. He can dowse over the practical ley hunter's map, even when all markers have been obliterated, and trace the course of a ley by the gyrations of his pendulum. The actual signal that the pendulum transmits varies from person to person, but in each case there is a marked change in the reaction to positive and negative, often a switch from a clockwise to an anti-clockwise swing. Working with a pendulum or rod, the dowser can also stand by an ancient ley marker and, by systematically quartering the ground and noting the reaction of his divining tool, work out the pattern and polarity of the energy that flows into, out of and, in some cases, round and round the site.

Occasionally, the dowser can pick up signals coming from a marker that has been

Above: dowser Tom Graves following the Glastonbury ley through St Leonard's churchyard in Butleigh, Somerset. Dowsers can trace the 'overground' – a term they use for the energy that, they believe, travels above the ground along ley lines – using either a pendulum, as here, or a dowser's rod

moved from its original position on the ley. Tom Graves, in his book *Needles of stone*, describes how he and another dowser, Bill Lewis, found a 3-foot (1-metre) high markstone just inside the churchyard wall of St Stephen's Church in St Albans, Hertfordshire. They had been tracing an 'overground', the dowsers' term for the energy that travels above ground along the ley system, down Watling Street, the present A5 road. At the crossroads by the church, they found that the overground, which ran up the middle of the road, did a sharp double bend to 'talk' to the stone in the churchyard on the right, before continuing on its way north.

Dowsers investigating cases of what seem to be deliberate non-alignments of particular sites have also found that often an energy stream flows from these places to one particular point on a major ley, forming tributaries that do not themselves fall into major alignments, but that feed extra power into the main system.

The difficulty in assessing the value of the concept of leys lies in the facts that there seems to be such a huge number of them, and that no particular pattern has yet been observed in their make-up. The problem is also complicated by the fact that leys are studied and theories propounded by large numbers of people from different disciplines, many of whom do not care to disguise their own biased viewpoints. Statisticians, computer programmers, engineers, philologers, dowsers, UFO enthusiasts, psychics and astro-archaeologists have all had a go at claiming the ley system as their own. No one who has read or thought about it with any degree of seriousness denies its existence. People continue to collect facts and make deductions but those who, without prejudice, face up to the questions involved are more aware of mysteries than of answers.

An evil in the earth

The power that dowsers can sense along ley lines is generally benign – but sometimes, as one Dorset farming family found to their horror, it can turn sour. ANNA PAVORD describes the causes – and the cures

EVE IS A SMALL, HUMOROUS WOMAN of about 35, married to a Dorset farmer. About five years ago, she moved with her husband and two young sons to a new farm where they intended to raise pedigree sheep and beef cattle. The house, a rambling building of stone and thatch, was 17th century at the core, with later additions sticking out in all directions. The land fell down steeply to a valley below. They had, they said, the best view in Dorset. They also had, unknown to them at that time, a 'black stream' – or negative ley – that ran across the farm from north-west to south-east, cutting diagonally right through the middle of the house.

'I know it sounds slightly mad,' says Eve apologetically. 'I thought it was when I first got involved, but I know now that these things do exist and that they can have a very nasty effect. It happened to me, you see.'

The ley system that covers the country with its network of strange lines has a sombre as well as a sunny side. Many people believe that leys carry an earth force overground between a series of conductors such as stone

Above: when Eve, a Dorset woman, and her family moved to this farm, in her native county, they had high hopes of success in raising pedigree sheep and beef cattle. But, unknown to them, a black stream – a ley line carrying negative, harmful energy – ran right through the farm, cutting diagonally through the house itself. Things soon began to go badly wrong for Eve's family, for no apparent reason – until Eve suspected the existence of a black stream, and called in a dowser

circles and standing stones. These tap the underground power and bring it to the surface. Certain circumstances may cause the ley power to become blocked and thwarted so that it turns 'sour' for the remainder of its path and becomes what is known as a 'black stream'. The 'stream' need not necessarily refer to a water course; it more usually denotes a stream of energy.

Eve first learned about black streams from a faith-healer who had helped her to recover from a serious car accident. She was interested but, like most people, sceptical about the notion. After all, nobody seemed able to pin down exactly what a black stream was. She forgot about it until three years later, when she and her family had already been at the new farm for some time. Things were not going well. Eve was bad-tempered and depressed. Her relationship with her husband deteriorated markedly. She hated being in the house, but felt that it could not have been the move alone that had upset her. After all, she had lived in Dorset all her life.

Quite by chance, she remembered her conversations with the faith-healer, and sent a map of the farm to a dowser. The map was returned within the week – with a heavy blue line drawn right through the house, coming from an old limestone quarry up on the western edge of the farm. A note on the map read: 'Black stream. You must do something about this.'

This prompted Eve to find out more about black streams, and one of the things she discovered was that any major disturbance of the earth – such as mining, quarrying or motorway building – can affect the currents of the earth force and change the benevolent aspect of the ley into a much more malevolent power. Not everyone is affected by this, but research suggests that those who are 'tuned in' may be prone to emotional disturbances and eventually to certain degenerative diseases, particularly cancer.

Healing the evil stream

Eve contacted the dowser and asked if he would come and deal with the black stream. He came about three weeks later and dowsed with a pendulum over the fields to pick up the line coming from the quarry. The reaction was strongly negative, and the dowser looked exhausted. 'Healing' the malevolence of a black stream is carried out using angle irons or stakes bound with copper, which are hammered into the earth. This particular dowser used a single angle iron. It is critical to the success of the operation that the stake enters the ground at exactly the right angle and in exactly the right place. The dowser first worked over the map, running his finger slowly over the line of the black stream and waiting for the pendulum to give an indication of the area in which he should work. When he had pinpointed the spot on a large-scale map, he returned to the fields and

slowly walked over the spot indicated on the map. The method could be regarded as a mystical game of hunt-the-thimble, with the gyrations of the pendulum indicating whether the seeker was getting 'warmer' or 'cooler'. It was a long, painstaking process, but when the exact position had been determined, the angle iron was hammered into the ground. The dowser thought that the polarity of the ley should reverse to positive within three days.

But Eve felt no better. She confessed, indeed, that she felt rather worse because the original problem was now compounded by the fact that she felt angry with herself for having been 'taken in' by the whole affair;

Peter F., a retired West Country doctor, was horrified when he discovered that a black stream ran through his new home. The stream passed straight through his house, passing between the main door and the window to the right of it at the front (below left) and skirting a tree in the back garden before continuing into the hills beyond (below). Peter called in a dowser, who confirmed that the black stream was about 18 feet (6 metres) wide, and 'cured' it by staking it with an angle iron. Peter has himself since become an expert dowser; using a pendulum (left) around the angle iron, he detects the point at which the ley turns from a black stream into a line of benign force

The geomancer's art

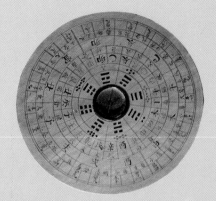

The concept of the earth force was very important to the ancient Chinese. They believed it was carried in channels in the ground, which they called *lung mei*, 'paths of the dragon', and divided them into two categories, *yang* and *yin*, the male and the female, symbolised by the azure dragon and the white tiger. It was vital to place sacred or imperial buildings where there was a proper balance of *yang* and *yin* – and so every building team included an experienced geomancer, one versed in the art of *feng shui* (literally, 'wind and water').

The value of the geomancer lay in his ability to select propitious sites. He would look for places in which the *yin* and *yang* elements were present in the favourable ratio of approximately two to three. The *yang* current generally flowed through mountains and hills; the *yin* ran along valleys and subterranean channels. The geomancer used a complex method including dowsing and consulting an elaborate compass like the one now preserved in the Science Museum in London (far left) to determine the attributes of the site; a woodcut from the Ch'ing dynasty (left) shows a geomancer at work with his assistants.

The official attitude to geomancy in today's Communist China is discouraging; but the tradition is still strong, and geomancers frequently advise on the siting of new buildings. It is their responsibility to ensure that the harmonious flow of the earth's energy is not disturbed – to prevent the creation of what the West calls 'black streams'.

after all, she said, even the dowser couldn't explain *why* it should work.

About a month later, she had a letter from the dowser, who had heard that the operation had not been a success. He asked to see the map again, and Eve was 'fairly staggered' when he telephoned to say that she had been right. Things had not changed. The dowser had not been able to check whether or not he had been successful when he first did the operation, because the various forces take several days to settle down and he had been unable to stay long enough.

He visited the farm again, resited the angle iron and added another one, then returned home. Eve by now thought the whole affair totally suspect. But after three days, the whole place felt quite different. For the first time, the kitchen was warm and the sitting room, which Eve had hated, was quiet and still. The healing had other effects too. She noticed that year that the trees they had planted seemed to grow much more strongly, whereas before they had barely made progress. The stock became healthier, and the lambing record improved enormously.

Eve's experience removed all traces of her previous scepticism, and she is now a dowser and healer herself. She holds that success in dowsing is just a matter of practice although, in the same way that a minority of people are tone-deaf or colour-blind, there will always be a minority who are unable to sense the earth force.

Dowsers in Britain have been working on black streams and their effects for more than

Below: *The dowser unmasked*, from a German work of 1704 in which the dowser is represented as a devil with cloven hoof, horns and tail. At this period, the Church was opposed to anything that could be regarded as challenging its authority – including 'paranormal' abilities

50 years. The poisons carried by the black stream are not tangible. They poison our emotions, images, ideas and produce a blackness of spirit that can act on our emotions without physically touching us and, through our minds, exert a degenerative influence on our bodies.

Leys and cancer

One doctor interested in unconventional methods of healing talked about a particularly unlucky house whose inhabitants he had been looking after for 25 years. Five different families had owned the house during this time, and the doctor felt that the disasters that happened to each new owner and his family went far beyond reasonable expectation: chronic alcoholism, mental breakdowns, a divorce, three cancer cases. His concern with his last patient from this house, the 33-year-old mother of two young children, led eventually to the discovery and correction of a particularly virulent negative ley, a black stream, which passed through the main bedroom of the house.

The effects of a black stream are not limited to people. Telegraph cables corrode more quickly on black streams than elsewhere. The owner of a stud farm near Axminster in Devon found that a black stream that was discovered running beneath his stables had been having a disastrous effect upon his horses. A high proportion of his mares either aborted, or else failed to conceive.

Chinese geomancers call these noxious

currents *sha* and believe that *sha* can operate destructively at many different levels, killing livestock, ruining health, causing decay. *Sha* arises when the balance is upset between the complementary forces of *yin* and *yang*.

The healing process has many different names: some call it 'environmental medicine', others 'land acupuncture'. The acupuncture analogy is a close one, for in acupuncture theory all the processes of the body – digestion, circulation, nervous system – are controlled by the balance of *yin* and *yang*. This interplay affects the whole body, but is most accessible on the skin, or just under it.

The *yin–yang* equilibrium runs as energy through a network of lines traced over the body, often called meridians. Each main meridian is associated with one major organ in the body. As long as the energy flow through the meridian remains in equilibrium, the body functions normally. Imbalance leads to ill health, and the acupuncturist chooses node-points along the meridian in which to insert the needles, which have the effect of restoring the energy flow.

It is not a difficult step to imagine the earth as a huge body, with its ancient sacred sites as the acupuncture points on meridians that are called leys. The angle irons or copper-sheathed stakes that the dowser uses to heal the land are the exact equivalent of the acupuncturist's needles.

There are many people besides Eve who can testify that the process seems to work. Sceptics dismiss the notion by saying that we believe what we want to believe. Indeed, the

Below: the M5 motorway, seen here at Failand in Avon, slices through the countryside of southern England, cutting several important ley lines. A growing number of people feel that black streams are a symptom of the arrogant way in which we choose to exploit the landscape of Britain without due regard for the subtle balances of nature

mind's ability to influence the body is a well-known phenomenon, but it is not too far-fetched to suggest that the will of the mind is itself shaped and influenced by earth forces.

Peter F., a West Country doctor, has twice had to deal with the disturbing influence of black streams on his life. He spent most of his working life in a county town practice with one other partner. His interest in alternative medicine is wide, and he has himself done a great deal of new work with migraine patients using techniques of ionisation. It was through study groups and conferences on healing methods that he first became aware of leys and black streams, but not until his partner had died of leukemia and he himself had undergone surgery for lung cancer did he suspect that a black stream may have been the cause.

Negative energy

Two experienced dowsers later confirmed that the doctors' consulting rooms lay on the junction of two black streams, and now Peter F. has no doubt at all that it was the long term exposure to the effects of this 'negative energy' that caused the cancer.

This is not the end of the story, however. When Peter F. retired, he moved with his wife 10 miles (16 kilometres) away to an old mill – a very pretty thatched building standing in a sheltered valley. Shortly after he moved in, he was horrified to receive a letter from the president of the American Dowsers' Association telling him that there was a black stream running through the mill room on the left of the building – the room that was to be converted into a study. A mutual acquaintance at a conference in the United States had passed on news of Peter's retirement. Idle curiosity had prompted the American to dowse over a map of the area round the doctor's new house, and this was how he had detected the black stream. It was dealt with in the same way as the one that had affected Eve's farm, and three dowsers who have since checked the area round the mill confirm that the house is now 'clear'.

The aim behind the ministrations of the dowsers is to restore the balance of our relationship with nature. The land healers fear that, with the arrogant assumption that we are in control of nature, we have scarred the earth with our reckless grubbing up of minerals, wrenching out of fuel, smothering of the land with tarmac and concrete. They warn us that, if we are to limit the destructive effect of our actions, we must start administering the cure now, before nature swamps us in the black streams of her disgust. This is why they feel earth acupuncture is so important for, as dowser Tom Graves says, 'In using it, we can heal not just the land and its energies, but also our relationship with nature and with ourselves as well.'

The secrets of the earth

Dowsers claim to sense a strong 'earth force' along leys – and scientific experiments appear to confirm its existence. But what is its nature, asks ANNA PAVORD – and how was early Man able to use it?

THAT LEYS EXIST is doubted neither by the practical nor by the mystical researchers into the subject. The question that neither side has yet answered satisfactorily is why. Alfred Watkins, representative of the practical school, supposed that the straight lines marked primitive trackways, but recognised that there were enormous flaws in this explanation, for leys led over impassable bogs or dropped over sheer cliffs.

Professor Alexander Thom, the engineer who surveyed over 600 megalithic sites and was the first person to document the precision with which they had been constructed, supposed that the monuments that stood on them had been experimental observatories. He noted that the sites aligned with other stones or landscape features, and surmised that these alignments were of astronomical significance. Alignments stretching from Stonehenge to Gibbet Knoll in the north west and to Figsbury Ring in the south east he interpreted as Moon sighting lines, and he saw the whole of the stone complex at Carnac in Brittany as an experimental site for refining the processes of astronomy. But there are problems with this explanation too. Why were the observatories built on such a massive scale when smaller ones might have given the same results? Why are there so many of these structures? Why, if early Man was simply building mathematical machines, did he go to such enormous lengths to import specific materials with which to build them? The answer to these questions is nothing but a resounding silence.

A large number of the present notions about the ley system centre upon the idea of a power, generally called the 'earth force', which provides a psychic as well as a physical alignment between ancient sites and which can be measured, not with the ruler, but with dowsing tools and the gaussometer. Another great question mark hangs over the nature of this power. Is it electromagnetic? Or is it some form of purely psychic force?

Guy Underwood spent more than 20 years of his life as a dowser before he died in 1964 at the age of 81. He firmly believed that there were lines of power over the earth, which he called geodetic lines, and which he could not classify as purely gravitational, rotational or magnetic forces. The system he devised was complex and involved the mapping and classification of several different types and patterns of the power that he was the first to call the 'earth force'. Underwood identified 'blind springs' at the points at which the primary lines of his system converged and noticed that the force formed spirals at blind springs, which usually had seven coils and which seemed to pulse with an annual rhythm.

The living countryside

Underwood believed that the primary geodetic lines were, in a geographical sense, fixed and that they were recognised not only by primitive Man, but by plants and animals too. He put forward evidence to show that pigs, sheep, dogs, hares, rabbits, tortoises, lizards, geese, owls and ants all used the lines of the earth force in some way. Badgers' setts and moles' nest hills were made over blind springs. Rookeries were built over them, gnats danced and ants made hills on them. Mistletoe and yew grew best above them. Willow, cedar and hawthorn were also sensitive to the primary lines.

Blind springs existed under megalithic

Professor Alexander Thom (above) was the first serious researcher to chart the precision with which early Man had constructed his early monuments, such as the stone circles in Britain and the extraordinary alignments at Carnac in Brittany, France (top). They were undoubtedly built according to some kind of plan – but what was their significance? Professor Thom suggested that they might be astronomical observatories – but if so, why are they built on such a massive scale? And why are there so many?

monuments, and were indeed the reason for their having been built at particular sites. Underwood also showed that the shapes of the enigmatic hillfigures that are scattered over Britain's downland were defined by geodetic lines. The eye of the White Horse at Uffington, Berkshire, lies directly over a blind spring.

The building of medieval churches and cathedrals also seemed to him to have been dictated to some extent by the lines of the earth force. The size and shape of a church-yard, the position of the lych gate, the alignment of the nave, all depended on geodetic lines, with a blind spring under the chancel steps.

Underwood's idea of an earth force that travelled along geodetic lines is very similar to the ley concept, which suggests that megalithic sites were chosen for a particular reason and that they were not only physically aligned but also connected by a measurable force that was allied in some way to the power of the mind.

The geographer Dr E. T. Stringer has proposed instead a telluric force, comparable to Underwood's earth force, but his theory

Dowser Guy Underwood (1883–1964) believed that early Man was sensitive to a mysterious force in the ground that flowed along channels that he called geodetic lines. Where these lines formed shapes of animals, he suggested, the ancients traced them on the landscape to form the famous hill-figures of England, such as the Uffington white horse in Wiltshire (below right). Underwood, himself sensitive to the geodetic force, discovered that the geodetic lines at Uffington (below) followed very closely the outline of a startlingly realistic figure of a horse; the familiar, curiously dragon-like figure that is traced on the hillside can be seen as a cryptic clue to the shape of the hidden power

(see box) suggests that geodetic lines and leys are 'evidence of the existence of a force produced by the Earth and its inhabitants acting in combination rather than evidence of a force emanating from the Earth itself.'

A tentative link has been suggested between the earth force and the orgone energy that Wilhelm Reich claimed that he had isolated as a pure, subatomic, primal force. Reich built orgone chambers constructed of alternating layers of organic and inorganic materials in which orgone energy could be intensified into swirling, spiralling patterns. Irradiation in an orgone chamber had, claimed Reich, the effect of releasing blocked energy flows in the body and of generally revitalising the system.

Spiritual energy

Many of the greatest works of the megalith builders, such as Newgrange in Ireland and Silbury Hill in Wiltshire, England, were constructed using carefully chosen layers of earth and chalk – organic and inorganic material. Newgrange lies on an alignment that also passes through a standing stone and an earth mound; Silbury also lies on an

important ley. John Michell has put forward the idea that some power similar to Reich's orgone energy may have been generated in the ancient sacred sites, and used by megalithic Man for a spiritually revitalising ritual, and that this power was perhaps transmitted along definite paths – ley lines.

It has also been suggested that the presence of quartz at megalithic sites may be responsible for the earth force. Quartz is one of the commonest of all minerals, so the fact that it occurs at megalithic sites is not in itself surprising. However, the remarkable thing about quartz is that it is *piezoelectric* – that is, it becomes electrically charged when physical pressure is applied to it. It is claimed that the amount of charge produced is sufficient to affect the ionisation of the surrounding air to such an extent that physiological changes can be caused in the bodies of living creatures that happen to be in the vicinity.

The presence of a particular kind of

crystal along the ley lines has also been put forward as a reason for the apparent connection between leys and UFOs. A writer in *The Ley Hunter* magazine suggested – rather improbably – that 'suitable crystals built into a ley, would provide the anode of an electric circuit, with the cathode in the UFO overhead; together they would provide something similar to a photo-electric beam – anyone stepping onto the ley would break the circuit and trigger off the reaction – in this case the embodiment of the UFO. In the laboratory, such a circuit produces coloured images similar to an Adamski saucer.' What are we to make of such claims? The statement that anyone stepping onto the ley would break the circuit is clearly nonsense: human bodies actually conduct electricity *better* than air – so the whole argument is destroyed.

The UFO connection

The correlation between leys and UFOs can be dated to the French UFO flap of 1954, when Aimé Michel published an analysis of the UFO sightings of that year. His conclusion was that UFOs travel along specific paths, which he called orthotenies. In the early 1960s an ex-RAF pilot and UFO enthusiast, Tony Wedd, made a tentative attempt to relate orthotenies to leys, but no conclusive evidence emerged before the whole orthoteny theory fell into disfavour. Nevertheless, it seems that UFO sightings have a tendency to cluster round ley centres like Warminster in Wiltshire, where 13 leys converge. Some people think that UFOs navigate by leys, others that they use ley power for their own propulsion, or else to overcome the gravitational pull of the Earth. Yet another theory suggests that UFOs are intended to draw our attention to leys so that we can once again utilise the ancient powers.

UFOs are not the only phenomena that seem to be attracted to ley lines. One researcher, Phil Grant, noted that in the Bournemouth area more than 90 per cent of all recorded supernatural manifestations occur

Wilhelm Reich (above) claimed to be able to produce pure primal energy in 'orgone' chambers made of layers of organic and inorganic material (below). It has been suggested that monuments like Newgrange in Ireland (bottom), built of chalk and earth, were also used to produce energy

on known ley lines. John Michell calls them 'paths of psychic activity'. Stephen Jenkins observes in his book *The undiscovered country* that various kinds of psychic phenomena appear to be triggered off at points where leys cross. He describes a phantom army, a Roman legion that he saw in Cornwall:

> The clumps and bushes were very still in the windless evening light when suddenly I experienced what I took to be a startlingly vivid optical illusion. Scattered among them, motionless but frighteningly distinct, was a crowd, a host of armed men. For a moment I stood stock still, unable to believe my eyes, then I began to run towards them. At once something like a curtain of heated air wavered in front of them briefly – and there were only bushes and stones.

This apparition occurred when Jenkins was 16 years old – and before he had ever heard of ley lines. Nearly 40 years later he returned to the same spot with his wife – and once again the eerie army shimmered on the ley.

Jenkins agrees with the dowser Tom

Lethbridge that some kind of powerful force can be triggered off at particular sites such as ley crossings, and that in these places the force exerts a particularly powerful effect on the human mind. Lethbridge also suggested that there may be worlds, not necessarily physical, that run parallel with our own, and that certain places act as 'trapdoors' that can suddenly precipitate us into one of these parallel realms (see page 1655).

Unfortunately there have been very few attempts to examine scientifically the nature of the power that dowsers and others can still feel in standing stones, stone circles and along the ley system. While researching for his book *Earth magic*, the author Francis

A balance of forces

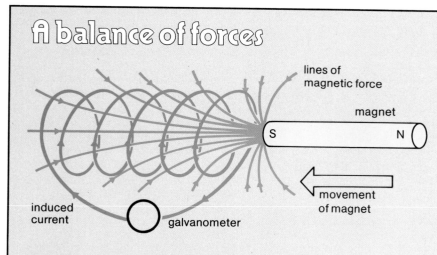

lines of magnetic force

magnet

S N

movement of magnet

induced current

galvanometer

In his book *The secret of the gods*, Dr E. T. Stringer puts forward an original – and seemingly plausible – explanation of ley lines. Like many others, he believes that leys are channels of an earth force, which he calls a 'telluric force' – from the name of the Roman earth goddess, Tellus.

The telluric force, he suggests, is induced by electric currents inside the Earth. Experiments carried out by Dr Harold S. Burr and Dr F. S. C. Northrop at Yale University show that all living forms – as well as the Earth itself – possess magnetic fields. And Faraday's law of electromagnetic induction states that, if a piece of material that conducts electricity is moved about in a magnetic field, then an electric current will be induced in it.

'The movements of the Earth . . . will obviously cause a rotation of all the electromagnetic fields,' says Dr Stringer. He goes on to claim that the rotation of the Earth induces a current in conductors within it; and 'the presence of this current in turn gives rise to a force, in accordance with the usual laws of electricity.' This is the physical component of the 'Planetary Telluric Force'.

What is wrong with this argument? It is plain enough to see that Dr Stringer has not given enough thought to what is moving and what is still in his application of the law of induction. He is perfectly right when he says that a conductor moving in a magnetic field will carry a current. But as the Earth spins, conductors and magnetic fields are all moving at the same speed – so no current can be generated!

Hitching set up an experiment that involved a Welsh dowser, Bill Lewis, a 12-foot (4-metre) high standing stone near the river Usk at Crickhowell in South Wales and a physicist, Dr Eduardo Balanovski from Imperial College in London. Bill Lewis claimed that the stone transmitted a force that he could sense and that seemed to wax and wane at intervals. He was interested to know if this could be scientifically proven.

The power of the spiral

Dr Balanovski arrived at the site armed with a gaussometer, an instrument that measures to an accuracy of thousandths of a gauss the magnetic field strength of the earth. In general this is very stable, averaging 0.47 gauss in Britain. The background levels of the site were checked and the meter set, but when the measuring device was pointed at the stone, the needle shot over the dial, showing a variation far greater than the few thousandths of a gauss that would have been reasonably expected.

In a later experiment that included Professor John Taylor of King's College in London, Bill Lewis marked a spiral pattern on the stone indicating the band where he felt the power to be at its strongest. The gaussometer showed that, on some parts of the spiral, the strength was almost double that over the rest of the stone. Professional reticence coloured Taylor's comment: 'These early results must be treated with great caution.' Balanovski, however, was more forthcoming: 'I do not personally believe

A quartz standing stone at Cregg, County Kerry, Ireland. Quartz is piezoelectric – it becomes electrically charged under pressure; it has been claimed that this is responsible for the power of prehistoric megaliths

Further reading
Francis Hitching, *Earth magic*, Picador 1977
Alfred Watkins, *The ley-hunter's manual*, Borgo Press 1986
Tom Williamson and Lin Bellamy, *Ley lines in question*, Trafalgar Square 1984

that the stone was accidentally chosen or accidentally placed,' he said. 'The people who put it there knew about its power, even if they didn't know about electro-magnetism.'

It seems possible, therefore, that megaliths act as transformers for some kind of energy, possibly electromagnetic in form, which they convert from sinuous underground streams to straight overground paths. It seems possible also that early Man instinctively recognised this force, and over thousands of years experimented with ways of channelling it and concentrating its random effects. He learned that the power could be amplified in the stone chambers of barrows, that it could be tapped by setting up huge rocking stones and stone circles along the power paths. He also learned that the power was influenced by the movements of the Sun, Moon and stars, and so experimented with methods of predicting eclipses and equinoxes using vast stone observatories. It is even possible that he harnessed the power itself to raise the huge stones.

Many see this period as the apogee of a civilisation obsessed with harmony and number that, using instinct as well as intellect, worked to combine terrestrial geometry with celestial movements, generating an energy that was natural and beneficent. Their monuments are in ruins, their rituals almost forgotten, their power system, the leys, tangled and nugatory. Behind the whole complex pattern lies a lost knowledge that, if we could rediscover it, might one day be the salvation of the entire human race.

On the right lines?

**Many cherished beliefs about ley lines are now being put
to the test by hard-headed statisticians who are rethinking
the mystical claims for these ancient 'lines of power'.
PAUL DEVEREUX describes their findings**

INVESTIGATION OF LEYS – alignments of ancient sites – can be carried out in two ways: by treating them as topographical features, using maps, fieldwork and archives to identify them, or as supposed lines of force, using dowsing and other techniques. Since the 1920s both these approaches to the ley enigma have been developing. Some of the most exciting research has treated leys as carriers of 'earth energies' – but, of course, as the discoverer of leys, Alfred Watkins, pointed out, leys must initially be identified as *physical alignments* before more speculative research is undertaken.

Ley hunting began in 1921 with Watkins's realisation that prehistoric sites – and later buildings associated with them – form straight lines across the landscape. Pioneer work was done in the two decades immediately before the Second World War, but it was not until the 1960s that ley theory caught the public imagination. Connections were seen by researchers such as Tony Wedd and Jimmy Goddard between leys and 'orthotenies' – straight lines that, it was believed, linked the sites of UFO sightings. This period marked a general rekindling of interest in leys and as such was important, but it was characterised by wild enthusiasm rather than hard research.

It was in the 1970s that the whole subject began to come of age. John Michell's *The old stones of Land's End* of 1974 was the first really careful, accurate study of leys as physical alignments. This work has subsequently been checked statistically by Chris Hutton-Squire and Pat Gadsby using computer simulation techniques. Some of the alignments between the standing stones of western Cornwall were found, from this statistical viewpoint, to be better than could be expected by chance. This result has been confirmed by two mathematicians, Bob Forrest and Michael Behrend, in work published in *The ley hunter's companion* in 1979.

One of the leys studied by Forrest and Behrend is the Saintbury alignment near Broadway, on the edge of the Cotswolds. It is about $3\frac{1}{2}$ miles (5.6 kilometres) long and appears to start at an ancient cross on an old, minor crossroads on the A46 near Weston-sub-Edge. This was a resting place for funeral processions on the way up to the next ley marker, St Nicholas's Church, which stands in an isolated position halfway up Willersey Hill near the village of Saintbury. The present church is Norman, and of a cruciform shape, but stands on the foundations of a Saxon church. It contains evidence of probable pagan origins in the form of a curious octagonal stone slab now preserved in the south transept, commonly known as the 'pre-Christian altar'. The hilltop above the church is crowned with the remains of a tumulus

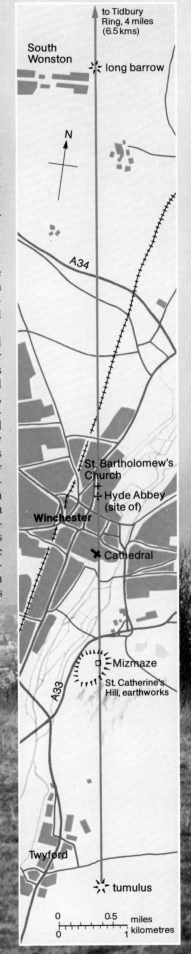

to Tidbury Ring, 4 miles (6.5 kms)

South Wonston

long barrow

N

A34

St. Bartholomew's Church

Hyde Abbey (site of)

Winchester

Cathedral

Mizmaze

St. Catherine's Hill, earthworks

A33

Twyford

tumulus

0   0.5   miles
0   1   kilometres

Previous page: Winchester Cathedral, seen from the Mizmaze on St Catherine's Hill to the south; and a map showing Winchester ley. The city of Winchester was the capital of England until 1278 but was also the site of several prehistoric settlements. At least one eminent historian believes that Winchester Cathedral is based on a megalithic structure that formerly stood on the site

'movement along a straight line'. Kimmis suggests that as the word evolved 'it extended its physical/spatial meaning in an abstract sense, so that straight linear movement became an analogue of honesty, justice, government and social order.' He lists words that suggest this, among them: reign, regime, regiment, regular, regulation and right. Kimmis feels that the expression 'the king's highway', *via regis*, reveals a genuine historical link between the use of landscape alignments and the institution of kingship. The word 'ruler' in modern English, for example, can mean a king or queen, or even a state leader, as well as an instrument for drawing straight lines. In French, *règle* – straight-edge or ruler – reveals the *reg* stem clearly.

If this preliminary research is on the right lines, it may denote that the practice of setting out leys degenerated into a secular procedure associated with government – the 'ruling of the land'. We can see that a similar situation existed in the Andean empire of the Inca in which the divine king, the 'son of the sun', ruled with the help of a network of 'royal roads'. Nigel Pennick, one of the

that also lies on this ley which, about a mile (1.6 kilometres) further on, passes over another hilltop marked by a Neolithic long barrow and encompassed by Iron Age earthworks. It is possible that the ley terminates here, though the line can be extended to pass through a pagan burial ground and Seven Wells Farm. Farms are not in themselves significant ley points, but wells can be, and this site is an ancient one recorded in the Domesday Book and it does contain seven wells. It is mentioned in Hugh Ross Williamson's 1948 novel *The silver bowl* in which a tale is recounted of a mysterious sacred relic that was hidden for a time at Seven Wells during the 17th century. From the air, the place is remarkable in that it is delineated by a perfect semi-circle of trees, which may indicate that there was once a henge structure there.

A pinch of salt?

Alfred Watkins believed that the names of ley sites were highly significant; noticing that many of them contained the words 'salt' or 'white', he conjectured that leys might have been salt trading routes (see page 1688). Such etymological enquiries are always fraught with dangers of misinterpretation; perhaps the most fantastic example is the Alaise mystery (see page 1722). But the need to see if language holds any clues about the mysteries of ancient alignment practices continues in current ley research. Jim Kimmis, for example, in an article in *The Ley Hunter*, has started a most promising line of enquiry into a group of Indo-European words that share the stem *reg*. Most have evolved through the Latin verb *regere*, 'to govern'. Apparently the earliest meaning of *reg* was

Above: aerial view of the north end of Saintbury ley in the English Cotswolds, showing the crossroads and a cross (in the foreground), with St Nicholas's Church in the background

Right: the so-called 'pre-Christian altar' in the south transept of the old Norman church of St Nicholas at Saintbury

Below: Seven Wells Farm on the Saintbury ley. Certainly an ancient site, the farm may have been built on a henge structure – and there really were seven wells

Below: map showing the major points on Saintbury ley in the Cotswolds. The ley, which is roughly 3½ miles (5.6 kilometres) long, begins at a 15th-century cross at the crossroads of the A46 and the main Saintbury road; it runs through Saintbury church, a Bronze Age round barrow, a Neolithic long barrow, a large Iron Age fort (part of which is now a golf course) and a Saxon pagan cemetery and ends at Seven Wells Farm. Alfred Watkins remarked that farmsteads occurred so frequently on leys that he hardly thought them worth recording; however, Seven Wells Farm had an attractively mystical name and seemed to be worth investigating

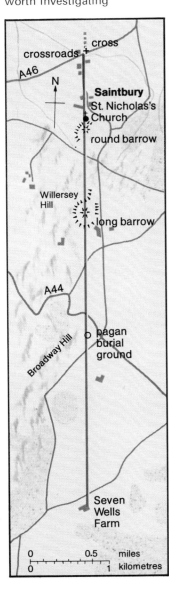

Luck and judgement

Ever since leys were discovered, controversy has centred on the question of whether or not these alignments appear accidentally in the landscape; it was in an attempt to provide an objective answer that statistics first became involved in ley research.

The most obvious starting point is to *assume* that leys are accidental, and then calculate just how unlikely it would be to find a straight line with a certain number of ancient sites – potential ley points – strung along it. It seems reasonable to interpret this assumption statistically by supposing that potential ley points are randomly distributed across the landscape; then, given the total number of such points, a simple calculation gives a guide to how likely it is that a ley with a certain number of points occurred by chance.

The problems start when you try to define what you mean by a random distribution. Statistically, a random distribution of a number of points on any particular map means that each point has an equal probability of appearing at any point on the map. But observation of acknowledged ancient sites quickly shows that their distribution is not, in this sense, random – it is well-known that they are, for instance, far more likely to be found on flat ground or at the top of a hill than on steeply sloping ground. What you need to do is to find a distribution that will model reality by assigning probabilities according to the steepness of the ground, plus other factors.

Unfortunately, this is a task that is beyond the scope of ordinary mathematics. What statisticians do in practice is to use computer simulation techniques on individual leys. Modelling the existing ley points and the surrounding topography by computer, they can then calculate an upper limit on the probability that the ley occurred by chance.

foremost researchers into leys and other aspects of geomancy, has uncovered some valuable evidence of a system extant at one time in Madagascar where certain straight roads could be used only by the king.

One of the first things the human mind seems to do is to search for patterns in data, and in the 1960s dramatic networks of supposed leys criss-crossing Britain were published in various magazines. Some modern ley hunters cringe when these are brought up today by critics as they are impossible to defend as true leys. Two of the best-known of these patterns are Philip Heselton's 'great isosceles triangle' and John Michell's 'St Michael line'. The apex of the 'triangle' is at the henge and stone ring of Arbor Low in Derbyshire, with its base angles respectively at the church in Othery, Somerset, and Mersea Island off the Essex coast. This gives the figure sides of around 200 miles (320 kilometres) in length. The St Michael line is even longer, stretching from St Michael's Mount off Marazion in Cornwall, passing through Glastonbury, Avebury and Bury St Edmunds in East Anglia to enter the North Sea close to Lowestoft (see page 771).

Such long lines were called 'primary leys' – but current research shows that they are simply *not* precise alignments between sites, which is the definition of a ley. In the case of the great triangular configuration, it has since been clarified by Philip Heselton that it exists more as an *idea* than a topographical reality. John Michell still considers his St Michael line to have merit; in some respects it may have, but it is not one single alignment. To cover all the claimed sites along its length the line would have to be in the region of a mile (1.6 kilometres) in width. This still makes it narrow for its 360-mile (580-kilometre) length, but it is a far cry from a narrow ley-type alignment. This and similar features could be called *geomantic corridors* to distinguish them from simple leys. A few may be worthy of study – most are figments of the imagination.

Another durable myth that has survived from the 1960s is that between 50 and 100 leys cross at Arbor Low ('Arbor' means the centre or fulcrum). In fact, only two have been satisfactorily identified.

The shorter the better

There is no acceptable evidence that serious modern ley researchers are able to find that supports the existence of very long alignments of the 'primary ley' type. Another problem is that the Earth's curvature causes map lines representing alignments longer than about 25 miles (40 kilometres) to become significantly inaccurate representations of their counterparts on the ground, and the accurate plotting of such long lines becomes a fairly sophisticated trigonometrical enterprise. It is now clear that convincing leys tend to be under 20 miles (32 kilometres) in length, with some of the best being less than 10 miles (16 kilometres) long.

What *does* seem to be true is that sacred sites seem generally to be related to nearby 'holy hills'. This pattern was discerned in British leys through comparison with Bolivian old straight tracks that converge onto sacred hilltops and the research of Dr Josef Heinsch, who detected church alignments directed towards certain hilltops in his native Germany before the Second World War.

In Britain, many 'holy hills' are identifiable by their prehistoric earthworks or structures, and are sometimes additionally marked by a hill figure. Somewhere near their bases there is generally an important shrine site – prehistoric or Christianised.

The well-known chalk hill figures of the Long Man of Wilmington, the Uffington White Horse and the Cerne Abbas Giant mark holy hills. At Wilmington in Sussex, the ancient church of Saints Mary and Peter aligns with the nearby Benedictine priory to the huge carved figure of the Long Man himself. The origin of this feature is not known, but is generally believed to date from the Bronze Age. The ley goes on over Windover Hill, on which the Long Man is situated, through a large prehistoric mound on its summit and on to a tumulus located on the other side.

The holy hill line at Uffington in Oxfordshire runs from the church of St Mary in the village, touches the curiously flattened Dragon Hill, passes through a long barrow on the slopes of Whitehorse Hill, through the prehistoric earthworks on top of the hill and on to a tumulus in the countryside beyond. The archaic outlines of the White Horse are to one side of the line. At Cerne Abbas in Dorset, it is again a church of St Mary in the village from which the line starts. The ley passes through a holy well known as the Silver Well – probably a pagan site, now associated with a St Edwold, that formerly had a reputation for healing – and the remains of Cerne Abbey before passing through the prehistoric earthwork known as the Trendle on top of Giant Hill. The Trendle used to be the site of the local maypole. Again the chalk hill figure – this

Above: the Cerne Abbas Giant – a Dorset hill drawing of ferocious virility and doubtful age; some experts argue that it dates back to the Romano-British period and others that it is only 300 years old. A ley line rises at the church of St Mary in the village of Cerne Abbas; nearby, a Benedictine abbey (left) was erected in the 15th century on a former pagan site, thus continuing unbroken centuries of religious activity at that particular spot

time the virile effigy of the club-wielding giant – is off the line to one side. At the earliest, this image is thought to date back to the Romano-British period, and Edward Waring in his *Ghosts and legends of the Dorset countryside* argues convincingly that the image may be a 17th-century folly. The line goes on over the long hill and ends, as is common with leys, at a tumulus beyond.

The old cathedral cities are generally associated with holy hills. Winchester, for instance, has St Catherine's Hill as its holy hill. A line runs through the site of Hyde Abbey in the city, through the cathedral – thought to be on the site of a former stone circle – and on over the top of the hill, which bears an earthwork, bisecting a curious and ancient design cut in the summit turf, known as the Mizmaze. Again, the line goes on to a tumulus.

At Hereford, the holy hill is Dinedor Hill, topped with prehistoric earthworks. The holy line runs through the ancient church of All Saints in the city, across the cathedral site and on to the hill's summit.

In all these cases, the lines are short. Alignments between a sacred site and its holy hill generally include other significant sites in the vicinity. In the case of the examples given here, *all* the major immediate sacred sites near the base of the given hills have been involved in the same lines.

Like beads on a thread

Research into the pattern of holy hill lines indicates that the orientation of the alignments tends to approximate to either north-south or east-west directions. All the lines described in this article have orientations close to north-south, but Dinedor, for example, also has a line that runs east from it to the prehistoric hill of Oldbury Camp, stringing three churches along its 7-mile (11-kilometre) length like beads on a thread. In London the holy hill of Ludgate, currently marked by St Paul's Cathedral but formerly by a pagan temple, is bisected by an east-west line running through the ancient sites now marked by St Clement Danes, the Temple, St Helen's and St Dunstan's in Stepney.

Critics argue that such lines are marked by features of such different ages that they cannot be valid. Ley hunters counter with the strong evidence for the retention and evolution of specific sacred sites through several different cultures right up to the Reformation and the remarkable regularity of the holy hill pattern. They also point to the precedent in Bolivia, where the landscape lines, obviously of pagan Indian origin, can be marked at one end by a Spanish church and at the other by a native Indian shrine.

There can be no doubt that a recurring pattern of alignments related to local holy hills exists in Britain. Throughout the world hilltops and mountains have been held by different cultures to be sacred: it is a constant motif in the nature mysticism that was

A shrine set up on an old straight track in the Bolivian Andes, where pathways have been cut perfectly straight through difficult scrubland for many miles. The Indians regard the tracks as both sacred and mundane, using them for worship and for everyday transport, just as English leys have survived the centuries with their alignments of holy places, wells, farms and commonplace roads

practised by many early societies.

For the last 60 years or so argument and abuse have been the only communication between archaeologists and ley hunters. In 1981, however, for the first time, calm, rational discussion commenced between ley researchers and a leading archaeologist. In issue 90 of *The Ley Hunter* Professor R.J.C. Atkinson, one of Britain's most prominent prehistorians, famous for his work at Stonehenge, commenced a debate on the merits of the ley theory. At this stage the Professor declares himself an agnostic with regard to leys – he neither believes nor disbelieves. Such an open-minded attitude lends hope that the increasingly accurate and reasonable ley research continued in Britain and Ireland will lead to at least a partial acceptance by the establishment of the notion that in prehistoric Britain sacred sites were ranged across local landscapes in straight lines. The overriding question then will be – why?

The Dragon takes off

Dowsers can often discern an energy in the earth that seems to travel along leys. But can this be detected using scientific instruments? PAUL DEVEREUX describes some successful attempts at monitoring ley sites

ALFRED WATKINS, the discoverer of leys, believed that the alignments formed by ancient sites were the relics of Neolithic traders' routes. But many subsequent researchers have felt that the explanation cannot be so simple: the alignments cross rivers, mountains, cliffs and swamps. However, this is now seen as an insufficient reason for dismissing the trackway theory: some straight tracks in Bolivia traverse the landscape without deviation for distances up to 20 miles (32 kilometres), seemingly disregarding the difficulty of the terrain. It turns out that these tracks are not used for secular purposes; they are rumoured in local Indian folklore to be pathways along which spirits travel. This is reminiscent of the Irish faery paths. It is interesting to note, too, that the ancient Chinese geomancers who practised *feng-shui* (see page 770) strove to *avoid* straight landscape lines for similar reasons – baleful spirits travel along them. This recurrent motif finds its echo in Britain in the energy that dowsers claim to be able to discern travelling along leys – a claim some ley experts have researched in detail.

It is difficult to determine exactly when it began to be suspected that leys might be associated with strange energy effects. The author Geoffrey Ashe remarks that the connection was first made by the occultist Dion Fortune in 1936; she described sacred sites as 'power centres' radiating 'lines of force'. Another early believer in the powers associated with leys was Arthur Lawton who, in 1939, published a pamphlet called *The mysteries of ancient Man*, in which he claimed that the layout of prehistoric sites reflects the presence of a 'cosmic force'. Lawton seems definitely to have been the first to link dowsing with leys.

Dowsing is, after mapwork, the commonest way of studying leys (see page 1691). Practitioners of the art interested in possible earth energies claim to have detected lines of energy, travelling in straight lines above the ground, that intersect at megalithic and certain other ancient sites. Tom Graves, himself a dowser, described his own evidence for this phenomenon in 1976 in his book *Dowsing*, but it had been known to many dowsers, among them Bill Lewis and John Williams, for some years. In his book *The pattern of the past*, published posthumously in 1969, Guy Underwood claimed that his dowsing revealed that ancient sites were located over 'blind springs' – apparent crossings of

Below: midsummer sunset at the standing stone of Ballochroy on the Mull of Kintyre, Strathclyde, Scotland. It has been argued that since straight lines are not to be found in nature, leys must be man-made. John Glover, however, has pointed out that this is not the case; this photograph, taken by him, shows the straight line of the apparent horizon

underground streams – and other dowsable features that he described as 'geodetic'. At this time, Lewis and others were finding that standing stones seemed to 'conduct' currents from within the Earth. These currents passed up the stones as helical sheaths. From certain points or 'nodes' on a stone, this energy, invisible to the eye but sensible to the dowser, seemed to be transmitted through the atmosphere. Other nodes were found to affect dowsers in different ways, such as causing their bodies to be thrown off a stone or to be twisted sideways. These corkscrews of force surrounding standing stones seem to change polarity according to the phase of the Moon, and can apparently be affected by a host of ambient electromagnetic and cosmic effects.

Some dowsers have found that these and other dowsable energy patterns associated

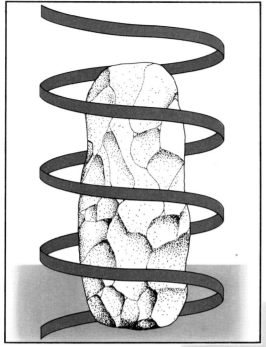

Right: Frank Connor dowses the Kingstone at the Rollright Circle, Oxfordshire. Many dowsers claim they can trace helical lines of force running close to the surface of megaliths (above). Certain points on the lines of force can be singled out as energy nodes. In an experiment carried out as part of the Dragon Project in 1979, dowser Bill Lewis was able, by touching an energy node on one of the stones of the Rollright Circle, to alter the reading on a voltmeter attached to the stone's surface (above right)

with megaliths can be deflected or made to disappear temporarily by the use of certain crystals. Geoffrey King, for example, can apparently affect the ground-level concentric rings of energy that dowsers can sense radiating from a megalith, by inserting crystal-tipped stakes at certain points. Many dowsers believe that the quality of a ley – whether harmful or beneficial – can be ascertained by using a dowsing tool known as a mager disc which, in effect, colour-codes the energies detected by dowsing. Negative energies can then be eliminated by driving stakes into the ground at carefully determined points (see page 1692). Wing-Commander Clive Beadon claimed that blocks of plastic containing specks of crystal, used on a plan or aerial view of a site, can be equally effective. It seems he is

practising a subtle form of psychokinesis.

In the United States, ley hunting is closely associated with dowsing. New England has many mysterious stones and chambered mounds that are not officially recognised as ancient sites. Consequently, they are not marked on maps, so American researchers are frequently obliged to use dowsing techniques to find what they believe to be lines of force in the landscape. These lines they call leys – but are they the same as Alfred Watkins's site alignments?

Research carried out by Sig Lonegren, a former editor of the *Journal* of the American Society of Dowsers, indicates that leys and lines of force do not always coincide. He has dowsed leys identified using a map and ruler in England and the lines at Nazca, Peru (see page 2002), and has found that only some features also carry a signal discernible by the dowser. He has also discovered, by dowsing, energy lines that are not marked in the landscape at all. It would seem from this that leys are *natural* lines of power, and that only some of them have been divined and marked by ancient peoples. It is all far from being understood at the present time. Lonegren is sure, however, that more careful terminology should be employed from now on: in an article in *The Ley Hunter* magazine, he has suggested that a dowsable energy line should be referred to as an 'E ley' – energy ley – to differentiate it from the kind that exists only on the map.

There has been some controversy among ley researchers over the question of whether leys are natural or man-made. There have been claims that all straight lines found in nature must be artificial, but John Glover, discoverer of shadow paths (see page 2717), has pointed out that straight lines *do* occur in nature – in light beams and the apparent horizon, for example. Another theory has been proposed by Brian Larkman, a leading ley theorist, based on an observation made by veteran ley researcher Jimmy

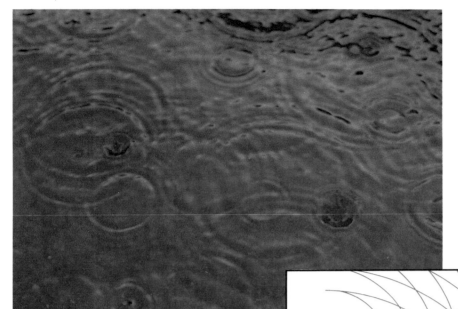

these two vastly different methods of enquiry. This was done because it was felt that dowsing encompassed a spectrum of related, subtle human sensitivities, ranging from the detection of minute physical cues to some form of ESP (as in map-dowsing): it seems to be a sort of bridge between physical and psychic modes of enquiry. Dr G. V. Robins was the consultant for the scientific programme, with Californian researcher Dr John Steele acting as the consultant for the psychic work. The present author took on overall co-ordination.

All sources of the earth energy legend – psychics, dowsers, physicists and tradition – agreed that the energy was associated with prehistoric megalithic sites, so it was decided to base the project at one megalithic site, and

lines of interference

meteorite A

meteorite B

shock waves

Goddard. He suggests that the sources of the phenomenon may be features originally formed by ancient meteoric impacts on the Earth and now eroded. Larkman suggests that these geological ripples could set up piezoelectrical effects in the crystalline structure of the affected rocks (see page 1698), which could give rise to powerful electrical epiphenomena.

But these are just theories. Because there is no objective method of assessing dowsers' findings, there is no check on their validity – unlike simple water divining, in which it is easy enough to check for hidden underground water. It became apparent to modern researchers that what was needed to check the various claims and ideas about earth energies was a wide-ranging study to see if scientific modes of monitoring could reveal unusual effects at ancient sites, and whether sites that showed such effects were also discernible by dowsers. In 1976, when the author Francis Hitching published the positive findings of physicists working with Bill Lewis at a standing stone in Wales (see page 1700), the need for a coherent study of this kind became pressing. For the Welsh incident added scientific weight to the claim of psychics and dowsers that ancient sites possessed unusual qualities. Folklore, of course, had been making such claims for hundreds of years: the old stones could heal, bring down thunder and lightning, were able to move by their own volition, and so on.

In November 1977, *The Ley Hunter* called together a number of dowsers, scientists, electronics and other experts to set up such a scheme – and so the Dragon Project was born; the name was a deliberate reference to the *feng-shui* symbol for terrestrial currents of energy (see page 770).

It was decided to set up two programmes, one measuring physical quantities, such as electric potential, and the other using psychics, with dowsing forming a link between

A drop falling into still water produces a characteristic pattern of concentric circles (top). The combination of two such patterns produces a series of straight lines (above). Ley theorist Brian Larkman has suggested that leys could have been formed by the combination of shock waves from ancient meteorites; the curious energies that have been discerned along ley lines could, he says, be piezoelectric effects set up along these 'geological ripples'

conduct exploratory investigations of other sites and control locations. The project was fortunate in being allowed use of the Rollright Stones in Oxfordshire by their owner Pauline Flick.

It took a year for practical work on the project to begin, but by the autumn of 1978 field work was well under way. The Rollright site has been subjected to three full-scale dowsing surveys, by Tom Graves, Bill Lewis and Major-General Scott Elliot. In addition, there have been dozens of other practitioners who have come along to add their findings to the project's overall investigation. Gradually a painstaking composite dowsing picture of the site was constructed, in the hope that the information gained would lead to conclusions about the relationship of dowsed lines with those found using scientific instruments, and with those identified with map and ruler. Work supervised by Steele aimed to find a link with the psychic impressions received by psychometrists.

Dowsing by pendulum, spring rod, aurameter and angle rods was undertaken as part of the project. Dowsing researcher Harry Lovegrove was also at the site to

Nazis in search of their roots

One of the more extraordinary episodes in the history of leys was the use to which the concept was put in Nazi Germany. The man who discovered the German equivalent of leys, quite independently from Alfred Watkins, was a clergyman, Wilhelm Teudt, a man with a passionate belief in the glorious past of the German nation.

In 1929, when he was 69, Teudt published his *Germanische Heiligtümer* ('German sanctuaries'), in which he announced the existence of a network of holy places, strung out over the German countryside 'like pearls on a string'. Unlike Watkins, he was quick to recognise the astronomical significance of the alignments. But he allowed the fervour of his nationalistic beliefs to lead him into confusion. For him, the discovery of the astronomical alignments of ancient sites was positive proof of the surpassing excellence in all fields of the primitive Germans. 'The more god-fearing the people, the more accurate was their science of astronomical orientation' – and since the Germans were undoubtedly the most god-fearing of all races, their alignments were naturally the best. Teudt and his followers were convinced that the Germans were responsible for every major human achievement. 'It seems ever more doubtful,' wrote one of his colleagues, Arthur Drews, 'whether astronomy arose in Babylon, or whether, as is far more likely, the Babylonian science originated in pre-Sumerian times from the genius of the German *Wandervolk* who were also responsible for the astronomical features of the Egyptian pyramids.'

Teudt's ideas were adopted with enthusiasm by Heinrich Himmler. He was eager to find a way of commemorating the great past of the German nation – and one soon suggested itself. The Externsteine, a dramatic rock formation that was regarded as the centre of the sacred heartland of Germany and 'the great racial generation centre' of northern Europe', was the obvious site. Pagan rituals had been performed there centring on the Irmensul, the German tree of life, until this was cut down in the eighth century by Charlemagne. Himmler planned to restore the symbol of the Irmensul to the highest rock and to make the entire site a monument to the glorious achievements of German paganism – and to the thousand years of Aryan domination of the world planned by his leader, Adolf Hitler.

Above left: the Externsteine, centre of the sacred heartland of Germany, planned by Himmler as a monument to the glorious achievements of German paganism. A carving on one of the rocks (left) shows the Irmensul, the German tree of life, bending in submission to Christ

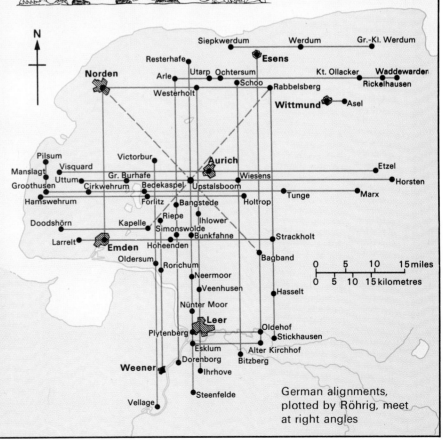

German alignments, plotted by Röhrig, meet at right angles

further, especially as it holds the possibility of using dowsing in conjunction with electronic methods of monitoring.

The dowsers at Rollright have themselves been monitored on occasion, by use of an advanced electroencephalograph known as the 'Mind Mirror', developed by biofeedback expert C. Maxwell Cade and Geoffrey Blundell of Audio Ltd. This instrument can measure the various brain rhythms produced by each hemisphere of the brain, and display them simultaneously on a monitoring device. These researchers have begun to recognise certain wave-pattern groupings that seem to be associated with various states of mind – like healing and dowsing. Sometimes the Mind Mirror reveals that a dowser can detect a signal before he or she is consciously aware

demonstrate his 'hasing' methods of dowsing. He used special angle rods and an array of devices employing 'charged' pieces of flint and various electrical components that seem able to lay down dowsable lines. Depending on the device used, these energy lines can be switched on or off at will, fixed temporarily or even permanently. If this is true, it may indicate that leys have been installed in the landscape by human action.

Dr J. H. Fidler, an energy dowser living in Scotland, has studied dowsable emissions from stone for many years and has succeeded in determining the wavelengths of the energy; his findings indicate that the emissions occur in the radio section of the electromagnetic spectrum. This is particularly interesting, as Dragon Project monitors have picked up anomalous radio signals at Rollright and certain Irish megalithic sites. It is an area which needs to be investigated

Top: a mager disc, used by some dowsers to colour-code the energies they can sense in standing stones

Above: an aurameter, a sophisticated version of an ordinary dowsing rod. The instrument consists of a weight mounted on a spring, an arrangement that makes it very sensitive to small movements

Left: Paul Devereux and Ian Thomson of the Dragon Project use a resistivity meter to monitor underground features that may affect the results of experiments at Rollright

of the fact, or before the dowsing instrument can amplify the dowser's muscular responses to the signal.

In June 1980 Bill Lewis visited Rollright to complete his site survey. Among a number of exciting results, he was able to demonstrate a dowser/machine interaction when he placed his hands on one of the 'energy nodes' on the circle's tallest stone, and clearly affected the readings being given by a sensitive voltmeter attached to points on the megalith. He was able to do this repeatedly. This gives project workers another hope that it may one day be possible to correlate at least some aspects of dowsing with standard meter monitoring.

A plethora of findings relating to earth energies has been produced by what have hitherto been considered arcane dowsing and psychic methods. The poor relation has always been the scientific investigation of earth forces, and it is in this sphere of enquiry that the pioneering Dragon Project has broken new ground.

What is the truth behind the tales that megaliths have paranormal powers? Can scientific measurement reveal the nature of their mysterious energy? PAUL DEVEREUX describes some experiments – and their startling results

LEY HUNTERS, DOWSERS and 'earth mysteries' researchers in general have long talked of an 'earth energy' – a supposed 'telluric current' that manifests itself at standing stones in particular, indicating that the ancients knew of its presence even if we are no longer, in general, aware of it.

The folklore relating to the old stones says that they possess unusual properties: they are the abode of spirits, they have supernatural powers of movement, they can heal, and they can bring down storms. Psychometrists have reported visions at ancient sites in which they see the stones being used as instruments for Druidic rites employing cosmic energies. There are also substantial numbers of accounts of apparently sane, reliable people sometimes receiving alarming sensations when touching megaliths – particularly sensations of tingling or shock.

And, just occasionally, there are dramatic events that draw public attention to the possibility that earth energies exist. One of these was the extraordinary geophysical display that centred on Arthur's Table mountain in the Berwyn range, mid Wales, on 23 January 1974. The full sequence of events is

Moel Ty Uchaf, one of the best-preserved stone circles in the British Isles, situated on the slopes of Arthur's Table in the Berwyn mountains in mid Wales. On 23 January 1974 Arthur's Table was the site of an explosion so powerful that it was registered on seismographic equipment as far away as Edinburgh. Some experts have suggested that megalithic sites are situated on spots where geomagnetic energy is concentrated. Could this energy have been responsible for the Arthur's Table explosion?

uncertain to this day, but there are clear reports of certain phenomena. An explosion and earth tremor were experienced in the vicinity of Arthur's Table during the evening: the explosion was heard over a radius of 60 miles (100 kilometres); the tremor was recorded on sensitive equipment by the seismographic unit in Edinburgh. Before the event, curious fireballs were seen both locally and nationwide. A blue ball of light was seen by an astronomer to be streaking westwards through the East Anglian skies, and it was observed disappearing over mid Wales. A white fireball was seen travelling south over the Isle of Man – again in the direction of Wales. Reports came in of multi-coloured lights over the Bristol Channel. From Llandrillo, the village at the foot of Arthur's Table, came accounts of red discs of light seen flying around the slopes some hours before the tremor.

It was generally assumed that an enormous meteorite had crashed into the Berwyn mountains. Police teams were sent up the slopes to see if anyone had been injured. Scientists came to search for the immense scar they expected to find on the mountainside, and to collect meteoric debris. But no evidence of a meteoric impact was detectable. The sequence of events became as mysterious as it was dramatic, and the whole matter disappeared from the headlines. It was, it seemed, another facet of nature that didn't fit into the neat theories of modern science.

But researchers into earth mysteries subjects noted one thing very clearly: on the slopes of Arthur's Table is Moel Ty Uchaf, one of the best-preserved stone circles in the British Isles. It is adjacent to one of Britain's most deep-rooted geological faults – the Bala fault.

Such strange events, along with the age-old legends and the claims from psychics and dowsers, have created a persistent idea of strange energies in the earth being harnessed by the megalith builders. To this speculation were added the findings of physicists at the

An ear to the ground

Crickhowell megalith, where magnetic anomalies were discovered (see page 1700). It was in an attempt to clarify this confused mass of information that the Dragon Project was brought into being in late 1977 (see page 1708).

While the considerable psychic and dowsing work already undertaken at megalithic sites provides the project's 'psychic archaeology' programme with a precedent on which to base itself, the physical programme has had to be an enormous pioneering effort. Its starting point was ultrasound – sound of a frequency beyond the range of normal human hearing. Some years before the beginning of the project, a zoologist had reported to *The Ley Hunter* magazine that a colleague of his had, while using ultrasonic detection equipment in a study of bats, noted ultrasonic emissions from 'a site you would call a ley point' – for which he could find no explanation. A similar anecdote came from researcher John Barnatt, who was approached by a stranger while surveying the Derbyshire henge of Arbor Low. This man mentioned that the skylarks singing overhead appeared to be attracted by ultrasound emitted by the stones. The Dragon Project's physical programme provided as good an opportunity as there would ever be for investigating such curious reports. In the months following the instigation of the project, limited funds were raised, experts were sought for consultancy in various spheres, and an ultrasonic detector was built by one of the project's electronic engineers.

So it was that, one grey October morning in 1978, the chief consultant for the physical programme, Dr. G. V. Robins, an inorganic chemist, found himself wandering around the Dragon Project's main field base – the Rollright Stones in Oxfordshire – carrying

This painting by the Irish nature mystic 'A.E.' – G.W. Russell – shows his impression of the energy field and spirits surrounding a dolmen. Folklore is full of stories about the supernatural nature of standing stones; one of the main aims of the Dragon Project, set up in 1977 to investigate ley sites, was to discover whether there are any scientifically measurable anomalies at these locations

The stone circle of Arbor Low, Derbyshire. Skylarks singing overhead appeared to be attracted by ultrasound emitted by the stones – which led the Dragon Project to monitor megalithic sites with an ultrasonic detector

an ultrasonic detector. Disappointingly, the detector registered nothing. But the zoologist whose experiences were reported in *The Ley Hunter* had apparently detected emissions around dawn. So Robins tried again a fortnight later, this time arriving at Rollright some time before first light. An hour before dawn, and still nothing had registered. But, half an hour before sunrise, the needle on the instrument's dial sprang to life. In two-second pulses, *something* was stimulating the detector.

Dawn flickers

It was from such mystifying results that the physical programme developed. With the assistance of volunteer monitors more ultrasonic emissions were recorded at Rollright, at the Castlerigg circle in Cumbria, at Avebury henge in Wiltshire and, to a lesser degree, at random sarsen stones from which the outer circle of Stonehenge was constructed. At control locations, such as concrete trigonometrical points on hills, no reaction was obtained. But it has been at Rollright that most of the work has been carried out. Sometimes no response was to be had on the detector; at other times the needle flickered dramatically. Two periods before dawn – about 30 minutes on some occasions and approximately 10 minutes on others – were the times when the instrument would most often spring to life. The effect would then last up to an hour or two after sunrise before fading away. Few responses were obtained during daytime and only apparently random 'spikes' of activity at night. The equinoxes provided more positive results than did the solstices. Preliminary correlations suggest that lunar phase and sunspot cycles may in some way be related to the apparent incidence of ultrasonic emissions.

If there is ultrasound at the old stones, how is it generated? Dr Robins, who was also involved with advanced orthodox work on what could be termed the energy states of stone, made an intriguing, but necessarily cautious, hypothesis. Could it be that

felt such an anomaly was worth a closer look, and by the beginning of 1980 intensive Geiger readings were being taken as part of the programme. But it was only with the end of the 1981 session that the remarkable findings that had been obtained were fully analysed. Many readings had to be taken at locations in and around the Rollright Stones, at other sites and in dozens of non-megalithic 'control' locations before deviations from a background norm could be clearly identified.

The picture that has emerged is startling, for highly localised spots of high Geiger counts have been identified at Rollright, at Moel Ty Uchaf and at megalithic sites near the Boyne river and Loughcrew mountains in Ireland. The circle at Rollright yields, most of the time, normal background counts, but on rare occasions certain points within it register sudden surges in Geiger readings. One day in August 1981, one of the identified 'hotspots' just outside the Rollright circle

microwave energy from the Sun is exciting the electron population in the lattice structure of the stones, causing a transduction of energy through the lattice that manifests as a pressure wave – namely, ultrasound? Theoretically, it is possible, but the Dragon Project found it difficult to obtain sufficiently sensitive ultrasonic detection equipment to test the idea at a stone circle. In 1980 and 1981 three additional types of ultrasonic detector were tried out, and two of these also picked up what appeared to be ultrasonic signals. Obviously, the accuracy of the experimental results must depend on the sensitivity of the transducer and the frequency at which the instrument is set, so it must be calibrated properly.

Sound that heals

If ultrasound *does* occur at stone circles, then it is possible that the geometry noted in stone circle layouts may somehow enhance this probably natural effect. The purpose to which the ultrasound was put is unknown, but it is worth noting that modern research has shown that ultrasonics can be used beneficially in healing human tissue and also in the enhancement of seed germination. The healing and fecundity legends associated with megaliths spring immediately to mind.

Another aspect of research upon which the Dragon Project's physical programme embarked was the use of Geiger counters. This was, again, triggered by an accidental observation: a few days after the Moel Ty Uchaf events in 1974, the geometer and architectural researcher Keith Critchlow happened to be surveying the site. While he was talking to a couple of scientists who were looking for evidence of a meteorite, it was noted that a Geiger counter casually switched on was recording a remarkably high count. This was apparently assumed to be an instrument malfunction, but when Dragon Project researchers heard of this story they

Above: Dr G.V. Robins, chief consultant for the Dragon Project's physical programme, tests an ultrasonic detector at the Rollright Stones, Oxfordshire. The detector registered pulses of ultrasound at several different sites in the period just before dawn

Right: Roy Cooper, local co-ordinator of the Dragon Project, monitors the Rollright Stones with a Geiger counter. Strongly localised areas of high Geiger counts have been found at many megalithic sites throughout the British Isles – but not at the control locations the Dragon Project has also monitored

yielded more counts per minute than when the Geiger counter was placed less than a yard from a radioactive isotope!

All these exceptional Geiger readings have so far been noted *only at or around megalithic sites*, and not at all at the control locations. It is known that uranium is present beneath some of the sacred sites of the North American Indians and the Australian aborigines. It *could* be that something similar is being discovered at prehistoric British sites.

Mystics and psychics have long believed that ancient standing stones emit powerful energies. As PAUL DEVEREUX explains, researchers on the Dragon Project seem to have found – and photographed – proof of them.

ALONGSIDE THE RESEARCH into ultrasonics and radioactivity that has yielded such spectacular results, the Dragon Project also conducted various other preliminary monitoring assignments. One of these was a number of attempts to photograph the Kingstone – the Rollright circle's outlier – by using an infra-red camera. Unusual but similar effects were obtained during three separate sessions, the most startling result at dawn one day during April 1979. On the photograph, a hazy glow is discernible around the upper part of the monolith, with an extremely subtle 'streamer' effect going off at an angle into the sky, cut off by the top of the negative's frame.

A member of the Dragon Project, a physicist at Kodak, examined and tested the negatives. No ordinary explanation was found that proved satisfactory; processing faults, heat from the stone, even freak refraction conditions were all considered but ultimately abandoned. The photographs remain unexplained. Deliberate attempts to reproduce the results artificially have failed. The effects were recorded at three separate

An infra-red photograph of the Kingstone menhir of the Rollright stone circle in Oxfordshire, England. The hazy glow round the top of the stone is said to be an energy emission; a research physicist from Kodak has examined this and several similar photographs taken by members of the Dragon Project and can find no explanation for the glow. In this photograph the Sun is well to the left of the stone and not, as might be imagined, immediately behind it

dawns, while photographs taken earlier and later on the same days yielded no unusual results – even on the same reels of film exposed at the same locations. The effect is not easily achieved – it is an anomaly. The results must, of course, be regarded with caution because insufficient work has been done on the method as yet, but it could well be that they indicate a worthwhile avenue of research.

An active – and constructively skeptical – Dragon Project researcher was R. B. Hale, an extremely experienced and well qualified electronics engineer. Among many of the experiments which he conducted, some involved a specially constructed radio receiver – a device receiving on a wide band but designed to pick up only local signals. Anomalous radio signals have been detected using the apparatus at Rollright and at a megalithic site in the Wicklow mountains in Ireland. Attempts at finding a source from which the Rollright signals may be emanating have so far been unsuccessful. Obvious sources like radio transmitters in the general district have been checked and ruled out. The signals are inconsistent and highly localised – like the Geiger results (see page 1713) – in areas only 6 to 8 feet (2 to 2.5 metres) across, something that is not to be expected with normally propagated radio signals. It is just possible that they may in some way be

Bursting with energy

to obtain traditional Kirlian photographs of a standing stone, but his efforts met with little success. Undeterred, Oldfield persisted in Kirlian experiments at Rollright – but using his new methods. On 4 April 1981, success was achieved. Shortly before dawn on that day, a stone in the Rollright circle was wired to a Kirlian camera and 'energised'. The camera – perhaps more accurately described as a 'device' – was there simply to induce an electrical current into the stone in question. This gave Oldfield a norm against which to measure fluctuations in the frequency or

associated with those dowsed by Dr Fidler (see page 1710) as coming from stones, but this hypothesis still awaits scientific investigation.

An important recent contribution to the Dragon Project has been made by the biologist Harry Oldfield. Oldfield has taken the problems associated with Kirlian photography (see page 1626) by the scruff of the neck and has fashioned the electrophotographic system into a far more usual method of investigation than before. He has shown that electricity is not necessary to produce photographs of the 'auras' around objects such as leaves – they will photograph *themselves* if sufficiently long exposure times are allowed.

A new diagnosis

Thus the criticism that the Kirlian method is simply displaying some electrical effect like corona discharge looks decidedly shakier than it did. Oldfield used advanced Kirlian cameras that, unlike earlier models, give repeatable results. But he has done much more than this. He has found that when a person is energised by a Kirlian camera, the body becomes both an ultrasonic and a radio 'beacon', and he has developed ways of monitoring this output. He is having great success in scanning patients, analysing their 'energy fields' on an oscilloscope and translating this into a physical diagnosis. The medical world is beginning to show considerable interest in the techniques involved. Oldfield's methods can apparently distinguish between cancerous and non-cancerous tissue in laboratory tests, and it is possible that a whole new era of diagnostic procedure is being foreshadowed by his work.

The Dragon Project suggested that Oldfield might try out his Kirlian techniques on megaliths. He raised an eyebrow and confessed that he hadn't thought of such an application, but the dark hours before dawn on 22 June 1980 found him at the Rollright Stones. The first experiment was an attempt

Top: author and ley researcher Paul Devereux monitors anomalous radio signals apparently emitted by the stones at a megalithic site (above) in the Wicklow Hills in Ireland. These strange signals – which are also found at Rollright – are extraordinarily localised, in some cases only about 6 feet (2 metres) across – the sort of 'behaviour' not expected from normal radio signals and certainly not understood, even by experts

amplitude of the current, which, it was hoped, would be affected by whatever energy or force might be at work on or within the stone. Such changes would be registered on an oscilloscope. In addition to this, a decibel meter was rigged up to pick up any sound emitted by the stone, and was set to be sensitive to frequencies reaching into the lower end of the ultrasonic scale – that is around 20 to 25 kHz. As the Sun broke the horizon, a distinct increase in the electrical field was seen on the oscilloscope. More energy was coming from somewhere to pass through the stone! This effect has been recorded several times since – but only at dawn. The experiment has also been tried during daylight hours – but without such changes occurring.

As always, early results have to be treated with caution, but it does appear that Oldfield's Kirlian techniques may be as applicable to the study of the energy states of megaliths as they are to the study of living systems.

Numerous other programmes of work were tried out within the scope of the Dragon Project. Different types of electrical measurement, for instance, were undergoing tests at various megalithic sites. Both electrical potential and sensitive current measurement in the stones themselves were attempted.

The most widely publicised rumour associated with supposed earth energies and ancient sites is the incidence of UFOs along leys. Research for *The ley hunter's companion*

A lasting impression

The subconscious – inspiration and intuition – plays a large part in ley research. Ley enthusiast and artist Chris Castle let his subconscious dictate when he engraved his *Visitation at Clew Bay* (left) in 1974. He 'saw' an elemental spirit in the guise of a winged lion guarding four aligned stones that pointed out into the Irish Sea. And psychics, such as Bill Lewis, worked closely with members of the Dragon Project to provide deeper insights into the sites that are being researched. Working with archaeologist John Steele, Lewis claims to have discovered a correlation between sacred sites and uranium deposits. He says the ancients believed uranium gave the earth added power, as long as it was left in the ground – to remove it would mean disaster. Did they somehow know that uranium would be an essential part of nuclear weapons?

in 1977 revealed the remarkable fact that 37.5 per cent of the leys being studied nationwide – essentially a random sample – had evidence of UFO phenomena somewhere along their lengths. It was, however, impossible to determine whether this association was with the alignments as such or the *sites* comprising the alignments.

A pattern of faults

But research *has* revealed possible reasons why stone circles, at least, might be particularly associated with the appearance of anomalous aerial lights. Paul McCartney, a trained geologist working on parts of the Dragon Project's physical programme, noticed that there was a surface fault – a fissure in the Earth's crust – running less than a mile (about 1 kilometre) distant from the Rollright Stones. He knew of the Moel Ty Uchaf incident and that the site was next to the Bala fault (see page 1711). Studying a geological map, he saw that one of Cumbria's major circles, Long Meg and her Daughters, was also within a mile (1.6 kilometres) of a surface fault. Subsequent, detailed research in England and Wales revealed that all stone circles are within a mile of a surface fault or an associated tectonic intrusion. In Scotland the pattern also seems to hold quite distinctly, except for one group of circles in Aberdeenshire that, perhaps significantly, have recumbent stones within their circumference.

A French researcher, Pierre Mereaux, has likewise found that the major megalithic complex around Carnac in Brittany is on an intrusion surrounded by fault lines. Moreover, his research, conducted over some decades, has shown that the Carnac rows largely delineate changes in the magnetic field.

Why should the megalith builders have

Harry Oldfield monitors the change in electrical resistance that occurs when a crystal comes into contact with healer Ken Shaw. Oldfield's development of Kirlian techniques has mainly been concerned with applications in medicine – but is now being applied, with fascinating results, to the study of leys and standing stones

chosen such geologically significant sites? The convenient presence of stone cannot be the answer, because there are too many cases of megaliths having been brought considerable distances to a site – as the bluestones at Stonehenge testify.

Could it be that there is a geophysical aspect to ancient sacred places? Recent evidence has suggested that movement along faults may produce aerial phenomena caused by piezoelectrical effects that are, in turn, produced by pressure on rock crystals adjacent to the faults. 'Earthquake lights' have long been noticed and even photographed. Michael Persinger and Ghislaine Lafrenière, two Canadian researchers, have suggested that a full-scale earthquake is not necessary to produce such atmospheric phenomena.

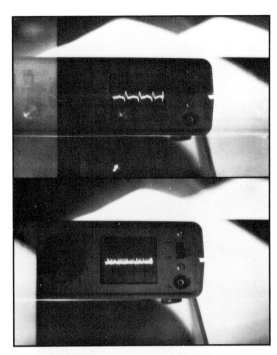

Left: oscilloscope readings showing the comparative behaviour of signals emitted by one of the Rollright Stones after it had been 'energised' by Oldfield's Kirlian equipment, just before dawn and (below left) just after – when the reading is obviously disturbed

Below and bottom: earthquake lights photographed during the Matsushiro, Japan, earthquakes of 1965 to 1967. The lights, which have been recognised as natural phenomena since the 1930s, are still largely unexplained. Modern ley research points to a connection between earth tremors and faults and the distribution of megaliths

This is one more of the mysteries that the Dragon Project began to uncover. As with all things which man does not understand, there are those who would wish to explain away many of the patterns and anomalies emerging from the research. But, unarguably, some of the results gained from the research are revolutionary.

Fieldwork on the Dragon Project began in 1978. Considering the enormous scope of the project and the fact that it operated on very slim budgetary resources, it was some time before any firm conclusions were announced. To add further complication, the phenomena being studied were not always present at the sites, and involvement of complex cycles necessitated extended study.

Dragon Project researchers allow themselves wry smiles when they read journalistic writers and over-zealous researchers making wild claims about UFOs and earth energies: they know that such matters will take a lot more research, frustration and perspiration before they are fully understood.

Further reading
Paul Devereux et al, *Earthlights revelation: UFOs and mystery lightform phenomena*, Sterling 1990
Tom Graves, *Dowser's workbook*, Sterling 1990
John Michell, *A little history of astroarchaeology*, Thames and Hudson 1977
Alfred Watkins, *The ley-hunter's manual*, Borgo Press 1986

Even mild geological movements create enormous exchanges of energy.

Because of their positions relative to geological faults, megalithic sites are likely to be bathed in seas of piezoelectricity every time there is a tectonic movement in their vicinity; this could be another form of energy input into the stones. Tectonic movements could be triggered by geological factors and also by the 'shear force' of the Sun and Moon crossing the horizon. This might account for the megalith builders' apparent obsession with astronomy.

Research carried out by Paul McCartney and this author has shown that the main incidence of UFO activity closely parallels the distribution of tremor epicentres in Britain. We are beginning to uncover a pattern that incorporates stone circles, geological faulting and anomalous aerial lights that could be mistakenly identified as UFOs. Could it be possible that the ancients were aware of this and incorporated such phenomena into their shamanistic rituals?

The phenomenal feats of mental computation achieved by a few remarkable people have astonished observers as being far beyond the normal human capability for calculation. ARCHIE ROY examines some of these supernova performers

IN TODAY'S AGE of the cheap pocket calculator many of us are in danger of losing whatever arithmetical skill we may once have possessed. In former times a shop assistant confronted with six similar items at 25p each would make an instant mental calculation that 25p × 6 = £1.50 and would punch that figure on the cash register. Nowadays in the same situation the shop assistant will solemnly punch 25p six times. Whereas children once mastered the 12 times table as a basic skill, they now use their trusty calculator to discover, say, what 4 × 9 equals.

Compared with previous generations most of us are arithmetically illiterate. But in past centuries there have been human beings whose calculating ability has so far outshone that of their contemporaries and predecessors that mathematicians, scientists and psychologists have been astounded. Appearing at random like meteors these 'lightning calculators' demonstrate that the human brain is capable of feats that remain largely unexplained.

Some of these lightning calculators have been exceptionally gifted in other spheres of human activity; others, in contrast, have exhibited a stupidity that threw their strange talent into bizarre relief. The only thing

Think of a numbe

common to most of them is that they demonstrated their extraordinary gift in early childhood. With some it lasted throughout their lives; with others it departed after a few years. Like the infant musical prodigies Chopin and Mozart, who played brilliantly and composed at an early age, the mathematical prodigies seem to have been either self-taught or simply endowed with their ability.

The Irish mathematician Sir William Hamilton (1805–1865) is a good example of someone with exceptional all-round ability. He began to learn Hebrew at the age of three, and by the time he was seven a fellow of Trinity College, Dublin, said that he showed a greater knowledge of the language than many candidates for a fellowship. By the age of 13 he knew at least 13 languages. Of his early mathematical ability a relative said, 'I remember him a little boy of six, when he would answer a difficult mathematical question, and run off gaily to his little cart.'

The German mathematician and scientist Carl Friedrich Gauss (1777–1855) demonstrated an exceptional early ability to carry out mathematical calculations in his head. A story is told of the first day he attended the arithmetic class of his school, when he was aged nine. Almost as soon as the teacher had finished dictating some problems young Gauss threw down his slate with the remark, 'There it lies.' At the end of the hour the slates were checked: only Gauss's answers were correct. By the time he was 13 he was excused from further mathematics lessons; and many of his most important mathematical discoveries were made between the age

Skill in mental arithmetic was once vitally important to scientists. Sir William Hamilton (below left) and Carl Friedrich Gauss (right) were many-sided scientific geniuses who were also mathematical prodigies. After the death of Gauss anatomists pronounced his brain to be far more complex than that of a labourer (below)

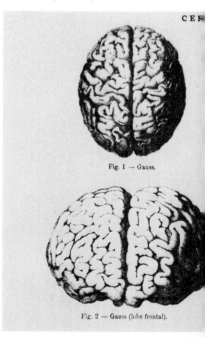

CER

Fig. 1 — Gauss.

Fig. 2 — Gauss (lobe frontal).

of 14 and 17. He became the foremost mathematician of his age, publishing his book on the theory of numbers when he was 24; he also made notable contributions to astronomy. Throughout his life he demonstrated an astounding ability to remember numbers and to carry out calculations in his head at uncanny speed.

The multi-faceted brilliance of Hamilton and Gauss tends to obscure their extraordinary arithmetical skill. When we examine such people as Tom Fuller, Jedediah Buxton and Zacharias Dase however, the real mystery of this peculiar power becomes evident.

Some of the 18th-century African slave-dealers seem to have surprised the Europeans with whom they traded by their mental agility in calculating intricate deals. However one of their victims, Thomas Fuller, outshone the best of them. He was shipped as a slave to America, to the state of Virginia, where he became known as 'the Virginia calculator'. In 1780, when he was 70, he was tested by William Hartshorne and Samuel Coates; among the questions they asked him were the following.

'How many seconds are there in a year and a half?' Fuller gave the correct answer in about two minutes.

'How many seconds has a man lived who is 70 years, 17 days and 12 hours old?' In a minute and a half Fuller supplied the answer. When his questioners told him he was wrong, he pointed out that they had not taken into account leap years.

Fuller died in 1790. He never learned to read or write.

Another 18th-century illiterate who was nevertheless a mathematical prodigy was Jedediah Buxton, the son of an English village schoolmaster. In spite of his father's occupation, Jedediah steadfastly refused to be educated, and as an adult he could not even scrawl his own name. He seemed to have no interest in anything apart from calculating. In 1725 he remarked that he was drunk with reckoning. This was scarcely surprising for he had just answered, after a labour of one month (and without pen or paper), the following mammoth question. How many barley corns, vetches, peas, beans, lentils and grains of wheat, oats and rye would fill a space of 202,680,000,360 cubic miles? And also how many hairs, each an inch long (and taking 48 hairs laid side by side to measure one inch across) would fill the same space?

His ability to solve this and similar problems earned him a certain fame and in 1754 he was taken to London to be examined by

Fig. 3 — Ouvrier allemand.

Fig. 4 — Ouvrier allemand (lobe frontal).

Tricks of the trade

Much of the labour of arithmetical calculations can be reduced by the use of a few simple tricks, and there can be little doubt that many of the famous lightning calculators used these. Those who professed not to know how they obtained their results may have used such methods subconsciously.

The following are some examples. If you want to test how much time and trouble they save, you should try solving the problems the long way – and time yourself!

What is the square of 97?
Instead of multiplying 97 by 97 in the conventional way, proceed as follows:
$$97 \times 97 = (100 - 3) \times (100 - 3)$$
$$= 10,000 - 300 - 300 + 9$$
$$= 9409.$$

Multiply 197 by 104
$$197 \times 104 = (200 - 3) \times (100 + 4)$$
$$= 20,000 - 300 + 800 - 12$$
$$= 20,488.$$

What is the square root of 3249?
Try approximate appropriate numbers:
$50^2 = 2500$ (too small)
$60^2 = 3600$ (too big)
Only 3^2 or 7^2 will give 9 in the last place. Try:
$$53^2 = (50 + 3) \times (50 + 3)$$
$$= 2500 + 150 + 150 + 9$$
$$= 2809 \text{ (wrong)}$$

Therefore the answer must be 57.
What is the square root of 92,416?
The required number must lie between 300 and 310, since 300^2 (90,000) is too small, and 310^2 (96,100) is too big. Looking at the last two digits, we find the number that gives 16 when squared (4). So the square root must be 304.
What is the square root of 321,489?
To find the appropriate numbers (in hundreds) around which to test, look at the first two digits (32). The square of 5 is 25 and the square of 6 is 36, so the square root will lie between 500 and 600. Looking then at the last two digits, we ask what number squared ends in 89? The answer is 67. So the square root must be 567.

Mnemonic devices can be used to remember numerical formulas that crop up frequently, such as the value of π (the ratio of the circumference of a circle to its diameter) to 12 figures. This is $\pi = 3.14159265359$.

The formula can be memorised by means of the following couplet, in which the number of letters in each word gives the number of each digit:

See, I have a rhyme assisting
My feeble brain its chore resisting.

Although dodges such as these have undoubtedly helped lightning calculators, they do not explain the astonishing ability demonstrated by many of them at such an early age.

the Royal Society. He visited Drury Lane theatre to see Shakespeare's play *Richard III*, but his response to this theatrical experience was to count the number of times each actor appeared and left the stage and the number of words each one spoke.

Travelling genius

A 19th-century mathematical wonder was Zacharias Dase, who was born in 1824. His extraordinary ability in mental arithmetic became evident quite early in his life, and as his fame grew he travelled extensively throughout Europe, becoming acquainted with eminent scientists such as Gauss and the German astronomer Johann Encke. Dase seems to have had wider intellectual horizons than Buxton and Fuller, and wished to use his calculating genius in the service of mathematics and science. Since he was able to multiply and divide large numbers in his head, he was able to create mathematical tables at incredible speed. By 1847 he had calculated the natural logarithms for every number between 1 and 1,005,000 to seven figures. The length of time he required for any mental calculation was dictated by the size of the numbers involved. In one test he multiplied together the numbers 79,532,853 and 93,758,479: it took him 54 seconds. Multiplying two numbers each of 20 figures took him 6 minutes; two numbers each of 40 figures took 40 minutes; and two of 100 figures each took him $8\frac{3}{4}$ hours! And all this was done without writing anything down.

Although he was anxious that his talent should be used to further the cause of science, he had, unfortunately, no ability beyond his gift. Many people thought he was stupid. One teacher tried for six weeks without success to teach him the basics of mathematics. Geometry was a closed book to him. And yet in spite of all this he did in some sense achieve his ambition. In 1849, on the

The son of a village schoolmaster, Jedediah Buxton (left) refused to learn to read and write but showed an extraordinary talent for mental computations. He excelled in very long problems that took weeks to solve, all without benefit of pen and paper. Archbishop Whately (below) was also a calculating prodigy, but his powers deserted him when he started school

The American child prodigy Zerah Colburn at the age of eight. He was exhibited by his father as a mathematical marvel, and astounded observers by his seemingly magical ability to answer the calculating problems with which he was bombarded

recommendation of Gauss, the Hamburg Academy of Sciences gave Dase financial support to create tables of factors and prime numbers between 7 million and 10 million. He was still at this colossal task when he died in 1861.

Other lightning calculators were Richard Whately (1787–1863), archbishop of Dublin, whose powers left him when he went to school, Vito Mangiamele, the son of a Sicilian shepherd, and the American boy Zerah Colburn.

Vito Mangiamele was aged 10 when he was tested by the astronomer François Arago before the French Academy in 1837. To the question, 'What is the cubic root of 3,796,416?' the child gave the correct answer in half a minute. It took him less than a minute to provide the answer (which is 5) to the question, 'What satisfies the condition that its cube plus five times its square is equal to 42 times itself increased by 40?' On being asked to supply the 10th root of 282,475,249, the little boy gave the answer '7', which is correct.

Zerah Colburn's talent seems to have appeared almost overnight. At first considered backward, he showed no sign of arithmetical ability at his village school; then one day his father heard him reciting the multiplication tables to himself without error. Soon his father was exhibiting young Colburn at various places in the United States, and he took him to England in 1812. Now eight years old, Zerah was bombarded with questions such as, 'What is the square root of 106,929?' Without hesitation he could

Born in 1806, George Bidder (right) was the son of an English stonemason. While still quite young, he was taken about the country by his father to exhibit his calculating prowess. People would test him with complicated questions such as: 'How many drops are there in a pipe of wine, if each cubic inch contains 4685 drops and each gallon contains 231 cubic inches, and assuming there are 126 gallons in a pipe?'

Bidder was highly intelligent, and his fate was quite different from that of other lightning calculators such as Buxton, Colburn and Dase. He not only went to school but subsequently attended Edinburgh University, where he won the mathematical prize in 1822. He became one of the foremost engineers in Britain, working both for the Ordnance Survey and later for the Institution of Civil Engineers, of which he became president. He is regarded as the founder of the London telegraphic system and is credited with the design of the Victoria Docks in London. An expert in civil engineering in an era when England's railway system was being created, Bidder was much sought after.

Unlike Archbishop Whately, who lost his outstanding calculating abilities at an early age, Bidder's powers actually improved as he grew older. According to a fellow of the Royal Society, he had 'an

The human slide rule

almost miraculous power of seeing, as it were, intuitively what factors would divide any large number . . . given the number 17,861 he would instantly remark it was 337×53.' He was not, apparently, able to explain how he did this; 'it seemed a natural instinct to him.'

Bidder passed on his gift to his son, George Bidder QC. Although not as brilliant a reckoner as his father, Bidder junior was a noted mathematician who could multiply a 15 figure number by another 15 figure number in his head. Two of Bidder's granddaughters also showed considerable dexterity in mental arithmetic.

The theory that the right hemisphere of the brain (the one less used by most, right-handed, people) might be more active in lightning calculators was put forward in 1903 by the psychical researcher Frederic Myers. As evidence for this he cited the fact that both Bidder QC and Edward Blyth, another 19th-century engineer and lightning calculator, were left-handed, indicating that their dominant hemisphere was the right one. However it is not possible to determine now whether any of the earlier lightning calculators were left-handed; nor is it possible to say with certainty that the gift can be inherited. The mystery remains, one facet of the larger mystery of the human brain.

---

answer '327'. To the question, 'What is the cube root of 268,336,125?', he could give the answer '645' just as readily. He was also able to say whether a large number was a prime number (one that cannot be evenly divided) or, if it was not, he could give its factors (the numbers that multiplied together give the original large number). For example, if he was given the number 4,294,967,297, he said that it was equal to 641 × 6,700,417.

Zerah Colburn never seems to have excelled in any other activity; he died at the early age of 35.

Common denominators

Dr E.W. Scripture made a study of such lightning calculators, and collected accounts of many more than those described here. As a psychologist he was naturally interested in trying to discover how such arithmetical prodigies achieve their astounding results. While his studies do not clear up the mystery completely, they do give us a glimpse behind the curtain, so to speak.

Scripture pointed out that in order to carry out their calculations and to store a multitude of numbers in their memories for long periods of time the lightning calculators need to have exceptional memories. Buxton, Fuller, Dase and Colburn all gave evidence

Mathematical prodigies are not all male. In 1981 ten-year-old Ruth Lawrence won an open scholarship to Oxford University in competition with over 500 students almost twice her age. She was assessed by the university as being possibly the most brilliant maths student ever seen in Britain

of possessing remarkable memories, often in areas other than computation. Possession of total recall would also enable the results of past calculations to be available for future operations, in much the same way that the 12 times table, once learned, is available to the ordinary mortal. Various conversion constants, such as the number of seconds in a year, or the number of inches in a mile, once assimilated, would be readily available for future calculations.

Scripture also suggested that other characteristics of the lightning calculator were rapid recall, a love of arithmetical computations and arithmetical short cuts, mathematical precocity and a good visual imagination. He concluded that a combination of these factors in a human being will produce a lightning calculator.

What he did not explain is why such characteristics are found in particular individuals such as Colburn, Mangiamele, Dase and Bidder (see box). If it is a question of heredity, what special constellations of genes would be necessary to create such persons? How is it that a few brains can perform supernova feats of computation that make the ordinary person's mathematical skills appear primitive? At almost any level of consideration, the lightning calculator remains an unexplained phenomenon.

'The cradle of all our science'

Radiating from an obscure village in eastern France is an invisible network of lines connecting places with similar names throughout Europe. ELIZABETH WATKINS explores its purpose and significance

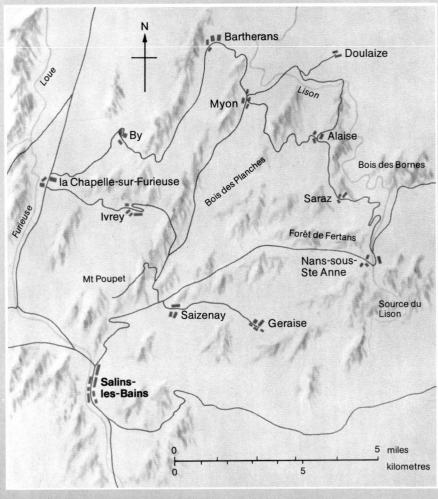

Salins-les-Bains nestles in a valley in the Jura Mountains, overlooked by the sites of ancient forts

TUCKED AWAY IN THE FOLDS of the Jura Mountains in eastern France, not far from the Swiss border, lies the little town of Salins-les-Bains. As the traveller approaches from the south, the road appears to be entering a cul-de-sac, so steeply do the cliffs rise on either side, each topped by a tumble of ancient fortresses. Straight ahead, to the north, stands Mont Poupet, at the head of a lion-shaped ridge. Salins-les-Bains stretches along a fast-flowing stream, the Furieuse, and straggles half-heartedly up the steep cliff-sides.

The tourist office stands in the magnificent 18th-century square. Its staff will proudly relate the history of the area. In the Middle Ages salt was synonymous with wealth, and the Chalon family exploited the salt of the mineral springs from which the town takes its name, using the wealth to develop the famous wine cellars at Beaune. No mention whatever is made of an earlier history of which there are so many proofs: the dozens of ancient tombs clustered on Mont Poupet; the many menhirs (four have been destroyed in the last 30 years alone); or even of the claim of nearby Alaise to be *the* Alaise, where Julius Caesar finally defeated Vercingetorix, the French equivalent of Boadicea. Still less is there any mention of the far more radical claims made for Alaise in 1935 by a Frenchman called Xavier Guichard: that the small area immediately north of Salins is the cradle of all our 20th-century science – the place where the Earth was first measured, geography was first recorded, and mathematics was developed to an advanced level.

Alaise is a sleepy village some 9 miles (15 kilometres) north of Mont Poupet. The present village lies well to the west of the

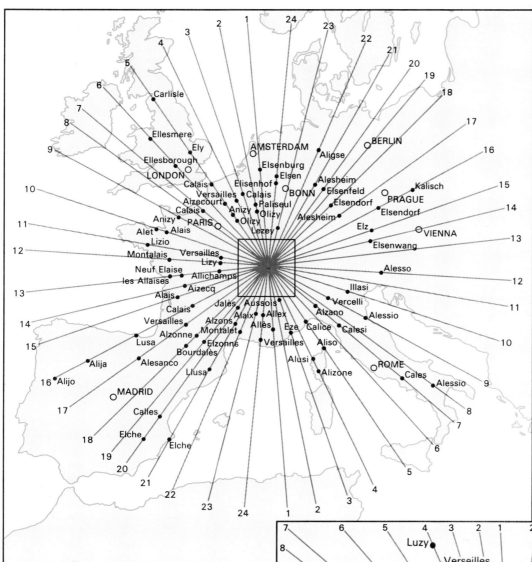

Left: the system of 24 'rhumb lines' that Xavier Guichard believed he had discovered. They span Europe from Britain to Greece and from Portugal to Germany, linking places with ancient names that he, as a philologist, believed were derived from the name Alaise. The lines radiate from Mont Poupet, near Alaise (below)

Following page, centre: one of the lines, charted in detail. Line 5 runs from Carlisle, near the Scottish border, to Aliso in Corsica. English names in italic type were not included by Guichard on his maps, but have been added here to suggest a possible relationship to Alaise

Following page, bottom: a chart of the Mediterranean, drawn on a single piece of vellum in 1626. It used a wind-rose system reminiscent of the prehistoric grid described by Guichard.

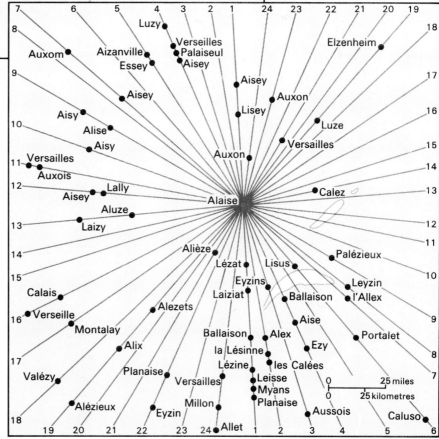

ancient Gallic town, Alesia, that stretched along the heights above the River Lison. About 3 miles (5 kilometres) still further to the west lies the village of Myon, directly north of Mont Poupet. On the highest point of Mont Poupet is a belvedere or look-out. Although only 2500 feet (800 metres) above sea level, it has one of the finest panoramic views in the whole of Europe. To the east and south-east the distant Alps can be seen, sweeping south in a great semi-circle. Even from 150 miles (250 kilometres) Mont Blanc stands out from its white-clad entourage. Comparatively near at hand, the pass that leads up from the Lake of Geneva to the Jura, the Col de Faucille, can be seen. To the west great plains stretch to the gentler hills of Beaujolais and Burgundy.

Mont Poupet, Myon, Alaise – Guichard spent a lifetime demonstrating that each of these places in turn was the centre of a direction-finding system, dividing Europe with invisible lines much as we divide it by latitude and longitude today. But since the ancients had no maps and used no writing, he believed that they marked their knowledge on the earth itself, just as we mark our boundaries today. These markers were places selected for their topographical features.

It was through philological studies that Guichard came to his study of prehistoric geography. The diffusionist theory of archaeology, which states that all knowledge and all civilisation was brought to Europe from the Middle East via Greece and Rome, did not fit the facts, according to his own researches into ancient European languages. The knowledge symbolised by the words and word-roots that he discovered, common to all European languages before they were Latinised, was far too sophisticated for a Europe supposedly inhabited by a scattering of warring, disparate tribes. There must have been a homogeneous culture based on considerable scientific knowledge, with widely spread religious beliefs and burial customs. Of course, this culture may have been disturbed by barbarian invasion even before the Romans arrived.

As a philologist, Guichard was well-read in the classics, which he combed for suitable references to ancient geography. But one of the authors he found most useful was Gosselin, a Frenchman who in 1786 won a prize for his comparison of the geographies of two Greek thinkers, Strabo and Ptolemy, who lived in the first and second centuries AD, respectively. Gosselin came to the conclusion that

in most of the geodetic measurements transmitted by the ancients can be

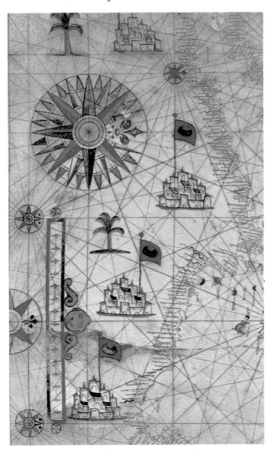

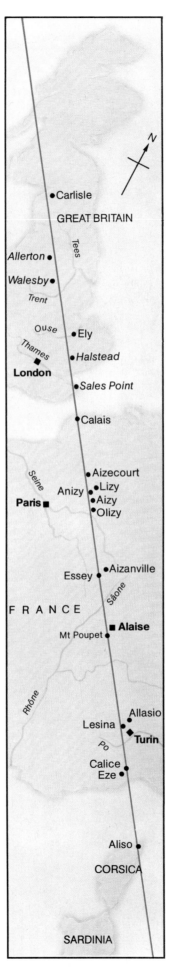

detected the vestiges of an astronomic science well perfected. The epoch during which the great work of fixing these measurements was performed is unknown. It appears that even in the time of Alexander the Great the memory survived only in a very vague tradition.

Guichard started by selecting three place-names used universally in Europe: Bourg, Antia, and Alaise. Bourg has been used since prehistoric times as a suffix in the names of human settlements; but it has been used in historic times as well, so Guichard discarded it. Antia occurs in such names as Florentia and Valentia, the ancient names of Florence and Valence (a town in south-eastern France). It has been used less often than Bourg in modern times, but the Greeks sometimes used it, so he discarded that, too.

An ancient name

Alaise had the qualities for which he was searching: widely used, very ancient, and yet showing no sign of having been used in historic times. Guichard found 382 place-names derived from Alaise, with a further 47 based on Calais (Cales, Calis, and so on); 37 were related to Versailles, Veiseille, Verceil, and so on. He found another group, nothing like so numerous, based on the words Myon, Millons, Milliers, Meilen or similar names. He stressed that Alaise is the ancient European form of the Greek Eleusis, and both came from the word 'hal', meaning salt.

When he marked places with these names on a map, Guichard arrived at some astonishing conclusions. Firstly, nearly all the places with names related to Alaise were situated on a wind-rose system based on the Alaise in Doubs. A wind-rose is the ancient way of describing a direction, dating from before the invention of latitude and longitude. Right up to the 17th century maps were drawn on this system. The rose was centred on some chosen point, while 'rhumb lines' led out from this fixed point in given directions. The compass was usually divided so that there were 16 or 32 rhumb lines. It was thus possible to describe a certain place as so many days' journey on such a line from the agreed centre.

Alaise is situated in the heart of Europe: lines running down from Scotland into Italy and across from Portugal into Poland cross here. Guichard believed that he could recognise 24 such direction-finding lines crossing at Mont Poupet, giving 48 rhumb lines to the rose. Guichard apparently overlooked the significance of the number of lines he found: one for each half-hour of the day and night. The interval between them should be $7\frac{1}{2}°$, but in fact is not regular. It varies between 6° and 8°, except between the seventh, eighth, and ninth lines, where the variations are still greater. Guichard thought these distortions had been made intentionally to give straight lines running down into Italy.

One line runs through Carlisle and Ely in

Surveying by the stars

Prehistoric geographers could have determined latitudes and longitudes by observations of the stars, Moon or Sun. The difference in latitude between Alaise and B, for example (below), is the angle marked in red. It could be found by measuring the angle between the

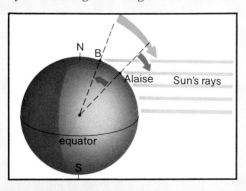

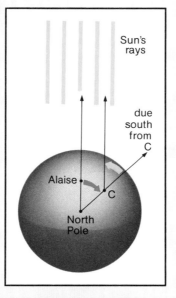

vertical and the noon Sun at Alaise (orange) and at B (green), on the same day. Subtracting one angle from the other gives the difference in latitude.

Longitude measurements (left) also required simultaneous observations at widely separated places. The difference in longitude between Alaise and C is the angle marked in purple. When it is noon at Alaise, the Sun is due south. At C the angle between the Sun and the local direction of south (yellow) equals this difference in longitude. The difficulty is to know the exact moment at which to make the measurement at C. Beacon fires could have been used to synchronise the observations. Or the measurements could have been made at the time of eclipses of the Sun, which are seen everywhere in the daylight hemisphere of the Earth virtually simultaneously. But co-ordination over a vast area would have been needed.

England, through Calais and eight other Alaise derivatives in France, to Aliso in Corsica. Another goes from Arklow in Ireland through another Calais, seven other places in France with Alaisian names, and four Italian ones (Vercelli, Alzano, Calesi, Cales). This line runs very close to Salisbury, but Guichard overlooks many British names. Another line runs from Aligo in Portugal, through Alija in Spain and four French Alaise derivatives to Elsendorf in Germany and Kalisch in Poland. Yet another runs from Alesanco in Spain through five French Alaises to Arlesheim in Germany.

A second system discovered by Guichard was based on solstitial lines, the directions of

Above: from a hill near the tiny village of Myon, prehistoric geographers observed the rising and setting of the Sun at midwinter and midsummer, according to Guichard

Right: present-day Alaise is a tiny village some distance from the site of the prehistoric Alesia, a hill settlement on which the most ancient of the geographical systems found by Guichard was centred

sunrise and sunset at midwinter and mid-summer. It was centred on Myon, to the west of Alaise.

Although the panoramic outlook from Mont Poupet is remarkable, it does not give an unobstructed view of the horizon all round the compass, and the summer sunset line is masked. In Myon there is a low hill from which the solstitial sunrises and sunsets can be freely observed, although the view to the south is blocked by Mont Poupet itself.

It was at Myon that Guichard made an even more surprising discovery. Each place with a name derived from Alaise was found to be a multiple of 10 Greek stades from this central Myon. In ancient Greece six units of length, all called the stade, were in current use. The stade that Guichard selected as fitting his system was equivalent to 1.15 miles (1.85 kilometres). In all, Guichard found 90 places at distances from Myon that were significant in terms of this unit. They included Alija in Spain (at 580 stades), Alijo and Milheros in Portugal (680 and 720 stades), and Caliso in Italy (500 stades). He was surprised to find that Meilen, which is in Switzerland, was situated too far away from Myon to make the 110 stades he expected – and then a Neolithic settlement was discovered under the waters of Lake Zürich, lying at exactly the correct distance. The very few Alaisian names that did not fit into the wind-rose system were all found to be precisely positioned in terms of stades.

So we have a picture of ancient Man mapping his immediate surroundings from an excellent look-out site in eastern France, using place-names to notate lines that extended in all directions. From now on, Man becomes aware of the importance of using solstitial lines, and moves his observatory a short distance to the north, whence the

Below: part of a system of longitudes discovered by Guichard in the positioning of ancient settlements. It extended beyond the area shown, eastward to Greece and westward to Spain

Bottom: place-names related to Alaise also fall on parallels of latitude, Guichard claimed

solstices can be more clearly observed. It is at this stage that Man starts to make accurate astronomical observations.

Yet even an astronomically based wind-rose map has its shortcomings. The further you move from the centre, the wider the spaces between the spokes, and the more difficult it becomes to express a position accurately. Guichard believed that the final developments in measuring the Earth, the introduction of latitude and longitude, also took place in Alaise, and that Alaise itself was on the first standard meridian. This invention is usually attributed to the Greeks, who placed the standard meridian first through the island of Rhodes, and later moved it to the far west, the Fortunate Isles (the Canaries and Madeira). Ptolemy is credited with measuring longitude for the first time in an experiment conducted at the time of the equinox, at Aswan in Egypt. But its accurate determination remained a problem until the invention of accurate chronometers some 1500 years later. Guichard's reconstructed lines of longitude, based on Alaise, are slightly less than one degree apart, an error that he attributed to the immense difficulties the ancients experienced in measuring.

Other searchers

Guichard was apparently unaware of his two contemporaries, Alfred Watkins in England and Wilhelm Teudt in Germany. All three men started from very different premises, yet reached much the same conclusions. Francis Hitching, the writer and student of the paranormal, makes an interesting comparison between Watkins and Guichard: both were convinced that their countries were criss-crossed with alignments, both based the alignments on place-names, and both were convinced that the alignments had come into being because of the importance of salt at these places. Alfred Watkins derived the name 'ley' or 'leigh' from place-names: Hitching asks whether this could be the English way of saying 'Alaise'.

The sad thing about Guichard's closely reasoned, scholarly, well-documented work is the extent to which it has been ignored. No publisher would look at it in the 1930s, and it was eventually published privately, by his friends. Yet later developments have made his work more relevant than ever. We know from the studies of Professor Alexander Thom of Oxford and others on Neolithic sites in Great Britain that sophisticated mathematics was in use in northern Europe at least a millennium before Pythagoras. It is now accepted that the alignments of Carnac in Brittany are older than those of Karnak in Egypt. What was the origin of the knowledge that went into their building?

On the highest point of Mont Poupet (top) you have one of the finest panoramic views in the whole of Europe. Xavier Guichard discovered sets of geodetic lines signposted by like sounding names (Alesias), which centred on this mountain. Guichard believed these lines were in fact mapping a network of salt springs, named when salt was important to Neolithic man in making the transfer from hunter to farmer, the first being centred on Salins les Bains (bottom)

The salt of the earth

Were ancient settlements along the Alaisian lines united by an esoteric yet highly practical religion – the worship of the Greek goddess Demeter? ELIZABETH WATKINS gives the evidence

THROUGH THE STUDY of ancient place-names Xavier Guichard became convinced that northern and central Europe had possessed a comparatively advanced civilisation long before the arrival of the Romans. He discovered complex sets of geodetic lines, signposted by place-names across the face of Europe. They consisted of: a wind-rose system centred on Mont Poupet; lines related to midwinter and midsummer sunrise and sunset, combined with distance measurements, centred on Myon; and a system of latitudes and longitudes centred on Alaise. These three places all lie in a small corner of land north of Salins-les-Bains, south of Besançon in eastern France.

The more Guichard studied, the more convinced he became that the ancients had possessed much knowledge that had subsequently been lost. He built up a consistent picture of this civilisation.

Knowledge had been handed on through secret societies. After initiation into one of these, novice membership could last as long as 20 years. Peace and order prevailed, affording this élite the time and opportunity to study. This peace was strengthened by universal worship of a mother goddess.

This civilisation was destroyed by invasions of barbarians from the east, particularly by the Gauls, who preceded the Celts and

Xavier Guichard believed that the most influential religion in pre-Roman Europe was the worship of Demeter (above right), Greek goddess of fertility and agriculture. In Greece her sacred rites were of enormous significance: initiation ceremonies lasted for four consecutive days, and the religious processions in her honour were so long that it took all day for the participants to leave Athens and make the 11½-mile (18.5-kilometre) journey to Eleusis. Over the years the Sacred Way of Eleusis (above) became associated with the burial of the dead and was lined with tombs of the great – for, as Demeter was believed to have said: 'Happy are those . . . who have seen these mysteries, for those who have not participated in them will not participate in life after death'

later intermingled with them. However, pockets of ancient tradition survived in the outlying areas: for example, in Britain in the Druidic colleges, which survived into Roman times; in Italy, where it gave rise to the Etruscan civilisation; and in Greece, where there was a sudden flowering of knowledge about 500 BC, owing to the fact that the Greeks wrote down the surviving scraps of learning from the earlier civilisation.

The least disputed part of Guichard's theory is that there was a widespread worship of a mother goddess, known at some times as a symbol of fertility, at others as the deification of nature. Guichard gives examples of this goddess taken from Troy, Denmark, Portugal, England and four different places in France. Since Guichard wrote, even more evidence has come to light about the universality of this ancient goddess, and very much more has been written about her. She appears in the temples of Malta, built about 2500 BC and now known to be the oldest free-standing stone buildings surviving anywhere in the world, and in the equally ancient tombs of Brittany. Professor Glob of Denmark is not the only archaeologist to believe that the most frequently occurring rock picture, the cup mark, is her symbol. In Greece she was known sometimes as Rhea-Cybele, more commonly as Demeter. She

was the daughter of Uranus, god of the sky, and mother of Proserpine, or Persephone, by Zeus. She was called by the Greeks the 'virgin', who symbolised life and watched over death.

According to the myths Pluto, god of the underworld, left his shadowy kingdom, emerging on the banks of the river Alesus in Sicily, where he found Proserpine and kidnapped her. Proserpine became his wife and reigned with him in judgement over departed souls.

Demeter, meanwhile, travelled the world

Above left: map showing ancient Greece, believed by Guichard to be the home of European agriculture

Above: the cave of Pluto at Eleusis, Greece, thought by some to be where the mythological Pluto, god of the underworld, abducted Demeter's daughter Proserpine (or Persephone), carrying her off to rule with him in his underground kingdom. Demeter travelled the world frantically searching for Proserpine, encountering such sympathy from the Eleusians that she taught them the secrets of agriculture in gratitude

Left: the elaborate burial ground of West Kennet long barrow, Wiltshire, England, dating from 3000 BC–1600 BC. The extraordinary care with which Neolithic man entombed his dead may be traceable to the rites associated with Demeter

seeking her daughter, and was received with sympathy by the people of Eleusis, in Greece, to whom she taught agriculture in return for their kindness. In a hymn dating back to Homeric times Demeter is quoted as saying: 'I myself have arranged these divine ceremonies, and after me you will celebrate them, and so you will earn my blessings. . . .'

Coupled with the veneration of the mother goddess went a belief in the afterlife, which gave rise to elaborate burial customs, at least for the great and good. In another hymn going back to the same time occur the words: 'Happy are those among men who have seen these mysteries, for those who have not participated in them will not participate in life after death.'

Mysteries of the afterlife

The evidence of megalithic tombs testifies to a similarity of burial customs all over Europe. Guichard believed that they survived in the ceremonies practised at Eleusis, which persisted almost unchanged for at least 12 centuries, into recorded history.

There were two sets of ceremonies at Eleusis. At the spring equinox there were quite brief rites to prepare initiates, lasting about four days, at a temple called the Eleusinon, in Athens. At the autumnal equinox the ceremonies lasted about two weeks, and it was then that the sacred pictures kept at the Eleusinon were paraded out to Eleusis, some 10 Greek stades ($11\frac{1}{2}$ miles or 18.5 kilometres) away. The procession was so long that, although it started at dawn, those at the end of it needed torches to leave Athens, and did not arrive until dawn the following day. The entire road came, over the centuries, to be lined with tombs of the great. The sacred rites were secret, and known only to the initiates; it is believed that one of the customs was to share cakes of unleavened bread on which the head of Demeter had been printed. But, significantly, there were mineral springs at Eleusis. Both 'Eleusis' and 'Alaise' are derived from 'hal', denoting salt, and Guichard thought the Eleusinian rites had to do with preserving bodies of important people in salt before burying them. Salt plays an important part in Guichard's explanations as to how the different Alesia locations (of which he found over 500) were determined. He dated the first Alaise – that in Doubs – to the early Neolithic Age, and thought that the most recent places with related names were settled in the early Bronze Age. The term 'Neolithic' is applied to the time when mankind was developing agriculture.

Man the hunter obtains all the salt he needs from animal flesh; man the herder can do the same, but has then to find supplies of salt for his herds, while man the agriculturalist needs salt for himself. As Guichard points out, the reason that large areas of Africa, Asia and Australia have always been sparsely inhabited was the absence of salt. And in Europe salt was also significant. It preserved food, thus enabling stock slaughtered in the autumn to keep the tribe alive throughout the long cold winter.

The meaning of Alesia

So Guichard thought the first Alesia had been established because of the magnificent salt springs at Salins-les-Bains – those same salt springs that in the early Middle Ages created so much wealth for their owners that they were able to found the great vineyards and wine cellars of Beaune. 'Alesia' meant a district in which salt was found, and Guichard insisted that all the Alesias have mineral springs, or other sources of salt, in their neighbourhood. Thus the first Alesias were in fact a network of salt springs, named at a point in history when salt was essential to enable the transfer from hunting to farming to take place. It was only later that the sciences of astronomy and Earth-measurement developed to the stage at which far-ranging alignments could be established.

It is a beguiling theory. Since Guichard published his researches in 1936, we have learned much that makes them seem more likely. For example, we know that the tombs in northern Europe, once thought to be clumsy copies of those of Mycenae in Greece, which date from 1500 BC, actually predate Mycenae by many centuries. We know the great megaliths of Europe predate both the oldest ruins of Greece and the pyramids of Egypt. We know that they were set up on a sophisticated mathematical basis, using extremely accurate engineering. We know that mathematics was highly developed in Britain, a millennium before its recorded appearance in Greece.

We also know more about surviving groups of primitive people than we did when Guichard commenced his work in 1910. Man usually starts herding after he gives up hunting, but before he takes to agriculture;

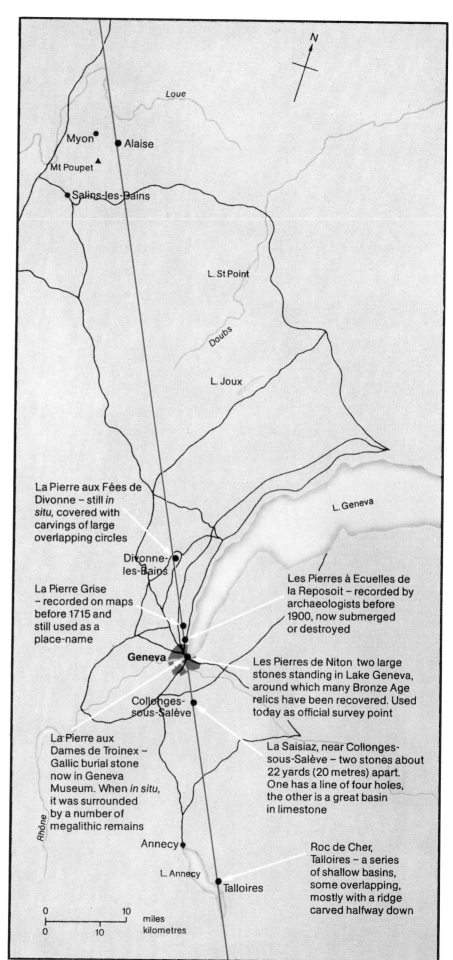

La Pierre aux Fées de Divonne – still *in situ*, covered with carvings of large overlapping circles

La Pierre Grise – recorded on maps before 1715 and still used as a place-name

Les Pierres à Ecuelles de la Reposoit – recorded by archaeologists before 1900, now submerged or destroyed

Les Pierres de Niton two large stones standing in Lake Geneva, around which many Bronze Age relics have been recovered. Used today as official survey point

La Pierre aux Dames de Troinex – Gallic burial stone now in Geneva Museum. When *in situ*, it was surrounded by a number of megalithic remains

La Saisiaz, near Collonges-sous-Salève – two stones about 22 yards (20 metres) apart. One has a line of four holes, the other is a great basin in limestone

Roc de Cher, Talloires – a series of shallow basins, some overlapping, mostly with a ridge carved halfway down

Myon
Alaise
Mt Poupet
Salins-les-Bains
Loue
L. St Point
Doubs
L. Joux
L. Geneva
Divonne-les-Bains
Geneva
Collonges-sous-Salève
Rhône
Annecy
L. Annecy
Talloires

0   10   miles
0   10   kilometres

studied them usually assume that they were used for ritual purposes, or were signposts, or memorial stones, or gave coded information – perhaps that certain minerals were present. Little of archaeological significance has been found near them: no burial remains, no traces of feasts or sacrifices, no weapons. The only finds that occur frequently are piles of ashes or fire-blackened stones.

Could these stones and petrogylphs have been first set up to lead nomads to the salt springs? Could they have been used later on for signals of a particularly significant kind? One of the problems in measuring longitude is the need for accurate chronometers. Right into the 20th century it was difficult to be sure of the accuracy of watches. It is interesting to note that in 1911 the *Encyclopaedia Britannica* was still telling surveyors to be sure to check their time by telegraph. Could these stones be ancient telegraphs, the places where signal fires were lit so that observers great distances apart could measure the positions of the stars at the same time?

A discovery of the Swiss geologist A. Jayet could be related to these standing stones and rock pictures. In 1940 he described an alignment of basin stones stretching from Talloires on Lake Annecy for some 25 miles (40 kilometres) to Divonne, north of Lake Geneva. In 1940 the French were too distracted to follow this up – but the line, prolonged, runs exactly to Mont Poupet.

Another fact apparently unknown to Guichard that supports his theories is the hiatus that occurs between the Neolithic and the Bronze Ages, a hiatus that Professor Colin Renfrew attributes to a deterioration in the climate. It is known that in a few centuries the Swiss lakes rose by more than 33 feet (10 metres). The amount of rainfall needed to bring about this enormous change might well have destroyed a newly established and tenuous system of farming. This climatic change might be responsible for the vanishing of the ancient culture that Guichard believed he had rediscovered. In the face of all the knowledge we now possess, it is time that Guichard's theories were investigated and put to the test.

and even when he does start to till the soil, he still remains nomadic, moving on to new pastures when he has exhausted one area of land. The lack of salt may well explain why, for example, the highlands of Kenya were so sparsely populated when Europeans first arrived there, while the much hotter, drier, scrubbier Rift Valley, with its chain of salty lakes, was overpopulated by nomads and their vast herds. In Uganda the lakes are not so salty, and salt is harder to find. In the west of Uganda lies a volcanic lake in which salty reeds grow. The tribe that learned to extract salt from these reeds by a complex procedure of burning them and washing the ashes was the only tribe in East Africa that did not need to live by hunting, herding or agriculture. With salt to exchange they could be sure of a steady supply of food for very little work. Is this how the ancients of Alesia found leisure for learning? After the disturbances in the Congo (now Zaïre) in the 1960s the craving for salt was so great that in Katanga rock salt and rough diamonds changed hands, weight for weight.

Guichard was also unaware of the number of standing stones and petroglyphs (rock pictures) that survive immediately south of Alaise, in both the Jura Mountains and Switzerland. Those archaeologists who have

Above: the pre-Roman Gallic burial stone known as La Pierre aux Dames de Troinex. Originally surrounded by a number of megalithic remains and positioned exactly on a major Swiss ley line, this stone is now in a museum in Geneva

Below: Lake Nyvasha, in the Kenyan Rift Valley. A salt lake, it has provided the focus for a number of settlements, even though cooler and more fertile land is close by

Further reading
Xavier Guichard, *Eleusis – Alesia*, F. Paillart (Abbéville) 1936
Tom Williamson and Lin Bellamy, *Ley lines in question*, Trafalgar Square 1984

Resting in peace

To most people the idea of being buried alive is pure nightmare. But some have perfected the art of staying buried alive for long periods – for fame and fortune, or even to gain enlightenment. BOB RICKARD looks at this curious way of passing the time

SOMETIME IN THE mid 17th century an astonishing incident occurred in the outskirts of Amritsar, in north-west India. Workmen, digging a ditch in a layer of brittle shale, found they had accidentally broken into an unsuspected tomb. Inside they found the dust-covered – and apparently mummified – body of a young yogi, sitting cross-legged in faded orange robes. They decided to bring the body to the surface and, so the story goes, when the Sun's rays first touched the body's dry skin, it began to change. The yogi gradually stirred and within a short time was talking to the workmen, seemingly not much affected by the ordeal of being buried alive. But he had an even greater shock to impart to his saviours. His name was Ramaswami, he said, and he had descended voluntarily into his tomb about 100 years previously.

Within a month news of the yogi's resurrection had spread far and wide in the subcontinent, and was taken by many Indians to be confirmation, if such were needed, of the reality of yogic powers. No one challenged Ramaswami, so universal was the belief in this feat. On the contrary, one famous historian, Arjun Singh, even journeyed to Amritsar to learn more of life in the previous century from one of its alleged former denizens. If Ramaswami was a charlatan, he was no ordinary one, because the historian came away impressed.

However, the story of Ramaswami, while providing the prototype for the phenomenon of living burials, is quite unsatisfactory as evidence. Further details are locked away in obscure publications in the Indian languages and are generally inaccessible to the Western researcher; and should one discover a reference it will almost certainly lack the kind of corroborative details that a Westerner would find convincing, partly because these have always seemed incidental to the Indian mind, preoccupied as it has been with philosophical or spiritual truths. Far more satisfactory are the records of a fakir called Haridas, who appeared in the Jammu region of India's north-west frontier in the late 1820s.

Haridas first came to prominence when Raja Dhyan Singh, a government minister, published a description of a four-month

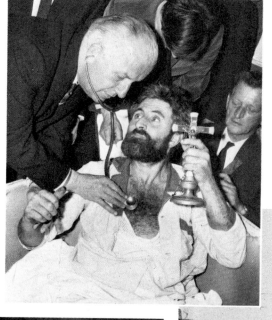

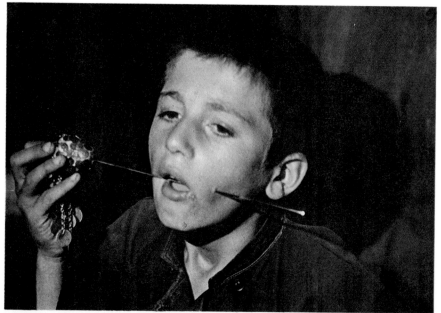

burial endured by Haridas that he himself had witnessed. This was independently confirmed by at least one European doctor. When news of further triumphs in Jasrota and Amritsar reached the ears of the Maharaja of Lahore, an educated sceptic, he invited Haridas to his palace for a carefully controlled experiment. Several English doctors, and French and English military personnel were also invited, the latter being asked to scrutinise the proceedings.

According to a lengthy account in the *Calcutta Medical Times* in 1835, the doctors had immediately discovered that Haridas had cut away the muscles under his tongue so that it could be doubled back to seal off the nasal passages at the back of the throat. For some days before his immurement Haridas consumed only milk and yoghurt and bathed in hot water. Finally he fasted completely, and before all the witnesses performed several extreme yogic ablutions to clean out his

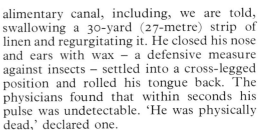

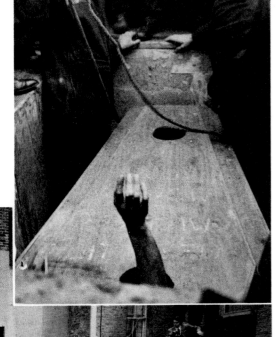

The capacity of Indian yogis – or holy men – to endure even the most hideous self-inflicted pain without flinching (bottom, far left), and to alter their metabolism at will, has long been the stuff of travellers' tales. But the mystic East does not have the monopoly of mind over body. In 1968 Mike Meaney, an Irish barman from Kilburn, London, was buried in a wooden coffin for a record-breaking 61 days. As the coffin was lowered he was in exuberant spirits (left); when he was exhumed, in front of an enormous crowd (below left), he was pronounced by a doctor to be 'in excellent condition' (far left). Others aim to get above ground as fast as possible – in 1955 escapologist Derek Devero freed himself from his manacles and a mailbag underground in Pollokshields, Glasgow, in just five minutes (above)

alimentary canal, including, we are told, swallowing a 30-yard (27-metre) strip of linen and regurgitating it. He closed his nose and ears with wax – a defensive measure against insects – settled into a cross-legged position and rolled his tongue back. The physicians found that within seconds his pulse was undetectable. 'He was physically dead,' declared one.

As the barley sprouts above

Haridas was wrapped in linen and placed in a large, padlocked chest, which was then sealed with the Maharaja's personal seal. The chest was buried and barley sown in the soil above it. Then a wall was built around the site and guards were posted around the clock. Forty days later the guests gathered again, this time to witness the fakir's unearthing. In the meantime, the barley had sprouted undisturbed, and the seal and locks had remained intact. Inside his shroud Haridas was found in the same pose.

According to one of the witnesses, Sir Charles Wade, the fakir had all the appearance of a dead man – his legs and arms had shrunk and were rigid, his head lolled on one shoulder, and there was no detectable pulse in arm or temple. Haridas was massaged all over for minutes before signs of life returned. Doctors pulled back his tongue, unbunged his nose and ears and inflated his lungs with bellows. He was back to normal within the hour. The Maharaja gave him a handful of diamonds; after that he was lionised and showered with gifts wherever he went – for a while. For despite performing several more times – without ever being proved a fraud – he was ignominiously drummed out of Indian high society for deflowering several of his female followers. He was never heard of again.

About a year after Haridas's successful performance at Lahore, there was a report in the *Indian Journal of Medical and Physical*

In the 1930s the United States and Europe were treated to repeated demonstrations of live burials by three Egyptians, Tara Bey, Rahman Bey and Hamid Bey. While in England Rahman Bey effected various 'mysterious' feats under the auspices of psychical researcher Harry Price, including a live burial at Carshalton, Surrey, in July 1938 (right). Although he emerged in good condition some time later (below right) his 'miraculous' abilities were later shown to be only average tricks by Harry Houdini, who outdid every trick the Beys performed

Below: the appropriately named Lucky, a tomcat, was found in a sealed drain in Bristol in June 1982. Workmen had blocked the drain five weeks before – with Lucky in it. His only injury was a stiff neck. After a hearty meal he was able to pose with kennelmaid Joyce Alsworth for the press

Science of August 1836 of a similar burial, by an unnamed fakir, at Jaisulmer. It might have been Haridas, for he too 'stopped the interior opening of the nostrils with his tongue' and made similar yogic preparations. This fakir was sewn into a thick cloth bag and placed in a stone cell lined with brick, which in turn was sealed with stone slabs, bricked up and guarded night and day. At the end of a 'full month' he was removed from his tomb perfectly senseless – and his skin was so dry and shrunken that he seemed to be almost mummified. His teeth were jammed together so fast that an iron lever was needed to force them apart in order to administer a little water. Even so, he too was fully recovered in a few hours.

In the 1920s three self-styled Egyptians – Tara Bey, Rahman Bey and Hamid Bey – aroused considerable interest in their tour of Europe and the USA. They performed live burials attended by newsmen and physicians, and in the ground of the witnesses' choosing. In what might be called the classic manner, they stopped their ears and noses with cotton, and consciously diminished their breathing and pulse rate. Tara Bey claimed this was achieved by willpower, together with pressure on 'certain' nerve centres in the head and neck and retraction of the tongue to the back of the throat. Recovery was aided either by the attentions of his assistants or through something akin to post-hypnotic suggestion. Despite achieving apparently genuine burials for short periods – for obviously they were not in the same league as Haridas – they were accused at every turn of trickery.

Houdini triumphs again

Their tour ended in a double disgrace. To scotch the rumours of fraud Rahman Bey agreed to lie in a coffin in the Hudson River, but for some reason came up after only 19 minutes, just a few minutes longer than the world record for breath holding. Harry Houdini saw his chance to expose the fakir as a fraud: using his own not inconsiderable powers of breath control, he spent one and a half hours in a steel coffin at the bottom of a swimming pool at the Hotel Shelton, New York. Tara Bey, too, was trounced, but by a Frenchman called Heuzé who was buried in an ordinary coffin for an hour. There was no need for mystical trances, he said, because by keeping absolutely still and breathing slowly there had been enough air.

It is easy enough to explain the burial feat by presupposing trickery, as openly advocated by the psychologist D. H. Rawcliffe in *Illustrated magic* (1931) – or as implied in Ottaker Fischer's speculation in the same work that fakirs must have dug concealed tunnels leading to hollow trees, or used coffins with false bottoms or sliding panels.

The fact that most of the mendicant jugglers and magicians calling themselves fakirs have been revealed to be cunning tricksters has not helped matters either. In 1955 the pioneering ufologist John Keel, then aged about 25, was a syndicated journalist drifting about India seeking out *jadoo wallahs* – performers of black magic and miracles. In his search for genuine mysteries, which was recorded in his first book *Jadoo* (1957), he saw very few and gradually became more cynical about the alleged accomplishments and motives of the self-styled 'living gods' and their ilk:

> Even though India is filled with tales about men who presumably equalled Haridas' performances, there is no solid record of them. Fakirs who tried the stunt afterwards were just imitators and they devised all kinds of tricks to do it. . . . More sincere holy men attempted the feat without trickery, and when they were dug up they were really dead.

These fatalities were so frequent that in 1955, while Keel was looking for someone to perform the feat for him, the Indian government was obliged to outlaw the practice.

But even the cynical John Keel found enough evidence to suggest that there were genuine fakirs with authentic powers – but they were solitary, secretive men who could not be found unless they wished it. This view had been confirmed by Louis Jacolliot, former Chief Justice in the then French Indies, who spent some time wandering through India in search of true fakirs. As Jacolliot explains in his *Occult science in India* (1884), he met several who, naked and without trickery or any kind of apparatus, demonstrated a variety of paranormal phenomena on demand.

If yoga is the means to the goal of *samadhi*, a superconscious state of union with the totality of existence, then the Islamic fakir and his counterpart, the Hindu *sadhu*, differ from more philosophical or spiritual yogis by

Right: an Indian fakir reclines on a bed of sharp nails, his emaciated body showing signs of previous self-torture. It seems that anything, from sticking knives in oneself to firewalking, is possible while entranced. The vital bodily functions can also be slowed until barely perceptible. It is under such conditions that yogis can remain underground for a considerable time

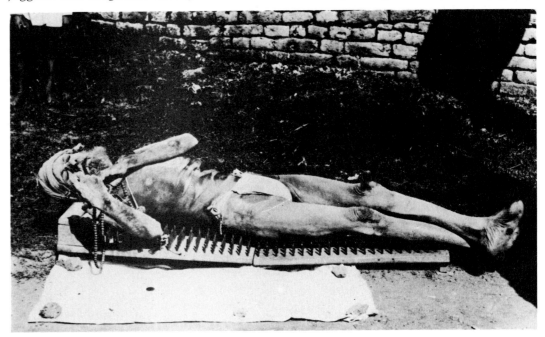

hibernating animal and can similarly be buried alive for days'. The comparison between the fakir's self-induced cataleptic state and animal hibernation was first proposed by James Braid, the physician who coined the term 'hypnosis', and the connection is clearly implied in the title of his *Observations on trance, of human hibernation* (1850), in which he discusses live burials. He concluded that yogis had perfected their control through the use of self-hypnosis, which released extraordinary subconscious powers.

This association with animal hibernation is an enduring and obvious one, and has engendered a splendid piece of American folklore, referred to by Ivan Sanderson in *Things* (1967), that from colonial times pioneer folk in the hard mountain winters would systematically chill their old folk in freezing draughts, then pack them in snow until the spring thaw. However, laboratory studies cited by Andrija Puharich in *Physiological psychology* (1950) show that although the yogi does indeed reduce his oxygen consumption and heartbeat, 'the two states are quite unlike.' For example, Puharich claims that in hibernation the basal metabolic rate is low and in yogic trance it is high; in hibernation blood sugar supply is much reduced whereas in yogic trances it remains more or less the same or can even rise. He concludes: 'Therefore, although trance and hibernation may appear to an outsider to be very much the same condition, they are, physiologically speaking, directly opposite conditions.'

Yet the fact remains that 'impossible' feats of suspended animation have been witnessed by many people of integrity over the centuries, in Africa as well as India.

concentrating on the means and not the goal. Their aim is nothing less than mastery of their immediate existence by absolute control of their bodies, minds and psychic forces. This, they claim, can be accomplished only by years of gruelling discipline bordering on self-torture. This single-minded persistence pays off with conscious control of the body's autonomic nervous system, which governs our involuntary functions, and through which the adept can demonstrably control his pulse rate, breathing, sexual function, metabolism, kidney activity, body temperature and so on. This fine control would extend to involuntary muscle functions; another form of the yogic ablutions used by Haridas to cleanse his alimentary tract is the reversal of normal peristaltic motion so that water may be drawn up through the bowel and bladder.

In *The living brain* (1953) the neurologist Dr W. Grey Walter agreed that conscious control of autonomic processes would enable an adept to reduce his body 'to the state of an

The buried fakir's self-induced cataleptic state seems to bear a resemblance to that of hibernating animals, such as the dormouse (above), or to the instinctive behaviour of some creatures, such as the Australian frog *Lymnodynastes ornatus* (right), that hide in the ground. Yet according to Andrija Puharich, the yogi's state is quite unlike that of a hibernating animal; for example, in hibernation the basal metabolic rate is dramatically lowered – but in trance it rises. Puharich summed up: 'they are, physiologically speaking, directly opposite conditions'

A grave condition

In Dahomey, West Africa, certain tribesmen are drugged, wound in a sheet (left) and buried for long periods. During this time they are supposed to be in touch with magical or archetypal forces that will benefit the whole tribe. Some Indian yogis, who go through similar ordeals, have been tested by Western scientists, such as Dr Elmer Green of the Menninger Foundation (below), and discovered to be 'elsewhere' mentally, and possibly aware of events outside time and space. The Russian mentalist Wolf Messing (bottom) apparently gained his bizarre gifts only after a prolonged, 'psychic' sleep, or trance

How can a man – even a trained adept, such as an Indian yogi – suspend his bodily functions in such a way that he is, in effect, simulating death? BOB RICKARD looks at the curious phenomenon of prolonged suspended animation that is still practised today

IT SEEMS IMPOSSIBLE to Westerners that men can deliberately put themselves in a state of suspended animation – by controlling their autonomic bodily functions, in a way not understood – and remain buried underground for hours, days, or – so it is rumoured – even years and emerge alive. Yet for centuries reliable witnesses have reported many such 'impossible' feats performed by Indian fakirs or yogis – but why do they choose such an extreme form of self-mortification?

The yogi has developed these disciplines to minimise inner and outer distractions (the latter by controlling his sensory channels) in his quest for the attainment of higher consciousness. But it appears that the Indian fakir uses them simply to control his body rather than to reach some nebulous *samadhi*, or ecstasy. To him the live burial becomes the supreme demonstration of his power over his body and mind. According to Andrija Puharich, the fakir is not unconscious in the ordinary sense, since one of his aims is to maintain full control of the four states –

waking, sleeping, dreaming and the biological shutdown of the 'false death' of catalepsy, which in the fakir's case is often self-induced. During the period of burial he does not lose consciousness but enters a deep state of meditation.

Just how and why the practice first originated is lost in the mists of time. The physician James Braid, at least, was sure of its antiquity. In his *Observations of trance, of human hibernation* (1850), he cites a passage from the *Dabistan*, a Persian classic on Indian religion: 'It is an established custom amongst the yogis that, when malady overtakes them, they bury themselves.' This implies that self-inhumation may have its

Augustine, for example, writing in the 6th century, described the ability of a priest named Rutilut, who could deliberately stop his pulse and respiration and who was insensitive to pain during his self-induced trances.

Whatever the origins of live burial, instances similar to those of India do occur in other countries where they are part of the physical phenomena of ritualised trance – as described in M. Eliade's *Shamanism* (1972). In *More things* (1969) Ivan Sanderson tells of a burial of an unnamed fakir for 24 hours under two truckloads of gooey earth in Belize City, British Honduras (now Belize), supervised by five doctors, including a British Senior Medical Officer.

And in Japan there existed a strange cult of self-mummification, described in Carmen Blacker's *The Catalpa bow* (1975). These Buddhists would vow to complete fasts lasting up to 4000 days, beginning with a severely restricted diet and gradually diminishing to a total fast with the goal of dying on the last day of the fast. At least two members of this 'interesting and now extinct' group are recorded as entering their tombs alive. Provided only with a breathing tube, they too

origin in attitudes towards death and illness, the technique being learned from the survivors who undoubtedly reported that the extreme form of isolation hastened their cure or enhanced their ecstasies. Comparisons might be drawn here with the therapeutic sleep of patients at the temple-hospitals dedicated to the god Asclepius in 5th-century Greece – such as the one that flourished at Epidaurus (see page 72) – and the practice, common in oriental mystery cults, of keeping an initiate in darkness or underground for a period of instruction, or in a trance-like sleep, induced by drugs or exhaustion, in order to obtain visions.

A different origin might have been the imitation of spontaneous instances of suspended animation – indeed the medical historians G. Gould and W. Pyle, in their *Anomalies and curiosities of medicine* (1896), compare the fakir's feat to cases of recovery from hanging or drowning involving either long periods of unconsciousness or the pathological form of catalepsy that has frequently led to the horrors of premature burial. This latter form, also called narcolepsy, contributed to the growth of the vampire legend (see page 3016). To this we might add the hysterical catalepsy that preceded the arrival of paranormal abilities in a significant number of cases, such as the Russian telepathist Wolf Messing (see page 2656) who was unconscious for three days.

Gould and Pyle discuss other cases in the literature of abnormal psychology from the 19th century either in connection with diseases or as 'spontaneous mesmeric sleep'.

The ability to simulate death is rare – though not unknown – in the West. St

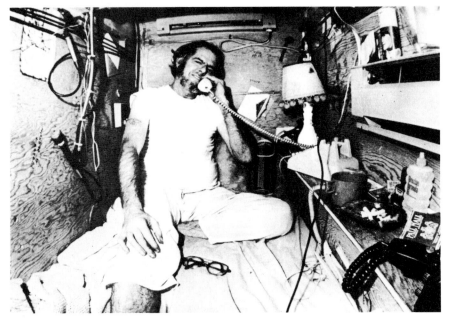

Top: in 1974 an Indian yogi buried his head in earth for many long minutes, with a pulse rate of just two beats per minute – but he survived. And a US stuntman, Bill White (above), attracted attention by staying underground for 134 days, two hours and five minutes in 1978, passing the time by telephoning the press – including the public relations officer of *The Guinness book of records* (in which he found a place)

eventually joined the ranks of mummified abbots in the temples on Mount Yudono.

According to the South African *Pretoria News* in late 1974, a Togolese jujuman, named Togbui Siza Aziza, was buried for three hours in Accra in an ordinary coffin. Stone slabs covered the box, then a layer of mortar topped with more slabs. After two hours the crowd began to panic and pleaded with Aziza, whose muffled voice could still be faintly heard. Finally, the ground shook and Aziza burst through the mortar, easily shoving the slabs aside. But the coffin was found nailed shut. Interestingly, Aziza, who tours with a group promoting African mysticism, Afrika Azzeu, says that he gains his magical

The legendary feats of Indian holy men include being buried with arms protruding from the ground (left), and keeping one's arms above one's head for 30 years (below). It seems likely that many such tales are mere rumour, but some of them may well be based on fact

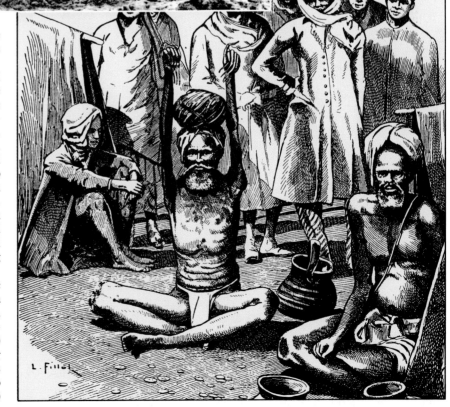

powers, which include the ability to heal the sick, understand animals and be impervious to pain, by meditating underground.

Among other accounts of suspended animation from Africa, mention must be made of the 'walkers for water', who were first drawn to the attention of Ivan Sanderson in 1932 by the British Resident Mr N. H. Cleverley in Calabar, British Cameroons. The Resident had dispatched a senior official and a sergeant of the Native Bush Police to investigate the refusal of several villages in the Ibibio tribal territory to pay their taxes. The villagers were nowhere to be found on their large swamp-surrounded islands, until the native sergeant doffed his uniform and went 'under cover'. Then he made a startling discovery.

Peering over a 6-foot (1.6-metre) cliff the sergeant saw 'the entire community (over a hundred souls, men, women and children, *and* their pets, which were confined in open-work baskets and appeared to be asleep) sitting motionless at the bottom of the water with their backs to the bank.' The sight of his sergeant shaking with fear – and failing to 'wake up' the villagers, in 8 feet (2.4 metres)

Stephen Pile's bestselling *Book of heroic failures* (1979) includes 'The most unsuccessful lying in state' and 'The funeral that disturbed the corpse'. The first concerns the 'late' Bishop of Lesbos who, in 1896, after two days lying in state, suddenly sat up and demanded to know what the mourners were staring at. In the second story a missionary called Schwartz who 'died' in New Delhi in the 1890s joined in the hymn singing from his coffin during his funeral.

In the context of Pile's book both are hilarious stories, yet premature burial was – and still is – a grim business. In the days when doctors merely felt the pulse

Death when is thy sting?

or held a mirror to catch the mist of breath, cataleptic patients had a horrifyingly high chance of being certified dead and duly buried – alive. In primitive areas knocking sounds emitting from freshly dug graves might be taken as ghostly manifestations and therefore ignored.

But, despite today's medical sophistication, the actual moment of death is the subject of hot debate; are we 'dead' if our hearts stop beating or only when our brains cease to register electrical activity? And is the heart that is transplanted an organ that is torn from the living or from the dead?

of water, was too much for the European, who fled back to Calabar. His report was not dismissed by his superiors, who were 'old Coasters' and well acquainted with the bizarre practices of the region. A second, more experienced team was dispatched, but by the time they arrived village life was back to normal and the sergeant had collected the taxes. This was not 'a yarn', Cleverley assured Sanderson; the incident had been soberly recorded at the Resident's court in Calabar.

This story is not unrelated to the live burial of fakirs. Either the African villagers could suspend their vital functions spontaneously, or they prevailed upon some shaman skilled in techniques akin to hypnotism. But there is a record of at least one yogi who performed a very similar phenomenon by an act of his own will in Bombay, on 15 February 1950, according to a report in the

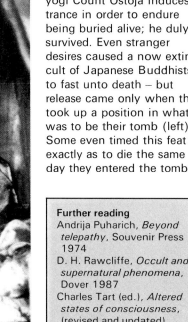

Above: December 1953, and yogi Count Ostoja induces a trance in order to endure being buried alive; he duly survived. Even stranger desires caused a now extinct cult of Japanese Buddhists to fast unto death – but release came only when they took up a position in what was to be their tomb (left). Some even timed this feat so exactly as to die the same day they entered the tomb

Further reading
Andrija Puharich, *Beyond telepathy*, Souvenir Press 1974
D. H. Rawcliffe, *Occult and supernatural phenomena*, Dover 1987
Charles Tart (ed.), *Altered states of consciousness*, (revised and updated) Harper SF 1990

Lancet for that year signed by a Dr R. J. Vakil. Before a huge crowd, and under Dr Vakil's supervision, 'an emaciated middle-aged sadhu called Shri Ramdasji' was sealed into a small underground cubicle for 56 hours. The chamber measured 5 by 8 feet (1.5 by 2.4 metres) and was made of concrete studded with large nails, and plugged with more concrete. At the end of the 56 hours a hole was bored in the lid and 1400 gallons (6400 litres) of water poured in through a firehose, and the hole re-sealed. The watery tomb was broken open nearly seven hours later and the sadhu discovered completely submerged. He had survived.

For 15 years after hearing the story of the Ibibio villagers from Cleverley, Sanderson tried to find out more about their astonishing feat, but in vain. 'Trouble is,' he wrote, 'I can't find anybody in our world who will even discuss the matter sensibly and from a scientific point of view. One would have thought that this would be a golden opportunity for liars and other storytellers. Perhaps it is too big a lie; perhaps they just don't have the imagination. Perhaps, however, it is the truth. . . .'